FOR THE GLORY

FOR THE GLORY

Two Olympics,
Two Wars,
Two Heroes

Mark Ryan

BOOKS

First published in Great Britain in 2009 by
JR Books, 10 Greenland Street, London NW1 0ND
www.jrbooks.com

Photos: page 1: top left photo: Scholz Family Collection, top right photo: Boys,
Colby E. 'Babe' Slater Collection, D-394 Box 3:18, Special Collections, University
of California Library, Davis, bottom photo: Scholz Family Collection; page 2: top
photo: Colby E. 'Babe' Slater in Snow, Colby E. 'Babe' Slater Collection, D-394
Box 2:63, Special Collections, University of California Library, Davis, middle
photo: Colby E. 'Babe' Slater, Mother Louise and brother Norman, Colby E. 'Babe'
Slater Collection, D-394 Box 3:20, Special Collections, University of California
Library, Davis, bottom photo: Press Association Images; page 3: all photos: Scholz
Family Collection; page 4: all photos: Cal Rugby Collection, University of
California, Berkeley; page 5: all photos: Scholz Family Collection; page 6: top
photo: Cal Rugby Collection, University of California, Berkeley, bottom photo:
William L. Rogers, photograph album and miscellaneous papers, 1924-91 (SC 616)
Stanford University Archives; page 7: top photo: William L. Rogers, photograph
album and miscellaneous papers, 1924-91 (SC 616) Stanford University Archives,
bottom left photo: Turkington Family Collection, bottom right photo: Cal Rugby
Collection, University of California, Berkeley; page 8: top two photos: Scholz
Family Collection, middle two photos: Virginia C. Slater; Colby E. 'Babe' Slater
with daughter Marilyn, Colby E. 'Babe' Slater Collection, D-394 Box 3:25; 3:22,
Special Collections, University of California Library, Davis, bottom photo: Paul
Dunn, *Monterey Peninsula Herald*, 1978, Cal Rugby Collection, University of
California, Berkeley.

ISBN 978-1-906779-25-2

1 3 5 7 9 10 8 6 4 2

Printed in Great Britain by Clays Ltd, St Ives plc

CONTENTS

OLYMPIC OATH

'In the name of all competitors, I promise that we shall take part in
these Olympic Games, respecting and abiding by the rules that
govern them, in the true spirit of sportsmanship, for the glory
of sport and the honour of our teams.'
*Written by Baron Pierre de Coubertin, the Olympic Oath was first taken
by Belgian fencer Victor Boin at the 1920 Antwerp Games.*

'I thought they were dead. We were sure it was only a matter
of time before they got their hands on us.'
*Norman Cleaveland, member of the US Olympic rugby team in 1924,
after French fans attacked Americans at the Stade Colombes.*

'The brightest entry scored on all the pages
of American international sports records'
*Henry J. Farrell, Sports Editor, United Press (UP) agency,
on the US rugby team's achievement at the 1924 Olympics.*

For Paul 'Boomer' Andrew – and Ned Turkington

If the true mark of a man is the courage he shows when his
health fails him, these fine men are giants among us.

introduction

BABE AND RUDY –
THE ODD COUPLE

Take two very different men, put them in a team and give them a choice: work together and win, or fall out and lose. Sometimes it can be a pretty close run thing, even if they have known each other a while.

Colby 'Babe' Slater was the tallest man in the Olympic team he joined, Rudy Scholz the shortest. Brown-eyed Scholz had a dark complexion, blue-eyed Slater was fair. Babe was the quiet type, Rudy could talk for America. Slater loved farming, while Scholz was a lawyer who got a kick out of big-city life. Babe rarely let anything annoy him too much; Rudy became irritated if the standards of others didn't meet his own.

Although they were the same age – born within two months of each other in 1896 – they might have been a little more alike had they ended up fighting in the same world war. But Rudy had to wait for the second round of global carnage to have his taste of hell on earth. There was still a mischievous innocence about him as a younger man, though he was also clever, driven and perhaps a little complicated.

Babe viewed life in far simpler terms than Rudy, having seen human beings reduced to their most basic form in 1918. His description of the dreadful aftermath on the the First World War battlefield of Passchendaele, Belgium, still has a haunting quality today.

He wrote in his diary in November, 1918: 'We saw the most ghastly sights imaginable – hundreds of men lying decaying in shell-holes – their bones within remaining – men lying where they fell with guns in hands and skulls in helmets. In some places the Germans and English would lie in the same shell-hole…'

When Babe began his Olympic adventures in the 1920s, he carried deep inside him many more terrible examples of what people can do to each other when countries engage in war. But he handled the burden well and commanded respect with ease. His long periods of silence were part of his nature anyway, largely because he didn't see the point in saying anything unless he really had something to say. Often he would keep his thoughts to himself, or write them down. On the rare occasions he did speak out, people stopped and listened.

His wartime experiences didn't leave Babe irretrievably solemn. Though he never forgot the fallen, neither did he allow himself to be defined by the slaughter he had witnessed, or crushed by the lingering memories. Slater was still young, and it wasn't so unusual to see a goofy smile break out across his plump lips.

Scholz was more than capable of causing such a smile; and his frivolous wit was apparent on the very first page of his 1920 diary for the Olympic trip to that same European country of Belgium.

He wrote: 'I apologize to myself for the misspelled words because I, myself know that it must be written at odd moments – if written at all – with no time to think of spelling but only the shortest possible route to putting thoughts and things on paper. As for the diction I can only say that a scholar of English would do well to avoid using the form apparent on the following page[s].'

Slater and Scholz would remain opposites in so many ways. The farmer and the lawyer thought differently, acted differently, and certainly looked very different. For an extraordinary period of the early 1920s, however, this odd couple shared the same dream and wore the same uniform to represent the USA in the same two Olympic Games.

The team sport they chose, described by Rudy as 'the finest true sport in the world', was so crazy and chaotic that even some of the players didn't fully understand the rules. It was called rugby, though no prior knowledge of the game is required to follow this story.

The Olympic adventure of 1920 was memorable for sporting excellence, as we shall see; but when Babe, Rudy and the boys became front page news from New York to San Francisco in May 1924, Americans weren't so interested in rugby itself. They wanted to know why their Olympians had been abused so badly. Some said the very future of the Olympics was at stake.

Blood had been spilled in the stands and on the field in scenes never witnessed at an Olympic sporting event before or since. There have been darker days in the history of the Olympic movement – both in Germany. There was the promotion of Nazism at the 1936 Olympics in Berlin; and the terrorist attack which resulted in the murder of Israeli athletes in Munich in 1972. But the violence at the 1924 Olympics was something else entirely, coming as it did in the stadium and sparked mostly by what the fans had seen on the sporting stage itself.

Sure, tensions off the field had contributed to the tinderbox atmosphere at the big match in 1924. Babe Slater and Rudy Scholz had both played their part in creating the conditions that would lead to trouble. But Babe and Rudy went to France to play ball, not to fight; they were in the French capital 'for the glory of sport', just as the Olympic Oath had demanded.

Most people associate the 1924 Olympics with a story featuring Rudy's famous sprinter-cousin, Jackson Scholz. The track races were full of sporting idealism and romance; and the tale of a Scottish runner called Eric Liddell was captured brilliantly in the movie *Chariots of Fire*. Few people know that the sporting venue for that true-life drama, the Colombes Stadium, had been bursting with hatred just weeks earlier. Babe, Rudy and their teammates were the objects of that hatred. And what they went through made the sprint rivalry between Jackson Scholz and British athlete Harold Abrahams seem almost insignificant.

Liddell, whose refusal to run on a Sunday made for such a touching storyline in the film, was also an international rugby player. But neither he nor anybody else would ever see another rugby match quite like the one between France and the USA in Paris early that summer.

Events at Twickenham just a week before those 1924 Olympics offered a hint of what was to come. However, no one could have suspected that a clash of sporting cultures – which first became evident in London but reached crisis point in France – would carry with it repercussions that last to this day.

—

chapter 1

THE BATTLE OF TWICKENHAM

AN OLD BRITISH COMEDIAN CALLED TOMMY COOPER HAD A JOKE about an injured man who told his doctor he thought he had broken a bone in two places. Without bothering to examine the patient, the doctor replied, 'So don't go to those places.'

If only sportsmen were so logical. Rugby players understand the risks they take, of course. The unfortunate men who broke bones at the Battle of Twickenham in 1924 were no different. But the US rugby team, led by captain Babe Slater, had taken a much bigger risk than usual when it challenged the Harlequins club of England to a game that spring.

Slater's team had the odds heavily stacked against them. Half the side had never played rugby going into this English tour. Even those who had played seemed to have forgotten some of the most important rules. On a technical level the US team was a joke. Yet Babe and his men were about to face one of the best English club sides ever assembled at the sport's spiritual home. Perhaps even more laughably, a few weeks later they were meant to compete for the Olympic Games gold medal by defeating the host nation, France, in her own backyard.

On the face of it, the leafy London suburb of Twickenham looked harmless enough. But rugby – a sport that could seriously damage your health if you didn't know what you were doing – had chosen to set up its headquarters there. And Twickenham wasn't somewhere the Americans needed to be at such an early stage in their team's development. At least one prominent US player wished he wasn't there at all.

Rudy Scholz had been around the block a few times, just as Babe Slater had. Unlike Babe, however, Rudy could already see why their Olympic dream might be destined to fall apart at the seams. A little reality would probably pop the stitches in no time. Harlequins had the firepower to expose any limitations the US team had. The English knew a bit about rugby, they had invented it. Now they were out to teach the Americans a lesson. If they succeeded, the fall-out wouldn't do much for what was left of the Slater-Scholz alliance.

This was southwest London on 26 April – just a week before the start of the Olympic Games in Paris. Twickenham was nowhere near as impressive back then as the colossal stadium that climbs so high into the sky these days. But the modest arena of the early 1920s was already the centre of the world for any committed rugby player. Twickenham was starting to take shape nicely, though covered stands along the sides meant that it didn't look like the 'open-bowl' stadia the American team was used to back in California, their home state.

In 1921 King George V had unveiled a war memorial at the stadium, in honour of the many international players who had lost their lives in the Great War. Babe Slater might well have been one of them. Somehow the US captain had survived the tail-end of that war, just across the English Channel. The rugby field at Twickenham – which had originally been nothing more than a cabbage patch – had played host to horses, cattle and sheep during the war. Now the animals were gone and the field was about to play host to human beings trying to do just about everything but kill each other.

The Americans, like the English, knew of the potential for bones to be broken. Rugby players didn't wear protective padding or helmets. Yet mercifully fatalities were rare. A Canadian player had died of a concussion sustained against the touring New Zealand All Blacks back in 1913. But you had to be very unlucky to lose your life playing this game. Normally, the harder you went in, the less chance you had of being hurt. The laws of physics dictated that it would be the other guy in trouble. In reality that was only true if you had the correct technique in the tackle to go with your aggression. Otherwise the tough-guy tactics could backfire.

The American rugby team's 'friendly' match against Harlequins needed to go well because they had lost their previous match against Blackheath. If the Californians lost again, there was little or no time to put things right. In a sense the tourists were lucky to have secured this fixture at all; they were relative unknowns in world rugby and had aroused suspicion at the sport's top table.

The tricky subject of what to do with these visiting Americans had been raised at a Rugby Football Union Committee meeting on 9 April 1924. Captain Stoop, who ran the Harlequins Club, sought clearance from the English game's governing body before he could finalise arrangements to play against the US team. At that stage he had no way of confirming whether they were truly amateur, as the regulations of the day demanded. He didn't know if the US team played rugby in the English sense at all.

The minutes of that RFU meeting revealed, 'Captain Stoop asked for guidance as to whether the Harlequins should play the California Team who were taking part in the Olympic Games, as he had not been able to get definite information about them. But [Rhodes Scholar Alan] Valentine, the Oxford Blue [he had represented the university against varsity rivals Cambridge] was one of the team. No objections provided the Harlequins took necessary precautions.'

Those minutes showed two factors at play. Firstly it was a good thing that the Americans had taken the extraordinary step of selecting Valentine without his attending any trial matches in the USA prior to the squad being finalised. The selectors clearly felt that anyone who had made a breakthrough in the English game, even at university level, would be good enough. Secondly Valentine had provided an important link between two very different rugby cultures. Without him the Quins might not have risked playing the Americans at all in case they weren't amateurs.

Professionalism was regarded as evil in English rugby circles. To play against a team motivated by money would have been decidedly dangerous for a London club seeking to uphold the noble traditions of the game. In fact all the Americans wanted from the gate money was this: enough cash to finance the rest of their journey to the Olympic Games, a sum that could be classified as 'legitimate expenses'.

All financial considerations were put to one side as Babe, Rudy and the boys warmed up for action. For the moment they had more than enough to worry about on the field. Slater and Scholz were the old hands among men who were at best rugby-rusty, at worst naïve. As a team, they were novices walking into the lion's den; and their annihilation appeared inevitable. After all, if you were trying to remember the rules while you were doing battle with the game's masters, it seemed there could only be one result.

Ah, the rules. What was rugby all about? Some of the American players might still have been asking themselves that very question as kick-off approached. Pierre de Fredy, Baron de Coubertin, could have reminded them. He was founder of the modern Olympic movement and a great fan of the game. De Coubertin liked to explain the basic objective of rugby like this:

> To gain the ball and carry it to the opposing try-line and touch the ball down behind the try-line as near as possible to the goal, which is made of two big posts linked together at half-height by a transverse bar. If he manages to do that, he scores a try which means a certain number of points [in those days three] for his team; the ball is then placed on the ground on a perpendicular line to the try-line starting from the place where the try was scored. The ball is placed at any point on this line and a player tries to kick the ball between the two posts and above the transverse bar. The try is thus converted, which adds [two] more points to the team score, and a total of all these points will decide the winner…

Not very different in essence from American football, you might think. However, as De Coubertin readily acknowledged, there was much more to the game of rugby than the basic rules of point-scoring. He had studied the sport as early as 1883 on a visit to Rugby School in England, the place where the game was conceived. What De Coubertin saw was the same sporting beauty that captivated the American reporter Harry M. Hayward, 40 years later. Hayward captured the aesthetic quality of rugby perfectly in 1923 when he wrote: 'As a game it has many attractive features lacking in the American brand of football…When a ball is swept from one end of the field to the other through a series of perfectly executed passes, participated in by every member of the team, it is beautiful and the enthusiast has every reason to revel in the sight.'

But rugby could be ugly too, especially when the tough guys clashed. Bart Macomber, an American football star of the day, was shocked when he watched a schoolboy rugby match in 1919. Writer Hayward observed, 'Macomber was considerably surprised when he saw the players upon the field with bare knees and no padding upon on their shoulders.' Then, once he had seen the biggest men from both sides locking horns for what is known as a 'scrum', Macomber was reported to have said, 'This is murder. I wouldn't play in that "scum" [sic] for a million dollars.'

The tangled mass of bodies becomes a human pin-ball machine. At first sight it looks like chaos and in a way it is. The most common reaction from anyone watching their first rugby match is: 'Rules? What rules?'

To many sports-lovers in the USA, rugby will always appear to be an illogical version of American football. The beauty of gaining any territorial advantage through the accuracy of a quarterback's bullet-pass simply doesn't exist in rugby. You can't pass forward – only to the side or backwards. Neither can your teammates block opponents who don't have the ball – even when they are clearly intending to level the player who does have the ball.

Being tackled is no fun. When your face is buried in the dirt and your limbs scattered in all directions, your biggest teammates – called the 'forwards' – have to get to the point of collapse as quickly as possible. It is not their job to help you up, rather to trample their way over you like a herd of rhino. The smallest guy on the team, called the 'scrum-half', (once the US Olympic side reached France it was Rudy Scholz) can then take the ball off what is left of you and give it to someone else who is feeling brave or stupid enough to want to put his body through what your own has just suffered.

So the big guys like Babe Slater are comparable to rhinos or even manic hyenas, feeding off the scraps of your carcass to take the ball further forward. And the hyenas on the other team look even uglier and even more ferocious, and they are trying to snarl their way straight through you in the opposite direction. Does it sound like fun so far?

Since you can't pass forward, there are only two obvious ways to get closer to your opponents' end-zone or 'try-line', where the objective of the game is to touch the ball down for a score. You can use clever passing combinations as you advance in a sweeping line together, or you can settle for a hefty, hopeful punt to clear your lines. Yes, confusingly, kicking the ball forward is allowed, even if you can't pass it forward with your hands. Therefore a desperate swipe of boot on ball is often the only sensible way to win territory or relieve pressure after an opponent's attack. Kicking the ball out of bounds is also the best way to gain a few seconds' precious rest. There are no time-outs in rugby, so the game requires tremendous stamina. And even when you have built up that stamina, the lungs often feel close to bursting.

To American football followers it might have seemed like a peculiarly English type of madness, that had spread to California in the late 19th century when someone wasn't looking. British colonies and even neighbouring France had to deal with a similar psychological contagion. Sanity had recently prevailed in the States and 'Gridiron' (American football), a game with a more obvious structure, had become the big favourite. If you were going to be dangerous on a sports field, you might as well injure people in a way that the spectators could understand, right?

For all that, there is far more method to the madness of rugby than first meets the eye. De Coubertin understood what really separated rugby winners from rugby losers. He explained,

> So many decisions require an agile mind and self-control, not least of which is being able to pass to a teammate who is better positioned than oneself. Discipline is the key to success. No team member can see the whole battle…What is admirable in [rugby] football is the perpetual mix of individualism and discipline, the

necessity for each man to think, anticipate, take a decision and at the same time subordinate one's reasoning, thoughts and decisions to those of the captain…[rugby] is truly the reflection of life, a lesson experimenting in the real world, a first-rate educational tool.

Despite rugby's virtues, Gridiron was simpler, more brutal, and gained the greater following in America. Rugby, it seemed, was history by 1919. But some die-hards couldn't entirely get the sport out of their system. And those who had left rugby behind were sometimes pestered by those who hadn't, until they agreed to make a comeback. In the end, California found enough rugby players to do something quite extraordinary, just when Gridiron was all the rage. They thought they would go and try to win the Olympic Games. And that's how 15 American players found themselves preparing to play the awesome Harlequins club of London. It was meant to be a warm-up match. To use a comparison from the sport of boxing, that's a little like Sonny Liston asking Cassius Clay (later Muhammad Ali) for a fight so that Sonny could have a gentle work-out before he faced someone good.

The Americans could have been forgiven for feeling a little punch-drunk. This was the third match they had played in six days – having previously beaten Devonport Services and lost to Blackheath. If Babe, Rudy and the others had expected an easy ride and a little pre-Olympic protection, they could forget it. *The Westminster Gazette*, a London newspaper, put it like this: 'The Harlequins paid their visitors the compliment of putting their strongest side of the season into the field, eight internationals being included, in addition to W. J. A. Davies, the old English captain.'

'Dave' Davies was 34 but a legend in the European game. He had captained England only the previous year. His 22 international appearances at fly-half – a key position almost like quarterback in Gridiron – was an English record, only to be eclipsed by Rob Andrew around 70 years later. Davies had more international experience than the entire American team put together. Half of the tourists had only been playing the game for a matter of months and had just two competitive matches under their belts.

If anyone could exploit American naivety on this spectacular stage,

'Dave' Davies could. Yet, as the *Gazette* had pointed out, he wasn't the only international. He wasn't even the only Davies. Captaining the Harlequins team would be Vivian Davies in the centre. The England international with the movie-star looks was full of pace and guile. His partner in the centre would be A. L. Gracie, the Scotsman who had played seven internationals for his country in recent years alongside Eric Liddell.

Meanwhile the classy England international player, R. Hamilton-Wickes, was waiting on the wing to punish any defensive lapses the Americans might show. He would hardly have been quaking in his boots when he saw his opposite number, the diminutive Rudy Scholz. He might have assumed that Rudy was fast, but then so was Hamilton-Wickes. All wingers were quick. You needed more than that to excel among the best. Rugby was about the sudden side-step, the stunning change in direction.

It was about brute force too. Among the giant Harlequins forwards was another England international called C. K. T. Faithfull. Another 'pack' member, Robert Collis, already played for Ireland, and his compatriot, W. F. Browne, soon would. In fact the entire Twickenham-based team was so full of ability that it would have struck fear into more knowledgeable opponents.

Perhaps it was just as well that Babe, Rudy and the boys didn't know enough about reputations in Europe to be excessively worried. Even so, word filtered through to the inexperienced Americans that they were facing one of the 'hottest' English club sides of all time.

A big crowd was expected – until heavy rain cut the numbers of spectators drastically. Already thousands of sports fans in the English capital had opted for an alternative venue and contest. Unfortunately for American coffers, the biggest soccer match of the year was taking place that very afternoon at Wembley Stadium. It was the 1924 FA Cup Final, in which Newcastle United were about to defeat Aston Villa 2-0 in front of 91,635 spectators. So the crowd that turned up at Twickenham was variously estimated between 3,000 and 8,000. The Americans would have to dig deep into their own pockets if they wanted to pay for that forthcoming stay in Paris for the Olympics. No cut of this gate money was going to solve their financial problems.

Still, the die-hard rugby fans who did turn up expected to be entertained; and they were not to be disappointed by the bone-crunching battle they saw.

As the rain subsided to a mild drizzle, the match kicked off. Harlequins immediately put their opponents under pressure out wide. It was a tactic they used time and again in the early exchanges, to stretch the defence to the limit. Soon the desperate Americans sustained a casualty. Lefty Rogers, playing on the opposite US wing to Rudy, collided badly with an opponent as he charged into a tackle. Lefty's fearless approach broke his own nose in two places. Blood poured out of additional cuts to the same shattered part of Rogers' face, and most men would have called it a day. But tough-guy Lefty didn't want to let his teammates down. Substitutions were not allowed in those days; and the Americans would have been reduced to 14 men. So Rogers stayed on the field and refused to let his injuries distract him. In fact, for the remainder of the game he was one of the USA's best players. How he managed to breathe properly under these conditions is not clear.

Before long it was the English who were a man down. One American player, a giant forward called Dud De Groot, was a newcomer to the game and wrote a journal about his strange rugby adventures. He explained later, 'Shortly after this [Rogers'] accident one of the Quin forwards [J. M. Currie] collided with Al Williams and the writer [De Groot] with such force that he broke his leg in two places.' It was an interesting turn of phrase to describe what sounded like a classic 'sandwich' tackle to eliminate an opponent. But De Groot insisted, 'It was a rough and hard-fought game, though scrupulously clean throughout. Our opponents told us afterward that it was the hardest match they had ever played, in spite of the fact that many of them had been playing the game for ten years or more.'

Tackling in American football was especially brutal because it had to be. Every 'gain' by the ball-carrying team was measured precisely in yards. If you were on defense, you either dropped your opponent the moment he took the ball, or the rival team soon made the 10 yards (9m) they needed to begin attacking you all over again. For the defending team, that was a recipe for relentless pain and eventual defeat. So the tackles went in hard; preferably so hard that the man with the ball went backwards, or didn't get up.

These American football tackles had never been seen on a European rugby field before. The methods they employed were quite shocking in their violent simplicity. An English match report suggested that the Americans were let off lightly for using tactics that the journalist regarded as foolhardy and dangerous. The report explained: 'It is fair to point out...that the closeness of the game was also due to methods which, in ordinary circumstances, would be much more severely treated than they were on Saturday.'

The Americans were apparently guilty of bad habits and a 'lack of appreciation for the Rugby Union rules. For that, one hastens to say, their teaching is entirely to blame. Nor need one emphasise too much the extreme robustness of their head-down charging and tackling, though it largely accounted for a most unfortunate accident to J. M. Currie. The Americans themselves suffered more than one injury, and the moral of it all was that finish [finesse] is needed in rushing and tackling as well as in running and kicking and passing the ball.'

Though the English journalist sounded patronising, his observations seemed to carry a warning. How would the French react a week later if the Californians flew recklessly into tackles, American football-style? Rugby, though naturally tough, was also a game of finesse and technique in Europe. The tackle was meant to bring down a player, not eliminate him completely for the rest of the afternoon. The American approach accepted none of this; and the clash of their culture with Europe's was already beginning to simmer under the surface.

In Europe, most of the tough-guy tactics were confined to the scrum-down; and in that department of the game the Americans were being overrun. When the rival sets of 'forwards' locked horns, the Quins were able to push harder and hook the ball out cleanly two times in every three. That meant they 'heeled' the ball backwards through their legs so that their three-quarter backs could begin a passing rush downfield towards the try-line.

Despite the size and strength of their forwards, the Americans were let down by a lack of technique and were shoved backwards. They had changed their scrum formation to the one used by most English teams. That meant three guys in the front row, grappling with their opponents. Then there were two middle-rank guys, who were unlucky enough to be wedged between the front three and another steaming trio behind them in the back row. This formation didn't work either, and the Americans suffered discomfort in the clinch. Sweaty bodies, awkward places, and the sort of uncompromising positions that would make anyone want to ask: who the hell invented this game? Rugby School and a boy named William Webb-Ellis had a lot to answer for.

The English newspaper reporter wrote, 'The American forwards, for example, waste a good deal of their undoubted strength in the scrimmages and mauls by an inability to heal out cleanly...'

All this meant a torrid day for Rudy Scholz, waiting out on the American wing for his share of ball and a chance to score. Instead Rudy spent most of the day chasing after the brilliant Harlequins backs, clever runners who enjoyed the lion's share of possession. Scholz often found himself heavily outnumbered as he tried to resist the fluent passing rushes of the British. The threat came from everywhere.

The first Harlequins try showed that even their forwards could be devastating with ball in hand. The English newspaper report described the home side's initial breakthrough like this: 'Pattison, who picked up on the run, started the passing move that gave Harlequins their first try: the forwards in this case did the passing, and one of them, T. W. Lowe, got the touchdown.'

That score threatened to open the floodgates, and De Groot acknowledged that the Quins demonstrated 'wonderful passing, coupled with their speed, knowledge of the game and ability to kick the ball to touch from almost any conceivable position was without doubt the finest thing of its kind we had ever witnessed.'

That wonderful passing rendered Rudy Scholz powerless as his opposite number, Hamilton-Wickes, romped over for a try. It was only when the British team kicked the ball 'into touch' (off the field) for a better restart position that the Americans could show their strength in the 'line-out' (when the ball was thrown back in). Babe Slater was heavily involved in this positive aspect of the Americans' game. When the ball went out of play, two neat lines of players formed, usually the tallest from each team. They would jump against one another for possession of the ball, which was thrown back in at height and straight down the channel between the rival players. The US team threw in American football style, with such power that the Brits were taken aback as it flashed over their heads like a rocket. Usually at the back of the line, Babe 'received' by jumping as high as he did in his best basketball matches for UC Davis, his college back in California. He caught the ball with such regularity that the USA team was dominating that area of the game.

An English newspaper report on the match made reference to Colby (Babe) Slater, 'the dangerous recipient of many a swift and well-aimed line-out throw from Caesar Manelli'. It went on, 'Cleverly mixed up with the ordinary lob in was an astoundingly swift and accurate pitch to a nominated player, standing quite twenty yards [18m] away. The curl and pace of the ball easily beat the men close in, and, unless well marked, the catcher at the extreme end of the line-out had a clear chance to get away or to pass back to his three-quarter backs. C. Slater, the captain, often was the catcher, and if he had not passed forward so often to another member of his pack, he would have been even more dangerous than he actually was.'

Babe Slater didn't accept that he had passed forward in any significant way and later criticised 'super-technical' British referees 'who we thought were crooks.' You could see why Babe would have wanted to lash out, as he too began to realise that the US team's Olympic dream might be a little far-fetched. In reality, however, the referee at Twickenham – a Welshman named Albert Freethy – was dishing out a good old-fashioned piece of sporting education.

In the USA, the benefit of the doubt went to the attacker if there was any debate about whether or not he had passed the ball marginally forward. This was probably because American football had already established itself in the national consciousness. However, in England it was considered a cardinal sin to pass even slightly forward in a game that was all about passing backwards while you advanced. Therefore the benefit of the doubt was given to the defending team if it seemed that a forward pass might have been committed.

Despite what for the Americans were new interpretations of rugby's rules, Babe and his team never gave up. A match report revealed, 'Just before half-time some bad fumbling in defence let in L. Farish to score an unconverted try for the Americans.'

Linn Farish, formerly of Stanford University and living near Babe Slater in Woodland, California, had a knack for this kind of opportunism. At Twickenham it looked as though he had started something.

One man down in the scrums, the English felt the pressure after the interval as the Americans tried to turn the tide.

But scores from Dick Hyland and John O'Neill were to little avail because W.J.A. Davies and W.F. Browne protected the London club's lead. The game ended 21-11 in favour of the Harlequins. De Groot, whose newspaper dispatches made him the official voice of the squad in many respects, almost like a narrator, took his defeat like a man. He maintained that 'although we lost, we learned more about the game of rugby football and how it should be played than we had learned in both our other games together…and although no American likes to take a licking in any type of a contest, to be beaten fairly and squarely by that sort of a gang was not half as bad as it might have been.'

Meanwhile Babe Slater also consoled himself with the glorious spirit of the contest itself. He explained, 'The sportsmanship of the players and spectators was wonderful.'

But Rudy Scholz sounded incandescent with rage when he wrote in his diary that night, 'We were defeated again and in good truth I never played on a more disorganized team. It is a case of every man for himself, the same spirit that prevailed on the boat [over here].'

That didn't sound like a player who was overly impressed with his captain, Babe Slater. A coach could determine tactics, but ultimately it was the captain who was supposed to inspire the right spirit out on the field. Babe hadn't done that, or at least Rudy didn't think so. Therefore it seems that Scholz couldn't give Slater his full support.

Ironically, Rudy's criticism therefore went against one of the central premises of De Coubertin's sporting philosophy – that each player should 'subordinate one's reasoning, thoughts and decisions to those of the captain.' But then again Scholz felt that the players, under Babe's leadership, were betraying the most important rule of rugby, also defined by De Coubertin – that individualism could only exist within a wider framework of self-control and unselfishness, so that each player was 'able to pass to a teammate who is better positioned than oneself.'

When he was venting his anger to his diary, perhaps winger Scholz was thinking of an incident also recalled by an English newspaper reporter, who wrote of the Americans, '. . .their passing was crude and obvious – once a centre threw away a try by not giving a well-timed pass out to his wing – but the running and dodging of men like R. ['Dick']

Hyland and N. [Norman] Cleaveland convinced me that here were first class players in the making – or the spoiling.'

It sounded as though Scholz had been denied a gilt-edged opportunity to score on the wing. And as De Coubertin and Scholz both knew, it was no use having flamboyant individuals like Hyland and Cleaveland if the Americans couldn't pass properly and work together as a unit. That was the only way to move forward against quality defences. Why wasn't this happening? Scholz never mentioned anyone by name when he complained to his diary about the inadequacies of the team. It wasn't his policy to do so. But the buck stopped with the captain, because a forceful leader inspired a unity of purpose among his players. Rudy was so disillusioned that he felt unable to help build the unity that he considered to be so lacking. Instead, his attitude was bordering on the subversive. It wasn't entirely fair, either.

Rudy may have had a point in offensive phases of the game; but how could it have been a case of 'every man for himself' in defence, when Lefty Rogers had played most of the match with his nose broken in two places? Had he been thinking only of himself, Lefty would have been halfway to hospital by the time play restarted after his accident. And the English newspapers marvelled at the unity the Americans showed in defence, as the big forwards tried to cover the smaller men among the backs. One wrote,

> …the way in which they break up and assist their backs to stifle attacking movements is beyond all praise. Time after time the Harlequins got the ball and started passing, but in the face of something they clearly could not quite understand, the Americans marked and brought down their men in no half-hearted manner. Even when brilliant and elusive runners like W. J. A. Davies and A. L. Gracie and V. G. Davies effected the breakthrough, individual Americans showed a remarkable sense of defence by covering beaten players. The result was that Harlequins missed three of four tries by inches, and two excellent wings like R. H. Hamilton-Wickes and H. C. Pattison found it desperately hard to find a way to the goal-line. C. Doe at full-back was surprisingly effective, both as regards fielding and kicking to touch.

Whatever reservations Babe harboured about the Welsh referee, Albert Freethy, it seems that the US team's manager, Sam Goodman, made a mental note of how tolerant Freethy had been of their heavy tackling. It never did any harm to forge a decent working relationship with the sport's top officials. You never knew when that might come in useful.

British hospitality didn't end with the match. Harlequins threw a party for the US team at the Princes' Restaurant in Piccadilly. It was a classy venue and made a fitting climax to a great day. The tables were heavily laden with champagne, wines and liquors – rare treats for the Americans when Prohibition was still very much in force back home. Although the tourists felt that the quantity of food didn't quite match the rivers of booze, they adored the occasion and were quite happy to participate as the game was played all over again, this time with words instead of actions. Quite happy, except perhaps for Rudy Scholz, who didn't want to play the game all over again. He hadn't enjoyed it the first time. Scholz left early, before conversation turned to the immediate future and the challenge the US team were about to face at the Olympics in Paris. And although there would doubtless be hurdles to overcome in the form of other competing countries, the greatest challenge of all was sure to come from hosts France.

Paul Andrew, a rugby fanatic who knew some of the 1924 Olympic team later in their lives, chronicled some of the events recounted here for the Bohemian Club library in San Francisco. Andrew wrote, 'The British advised the Americans not to let the French get ahead or to let [their star player, Adolphe] Jaureguy out on a run.'

Quins players Collis and Browne hadn't been playing when Jaureguy twice scored doubles against Ireland to secure victories for France, in 1920 and 1923. But they didn't need to have played to understand how one Frenchman had dented their nation's sporting self-esteem almost single-handedly. So the advice was simple: stop Jaureguy and you had an outside chance. Harlequins fly-half W. J. A. Davies had first faced Jaureguy in 1920 at Twickenham, when the English had managed to keep the young man relatively quiet during an 8-3 victory. Deny him space; that was the way to do it.

As he listened, Slater would have concluded that the advice from the

English, although offered along with copious amounts of champagne and wine, was fundamentally sound. He and Rudy Scholz knew about Jaureguy already because they had played against him four years earlier in a post-Olympic tour of France. But it wasn't just Jaureguy who would have to be subdued; it was the entire French team.

An England side that included 'Dave' Davies had almost been undone by the French at Twickenham just two years earlier, having thought they were home and dry. A versatile hard man called Felix 'Rene' Lasserre had scored one of three French tries in the second half that day, as they stormed back to draw 11-11. That was what happened when you let the French believe in themselves. And Lasserre would be out to promote that self-belief at the Olympics in Paris, for he was due to lead France at the Games.

Even so the Harlequins had seen enough in the American team to believe that they had a fighting chance against the French at the Olympics. England had already beaten France that year, 19-7 at Twickenham. Therefore if the Americans could use their physical qualities and tough tackling to knock the French out of their stride early on and apply some kind of stranglehold, they might just be able to pull off a shock. It was improbable, but not impossible.

The Americans' reward for taking their defeat in London like men was that they would leave armed with the seeds of a game-plan that might just make the difference in Paris. The English had taken these Californians to their hearts and the feeling was mutual.

The Harlequins players couldn't take on the French themselves, because Great Britain wasn't sending a team to the Olympic rugby tournament. The English adhered almost religiously to the parameters of their rugby season. April was a month for rugby, like any month with the letter 'R' in it. May was most definitely not. That was the first month of the cricket season. There was to be no overlap between these two quintessentially English sports, and the very idea of rugby in May was regarded as sacrilege by sporting conservatives. Nevertheless, that didn't spoil the instant rapport between the Americans and their hosts.

Never was the Anglo-American alliance warmer than on that memorable night of comradeship after the Harlequins match. De Groot, the big American forward who had studied at the prestigious Stanford University in northern California, said later, 'We all went back to our hotel with the one thought and feeling in our minds and hearts – never had we met a finer bunch of men than the group that had that afternoon defeated us.' Team manager Sam Goodman said of the Harlequins experience, 'We learned a great many things which were destined to be of great service to us later in the Olympic matches.'

The next night it was the turn of the British Olympic Association to play host to the tourists in Piccadilly. An American newspaper article gave a good indication of the spontaneous warmth of feeling that had developed between the Brits and the Yanks in such a small space of time. 'Sparrow' Robertson wrote:

> Lord Decies, who presided, apologized for the short notice which had been given for the dinner, but short as the notice had been, he said, the pleasure of entertaining their guests was just as great as if several weeks' notice had been given. The United States, he said, in organizing a team and coming thousands of miles in support of its friend and ally, France, in her efforts to make the eighth Olympics the greatest possible success, had shown a wonderful and at the same time a very broad-minded spirit, and the action was worthy of the highest praise.
>
> Mr Sam Goodman, the manager of the American team, replied by saying that the way in which the British Olympic Association and the Harlequins had come to them and taken them under their wing, when they heard that they were more or less on their own in London, had appealed to and touched them very much. He said he was sorry his team was not to have the pleasure of meeting any British team in the Olympic Games, because it was by meeting such fine teams that the younger members could pick up and learn the finest of all games. He thanked everyone again for their kindness and hospitality. The proceedings ended by the playing of the American and British National anthems.

In reality the evening hadn't been as formal in tone as that description of the speeches made it sound. Four years later, when the American Olympic rugby team of 1924 had its first reunion, Norman Cleaveland's topic for a witty after-dinner speech was entitled: 'How I broke into the upper 400 by teaching the English nobility college yells.' The implication was that Cleaveland felt he had joined society's elite by introducing some of the titled guests to the bewildering college yells which had become signature-chants at top American seats of learning. And you can just imagine the English aristocracy listening in open-mouthed astonishment to the Stanford Ax Yell, for example, which went like this:

> Give 'em the ax, the ax, the ax!
> Give 'em the ax, the ax, the ax!
> Give 'em the ax, give 'em the ax,
> Giv 'em the ax, where?
>
> Right in the neck, the neck, the neck!
> Right in the neck, the neck, the neck!
> Right in the neck, right in the neck,
> Right in the neck! There!

It must have been hilarious for the Americans to hear the clipped, plumby tones of the English upper classes trying to repeat this less-than-subtle refrain. The Lords were probably invited to master even more nonsensical college yells – and there were plenty – as the champagne flowed. They accepted the challenge and enjoyed it. Slater and the boys appreciated this willingness to open their minds to an entirely different culture. Thanks to their efforts, the Americans were feeling right at home. When Jack Patrick, a star US player, later talked about these experiences, he 'paid great tribute to the British sportsmen, and told how well they were treated in Great Britain…'.

So the 'special relationship' between the British and Americans was never stronger than in Piccadilly in late April back in 1924. The evening had been so enjoyable that another event was hastily arranged for the following day, so that the tourists could see the best of all things British on show that weekend. The official BOA account confirmed: 'Arrangements were also made for the Americans to visit the Empire Exhibition on the only day they had available before leaving for Pairs, viz. Sunday. Although the Exhibition was closed to the general public, the authorities kindly consented to permit the Americans to enter and to view the buildings, etc.'

Amid all the hospitality, it was easy to forget just how much was still wrong with this US squad. Babe privately blamed British referees for the defeats in England. He therefore seemed to be in denial over the failure of the American team to fully grasp and then stick to the rules of rugby as played in Europe. Meanwhile one of his most senior players, Rudy Scholz, had lost all enthusiasm for this Olympic adventure. He didn't even want to play in such a disorganised side, because he considered it to be so lacking in team spirit.

Time was perilously short before the biggest test of all, those games in Paris. For all their kind words and good intentions, the British were not entirely confident that their American guests would actually win the Olympic rugby tournament. If the Americans could land a humiliating blow to French pride at the start of their Olympics, England would of course be delighted. But could Babe Slater and Rudy Scholz reunite and turn American fortunes around? It seemed unlikely.

A complex dynamic existed between Babe and Rudy, who were both strong characters and natural leaders. Only one man could be captain; and in 1924 it was Babe. Yet Rudy probably thought he should have been captain, because he had worked so hard to make the Olympic trip a reality through his tireless administrative and fundraising work. Something else may have made Rudy's lack of authority harder for him to take, given that Babe had been elected team leader. Babe had lived one of Rudy's dreams already – he had been to war and he had come home a hero in the eyes of many.

Rudy loved the military. He would spend a lifetime loving the military. Yet it was Babe who had been shipped off to war; Babe who had acquired 'veteran' status; Babe who was still taking centre-stage even now. If envy was creeping into the equation, you could almost understand it. However, had Scholz been able to read Slater's war diary, he may not have felt so sore at being stranded elsewhere while Babe began his march into hell on earth.

chapter 2

From Earthquake
To War

Anyone born in the San Francisco Bay area, as the 19th century prepared to make way for the 20th, was likely to be touched by disaster at a tender age. So it was for Babe Slater, born 30 April, 1896, though life was idyllic enough during his earliest years. The youngest of four siblings in Berkeley, California, Babe was never going to settle for being the runt of the family. He began growing right away, and wouldn't stop until he reached 6ft 3in (1.9m) and weighed 220lb (100kg). The long journey to adulthood would be full of emotional challenges; and it wasn't hard to see where his resilient nature might have come from.

Babe's father, Captain John Slater, worked for a steamship company called Boudrow and Mighell. He did well enough to own two houses in Berkeley – one at 1335 Shattuck Avenue and the other at 1426 Spruce Street. Life with his wife Louise and four children, Marguerite, James, Norman and Colby – or 'Babe' as he became known – was comfortable and happy at the big house in Shattuck Avenue. While John was away at sea, Louise, a talented artist, would turn her hand to wood carvings and painting. Unfortunately, the rhythm of life in and around San Francisco was about to be rocked by one of the great natural disasters of all time, and the Slater household would never be quite the same afterwards.

At 5.12am on Wednesday, 18 April 1906, a massive earthquake ripped San Francisco apart, and 80 per cent of the city was destroyed in the subsequent fires. Babe's nephew, Norman Slater, was told by his own father, Norman senior, what it was like for the children across the bay in Berkeley. He said in 2007: 'They saw smoke for several days, even a week I think, coming over to Berkeley from San Francisco. They didn't go over there, but my father was very conscious of what had happened in San Francisco, and he was upset over it. Babe was ten years old, and at that age he would also have been cognizant of the disaster unfolding over the water.'

Newspaper reports of 375 deaths, and the reaction they must have generated among adults who already knew something terrible had happened, told the children that they were close to a truly dreadful event. In fact the death toll had been played down, and modern estimates put the figure at closer to three thousand, on a par with the 9/11 terrorist attack of 2001.

Furthermore, between 225,000 and 300,000 of San Francisco's population of 410,000 were left homeless. Half of these evacuees fled across the bay to Oakland and Berkeley. Norman Slater revealed in 2007: 'Babe's mother and father took in refugees from the San Francisco fire. Their house in Shattuck Avenue still stands today, it is quite large; and so Babe, my father and the rest of the children suddenly had new people living with them in the house. My maternal grandparents took in an opera singer and a music-writer, as I recall. Everyone who had some room took people in at that time.'

Refugee camps were set up in locations like Golden Gate Park, and some of them were still in operation two years later, in 1908. That was the year that Babe's father, Captain John Slater, died.

Suddenly Babe's childhood became more complicated. Apart from the obvious grief that a 12-year-old would feel at the loss of his father at such a sensitive age, there were other changes that must have been tough to bear. Without him, Captain Slater's family fell upon hard times, and the children must have had to grow up quickly from that point onwards. Still, whenever life offered sink-or-swim choices to Babe Slater, he swam.

Even as early as 1910, just two years after his father's passing, and when Babe was aged no more than 14, there was something supremely confident about the way in which he posed for a sports photograph with his brother Norman and three friends. No one would have guessed what troubled times he had already been through. Neither could anyone have foreseen that, by the time Babe doubled his age, the same two brothers would be lining up for another group photograph – on their way to the Olympics in Paris.

Back in 1910 Babe didn't have the muscles which made his arms and legs such formidable sporting weapons in later years. Those muscles were already visible in his elder brother Norman's sturdy limbs, and few doubted that Babe would quickly catch up.

Emotionally the future seemed less certain, and there had been fresh developments to deal with at home. Louise Slater had remarried, though it appears that any happiness with her second husband, Edward Phillips, was short-lived. Norman Slater commented in 2007, 'Having a substitute father would have been difficult for everyone, but they just got on with it. I never heard Babe being critical of that gentleman or praising him either.' Within two years, however, fresh tragedy had struck because Babe's stepfather killed himself. Aside from the huge trauma that such a dreadful event must have brought to the family, there were ominous financial realities to face too. Babe's mother was forced to sell the big family home in Shattuck Avenue, which had been so welcoming to strangers after the great fires. Now other strangers had taken over that family space for good, while Babe's grandparents were living in the Spruce Street property. Louise therefore moved her children into far more modest accommodation at 2317 Haste Street.

If Babe Slater felt any frustrations at the way his family life had taken such a sad downward turn, he had the perfect outlet for them – the rugby field. By the time he was 15, Babe had joined his brother Norman in their first great sporting double act. They set Californian rugby alight by inspiring Berkeley High School to the county, regional and state rugby titles in 1911 and 1912. But the Slaters weren't at the top of the rugby food chain yet, and they would have realised just how far they had to go in the second of those years. For in 1912 a touring team from

Australia, the 'Waratahs' of New South Wales, produced such a dazzling display of running rugby that they couldn't help but capture the imagination of every young player in the State of California. One of their players, Danny Carroll, had won Olympic rugby gold with Australia at the London Games of 1908. In 1920 he would become one of Babe and Rudy's teammates at the 1920 Olympics in Antwerp.

Rugby was a sport which allowed the Slaters to make full use of their brawn; but great players, they realised, needed speed and guile too. Babe was further inspired when he witnessed part of a tour to California by the magnificent New Zealand side of 1913. The best team in the world, they played in black and terrorised opponents with their running power and steely aggression. The 'All Blacks', as they were known, also had a crowd-pleasing pre-match routine, one which was guaranteed to thrill any rugby-loving adolescent. They performed the 'Haka', a fearsome war-dance learned from the Maori tribesmen who first ruled New Zealand. It was designed to strike fear into the hearts of opponents; and it worked.

The All Blacks romped through California unbeaten, and showed their American hosts the way the game should really be played. The Olympic Club of San Francisco put up the most respectable fight on 4 October 1913, at Saint Ignatius Field. They only lost 19-0. That defeat became more admirable when the All Blacks beat the strongest combined team their Bay Area hosts could muster – 'All California' – by 51-3 at Berkeley. Though the game wasn't an official international it is sometimes described that way. The 'All California' team actually featured Danny Carroll from the previous year's Waratahs of Australia. Carroll had fallen in love with California and since made his home there. Without his fellow Australians by his side, Carroll could make little impact on those awesome All Blacks though. These New Zealanders were the superstars of the world game. Their level of performance was something to which Babe Slater could aspire. Trying to be like the All Blacks would soon turn Babe into a great player too.

For all that, Slater had developed another passion, beyond the spectacular world of sport; and that passion would determine his next move. 'He was a born farmer,' said nephew Norman, 'even if he was raised in Berkeley.' Such was his enthusiasm for all things agricultural that he didn't even wait to finish high school before enrolling in Davis, or University Farm School as it was known at the time. Davis was an hour or two inland from fast-moving San Francisco and it belonged to another world. As a branch of the University of California's College of Agriculture, it offered a three-year course in all the principles and practices of farming – and Babe couldn't wait. He didn't want to be a city slicker; the slower-paced life of a country boy would do him just fine.

There can be little doubt that he intended to play a good deal more rugby throughout his academic career at Davis. But in 1915 the university dropped rugby as its flagship sport and reinstated American football instead. Undaunted, Babe turned up to try-out for Gridiron. Only 17 others joined him from a student body of 296. Coach Robert E. Harmon spotted Slater's talent immediately and built the team around him. That faith was soon justified, and Davis fans who paid 25 cents to see something special in the university's first match were richly rewarded. Even though 'the Farms' narrowly lost that first clash to the more experienced Saint Mary's team, there was only one star of the show. Slater's running power and tactical punting were deeply impressive. Davis were denied by a score in the final quarter, but Babe had made a lasting impact.

Slater didn't restrict himself to American football. He starred in baseball, playing left field; and he stunned the crowd with a memorable moment in a 3-2 win over the University of California – better known as 'Cal'. Babe made what was described as 'a diving shoe-string catch with the bases occupied', to seal his team's triumph.

He was also inspirational as captain of the 1915–16 basketball team. His play was described as 'indomitable' and 'splendid' – and not without reason. In one match alone he notched up a personal tally of 21 points and 'left his small defenders running in circles'. In another game, against Reno YMCA, he landed two audacious baskets from the centre of the floor, and finished with a decisive 13 points in the hard-fought 23-21 victory.

For all that, it was American football that drew the biggest crowds, and 1916 marked the sporting peak of Babe's collegiate life. He took centre stage for American football's 'Big Game' on Thanksgiving Day, between the University Farm School of Davis and their rivals 'Cal' (University of California, Berkeley).

Hundreds of Davis supporters took a train to Berkeley for what promised to be an epic showdown between the two emerging giants of the sport – Babe Slater and Cal's 'Crip' Toomey. Babe was already ahead in the personal duel, because during the first match in Davis he had eclipsed Toomey's two field goals with a touchdown pass of 35 yards (32m), the first recorded 'long pass' in the history of the game. He had followed up with the winning drop-kick from 35 yards to earn UF a famous 10-7 victory that afternoon.

On Thanksgiving Day, however, Toomey took his revenge, his second-half field goal proving decisive. Babe's talent still shone brightest though, and he dazzled both sets of supporters in a huge crowd with his storming runs, long forward passes and telling punts. Slater was described by one writer as 'a whirlwind going through Texas', though he would probably have swapped such plaudits for a win. Still, with 40 points and six touchdowns in a near-perfect season, defeat wasn't a feeling with which Babe ever became too familiar. And in one memorable match, a 24-6 rout of Nevada, he dived over for a touchdown after just two minutes. Not content with that, he ran 62 yards (59m) for an amazing interception score to take 'the Farms' out of reach.

Despite his athletic prowess, Babe was quiet and unassuming, and that just made him even more popular with his peers and teachers alike. Whatever position of leadership and responsibility they could give him, they did. So he became Junior Class President, House Manager for the Agricultural Fraternity of Calpha, and Thanksgiving Day Special Chairman. He took on responsibilities for Picnic Day, a hugely important event in the University Farm calendar, which was comprised of a top livestock parade, sports tournaments and many other peripheral activities. It was the chance for the university students to show the surrounding community what they could achieve; and it wasn't a day to be trusted to anyone who lacked organisational ability. In 1916 Slater was appointed Picnic Day Parade Chairman, and the following year he became General Parade Chairman. That said everything about the high esteem in which he was held in this specialised community.

Given the dark drama of world events in 1917, there was something deliciously idyllic, charming and even naive about some of the events that Slater and his colleagues helped to put on for the '9th Annual

University Farm Picnic Day' on 28 April that year. Several hours before the big baseball showdown between Stanford Varsity and University Farm, for example, the Athletic Field at Davis was treated to events such as the '35-yard Dash, Girls, (8 years and under)' and the 'Three-Legged Race – Open to any couple'. Elsewhere there was an 'Ice Cream, Cheddar Cheese and Jack Cheese making' demonstration by a certain Professor Baird. Wisely, Babe had realised that the day was not just about the athletic elite, but also about families. He cut his cloth accordingly, and he didn't disappoint.

Perfect days, however, would soon be in short supply. The previous month German submarines had sunk three American ships in the Atlantic. It was an act of provocation after the US had repeatedly warned the Germans against using their U-Boats to attack passenger and freight-carrying vessels. On 6 April America had declared war on Germany, with President Woodrow Wilson describing this grave measure as 'an act of principle and idealism'. He told Congress that 'the world must be made safe for democracy.'

Even as he graduated from University Farm School on 18 May, at the end of his three-year course in agriculture, Babe Slater must have known that his life was about to change. He and his contemporaries had been awarded non-degree certificates and were urged to serve their country at the earliest possible opportunity.

That same month the United States House and Senate had passed a selective service bill in order to recruit a large army. The obligation to serve was spread among all qualified men aged 21 to 30. Babe had turned 21 on 30 April, and wasn't about to shirk his duty. 'Not many men want to go to war', said Babe's nephew Norman Slater in 2007. 'But patriotism just takes over I guess, and that is how it was for Babe.' By early June over nine million men, including Slater, had registered for the draft.

The British had been fighting the Germans since 1914; casualties had been horrific and had run into millions. Between July and November of 1917, as heavy rain turned the trenches into a deathly quagmire, British forces conducted a new offensive. It was mounted against German lines near Ypres in Belgium, where there was mass-slaughter at the Battle of Passchendaele. On 23 September, while the violence continued in Northern Europe, Colby Slater officially joined the United States Army. Given the positions of authority Babe had already held, it was no great surprise when he was promoted to Corporal on 1 November. By May 1918, he had been put in charge of 42 Yolo County recruits, known as the 'Liberty Boys'. They were assigned to Camp Lewis, American Lake, Washington, for the sort of intensive training that might later save their lives in war.

Despite his determination to fight on the Anglo-American side in the First World War, Rudy Scholz was actually German by blood. His father, also named Rudolph, came from Bavaria, a part of Germany known for the appealing nature of its people. With its beautiful woods and spectacular mountains, Bavaria was the jewel of southern Germany, and its inhabitants were widely considered to be warmer and more relaxed than some of their compatriots. Though more than capable of tapping into the legendary German capacity for discipline when necessary, the Bavarian German also knows how to live life to the full. So when Rudy junior was taken there as a six-year-old, he was made welcome by the local people. He adapted easily to his new life, and he picked up the language too.

His father's motivation for taking his family to Europe for a year was touching. It seems that the driving force for leaving America, albeit temporarily, was Rudolph senior's love for his wife, Catherine Bayer. Another German by blood, Catherine had met and married Rudolph in the very American setting of Chicago. Like any good husband, he wanted to help her develop her own considerable talents, in music, to the full. But Rudolph was prepared to go much further than most husbands to ensure that this happened. To please his wife, he was willing to leave plenty of success behind him too.

Rudolph had been a baker in Kewanee, Illinois for six years, and it was there that Rudy was born on June 17, 1896. His father did so well he could afford to build new premises for his business on Second Street. While he supervised an army of bakers downstairs, the smart new brick building offered room upstairs for a music conservatory. Rudolph was working so hard for a reason, it emerged. In an impossibly romantic gesture, he sold his business to fund his wife's artistic dream. The local Kewanee newspaper reported how the

Scholz family would 'leave for Europe, where Mrs Scholz will enter one of the leading conservatories for a year's study in music. Later, they will return to America and purchase an orange grove in Southern California.'

It sounded so perfect. Sure enough, Rudolph, Catherine and their sons Harry and Rudy stayed in Germany the full year as planned. Catherine lived her musical dream for those 12 months, and then prepared to cross the Atlantic once more.

On their return to the United States, the Scholz family headed out west towards California. Then, in a move which reflected the exciting, adventurous times they lived in, they suddenly changed their plans along the way. Rudolph heard about silver mines in Idaho, and took his family off the train at Nampa instead. He intended to cash in on the silver boom by working as a baker while investing in a mine. But this time his appetite for adventure backfired on him. Rudolph invested too much money in the mine without seeing sufficiently swift returns.

Pretty soon he had to send for his stepbrother, Raimond Helmstetter, to come over from Europe and bail him out of trouble. Together they established the Nampa Bakery, and might even have stayed there had their story not taken a tragic turn. Just a day after Rudolph went to work at a silver mine in Thunder Mountain, leaving the bakery in the capable hands of Catherine and Raimond, disaster struck. Helmstetter was laid low by typhoid fever; and although his condition wasn't initially regarded as life-threatening, he deteriorated rapidly. The unfortunate German died in the Catholic Hospital in Boise two weeks later. It must have been a shocking moment for a young Rudy. Like Babe Slater, he had learned some of life's harshest realities at a tender age. After mourning their loss, the family felt that a change of scenery would best help those who had suffered and survived the tragedy. So they headed on west as originally intended.

By 1909 Rudolph Scholz had moved his family to Medford in Oregon, where an order of German Benedictine priests ran the Mount Angel Academy. A 13-year-old Rudy Scholz was enrolled and fitted in just fine. He excelled at sports, as he had done from the moment he could run, but that was only half the reason for his happiness. Instead of rebelling against it, as many teenagers do, he enjoyed the strict discipline that underpinned the Mount Angel regime. The atmosphere never became oppressive enough to dent his confidence or hinder his ability to express himself. To Rudy the rules, designed to eradicate selfish behaviour, were helpful and sensible. As a result of his mature approach to the regime, he positively thrived.

The German priests gave him a solid grounding before his next move, to Columbia Prep – the University of Portland's predecessor. Again he quickly proved himself to be talented at just about every sport he tried – baseball in particular. His brilliance gave him the chance to gain a Baseball Scholarship to a seat of learning that would always remain close to his heart. In August 1913 he enrolled at the oldest college in California – Santa Clara. To be more precise, he enrolled as a senior in the Jesuit high school programme that was situated on the same campus as the college in those years.

Founded in 1851, Santa Clara was an inspirational sight from the moment any new student came up the elegant driveway and first laid his eyes on its solid, sandy-coloured church and tall, welcoming palm trees. It was run by Jesuit priests, men who loved God first and then the sport of rugby. It wasn't such a strange combination. Rugby was considered to be character-building; a tough game that taught a boy how to persevere in the midst of suffering, without actually killing him before such an important lesson was learned.

Eighteen tragic deaths from injuries sustained during American football matches had prompted President Theodore 'Teddy' Roosevelt to threaten to ban the rival Gridiron game completely in the first decade of the 20th century. Between 1906 and 1917 the authorities in California and Nevada quietly ensured that American football teams were either disbanded or severely limited as competitive forces. Rugby was played instead, and Rudy Scholz took to that sport just as easily as he had adapted to any other ball game.

Rudy began to learn rugby in the second or third week of September 1913. He showed promise and was destined to make the Santa Clara Varsity Rugby Team while still a high school student. Incredibly, however, there was a far greater challenge on the near horizon. Within six weeks of first picking up a rugby ball, Rudy played against the greatest team in the world – the New Zealand All Blacks. Santa Clara's college boys took on the iron men of New Zealand twice – on 22 October and 12 November. Unsurprisingly they lost both games, by scores of 0-42 and 0-33. Unusually for the time, substitutes were allowed in these games. Rudy, a substitute scrum-half, sprang off the bench to play the second halves of both these matches when the going got tough for his team. Though he couldn't turn the tide, he did sample the All Black magic and witnessed close up the pulsating brilliance of a team in perfect harmony. Babe Slater may even have been watching from the sidelines as the students were taught a harsh lesson by the masters of the game.

Rudy retained a healthy respect for the All Blacks for the rest of his life, and even in 1942, when asked to name the greatest players he had ever seen, he said, '…there was Roberts of New Zealand, a center three, and was he a slicker at the game! You also have to go for Jim Wylie, now coaching at Stanford.' Wylie played in that 1913 All Blacks team and loved California so much that he too decided to stay there, just as the Australian, Carroll, had done the year before.

The locals loved the Antipodeans and saw them as sporting gods. However the All Blacks tour, in particular, didn't do much for Californian rugby's self-confidence, or instill a widespread belief that men from the West Coast could one day become world-beaters. Some said rugby in America never quite recovered from the drubbings handed out by the All Blacks that year. Others maintained that it all depended on how you looked at the defeats. Sure, they represented a reality check – and you could almost understand the pessimism of some doom merchants – but more resilient characters knew that the New Zealanders, and before them the Australians, had provided priceless experience for those who were willing to swallow their pride and seek sporting greatness themselves in the fullness of time.

Rudy and his teammates certainly had no reason to feel ashamed of the Santa Clara score-lines because they were quite normal in the context of the tour. That 1913 All Blacks team played 13 games on the West Coast, including two with Stanford, three with the University of California and two with Santa Clara. 'Cal' was one of only two teams to score against the All Blacks, losing 3-38 in one of their games. The other was the 'All-America XV' in that 3-51 defeat at Berkeley in the 'unofficial international'.

These scores were consolations. After playing three games in Canada, the All Blacks returned home to New Zealand with a record of played

16, won 16, points scored 610, points conceded 6. Perhaps the most startling aspect of the entire tour, looking back, is that a 17-year-old American with virtually no rugby experience whatsoever did battle with the mighty New Zealand. What happened may even be unique in the history of the game. There could have been no more vivid an illustration of Rudy's aptitude for rugby than for him to have played as a rookie against one of the greatest sides in the history of the sport.

For those who responded positively to heavy defeat and were determined to improve, the lessons handed out by the Australians and New Zealanders in 1912 and 1913 were learned so thoroughly that they lasted a lifetime. Scholz certainly wasn't ready to throw the towel in. More than 30 years later, Rudy would still be playing rugby with the same passion.

This long-term love affair with rugby did not exclude other sports, especially when Rudy was young. Those wishing to take advantage of his genius for baseball, for example, didn't give up easily. A Western Union telegram from a gentleman by the name of Joe Maher on 13 August 1914, asked 'R Schulz, Sisson, California', quite bluntly: 'Would you consider going to St Marys if better terms are offered you?'

The message was clear. Scholz was already being tempted with the sort of incentives enjoyed by semi-professional baseball players, if only he would just agree to attend a rival seat of learning. He chose not to do so and continued to hone his baseball skills by representing Santa Clara instead. In fact Rudy was so good that he once helped his team beat a visiting side from the famous Chicago Whitesocks. But baseball never seduced Rudy quite like rugby did.

By 1915 Scholz was captain of the Santa Clara rugby team too. He learned how to play in a variety of positions on the field, including the one he had adopted as a rookie against New Zealand – 'scrum-half' or 'half-back'. This pivotal player links the two elements of any rugby side: the brawny forwards, who are the team's tough guys and spend most of their time fighting for the ball; and the backs or 'three-quarters', who are usually the more graceful movers and are generally quicker. The job of the backs is to conjure enough magic to wrong-foot the opposing defence. In that way, they cut through the gaps they have created, and score most of the tries. Usually the objective is to pass the ball out to the 'wingers', the glory boys and fastest men of all, who are waiting out wide to dash over the try-line (rugby's equivalent to the end-zone) to score.

Traditionally, forwards think that the backs or 'three-quarters' in their team are soft prima donnas. Backs, meanwhile, like to think that forwards have fewer brain cells and less skill. Somehow the scrum-half, usually the smallest guy on the team, has to keep the peace and encourage unity and continuity among the 15 players. Scholz handled the diplomatic role well, but he was also fast enough to play on the wing.

When a 20-year-old Rudy Scholz enjoyed one of the highlights of his collegiate career – the 'Big Game' of 1916 between Santa Clara and Stanford – he was on the right wing. Charlie Austin, a Stanford graduate who had played against the All Blacks in 1913, had been brought over to train Santa Clara that year. It proved a wise piece of poaching. Already developing dark bags under his eyes and losing his hair, Austin was a deep thinker about sport, and demanded similar intensity from his charges. They responded well and Rudy Scholz – at a mere 145lb (65kg) – learned to punch above his weight. Against all expectations, little Scholz led his Santa Clara team to a thumping 28-5 victory over a Stanford side previously regarded as unbeatable. John O'Neill, who would play on the 1920 and 1924 Olympic teams, also starred in that Santa Clara line-up, as did the Muldoon brothers, John and William, who would be future Olympian 'ruggers' and the victims of many a Scholz practical joke.

The resounding defeat of Stanford rounded off a perfect Santa Clara season of ten victories and no defeats. At the same time it ruined their opponent's previously unblemished record, which made the 'Big Game' win all the more satisfying. Coach Austin's ability to master-mind such an upset, together with his obvious links to both colleges, would be remembered in 1924, when the US team was looking for an Olympic coach.

In 1917, however, Rudy's thoughts found a new focus. He began to turn his attentions away from sport towards the war in Europe. Despite the ongoing horrors in the trenches of northern France and Belgium, where millions of young men were still losing their lives, there was no end to the war in sight. It was becoming increasingly probable that the USA would enter that war, as her ships continued to suffer at the hands of German U-boats. Rudy Scholz was determined to play his part if he got the chance.

Military life, with its discipline and rigorous physical demands, had always appealed to Rudy; and he possessed the courage and confidence to want to test himself in the most hostile environment. Rudy's German heritage doesn't seem to have complicated the situation for him one bit. If he ended up having to fight and kill distant relations, that was too bad. It was a risk he was willing to take in order to serve his own country – the USA. This was war; there was no room for doubt.

First Scholz became student Major of the Reserve Officers Training Corps at Santa Clara. As usual, he soon set his sights ever higher – and tried to land a place at America's elite military academy – West Point. A family contact in Washington DC called Chas L. McNary advised Rudy on how he could take the official route towards West Point. He sent a telegram on 16 February 1917, which read:

'Rudolph Scholz Medford Oregon

Competitive examination applicants for West Point to be held Feb 23 at Post Office Medford 9AM wish you success.'

But even if he passed the exam, Scholz knew the West Point application system could take years. By the time he graduated the war might be over.

In April 1917 the USA entered that war as expected. Men were being readied for action and Rudy didn't want to miss out on the call to arms. If strings could possibly be pulled to fast-track Scholz into military service, he didn't see anything wrong with pulling them. On Rudy's behalf, therefore, a family friend named J. E. Barkdull of Medford, Oregon, tried to harness the support of an Oregon Senator called George E. Chamberlain, who just happened to be Chairman of the Committee on Military Affairs. Barkdull wanted Scholz pushed to the front of the military queue, and seemed to think that Chamberlain would oblige on the basis of another case in which the senator had apparently intervened.

The letter that came back, dated 18 June 1917, was polite but firm. '…In reply permit me to say that the Oregon boy who has just entered the Military Academy was appointed by me last year, but had to wait for the proper time to arrive for his entrance. He secured the nomination as the result of an open examination held at Portland. Unless the two boys now there whom I appointed fail to pass their annual examinations it will be 1919 before I have a vacancy to fill, but you may rest assured that if your young friend Rudy Scholz does not secure a nomination before that time I will do my best for him directly an opportunity occurs…'.

Scholz realised that 1919 might be too late for him to fulfil his military ambition. He was now involved in a race against time. On 8 January 1918, US President Woodrow Wilson set forth his historic 'Fourteen Points', a road map to peace whereby the warring European nations might live peacefully together in future. Wilson's speech was not warmly received in Europe, since the various powers had not been consulted. Even so, it seemed that the countdown to peace had begun.

Rudy achieved a breakthrough of sorts in the early summer of 1918, when his persistence finally won him a prized military move eastwards, one he saw as the springboard to Europe and the war. An Oregon newspaper got hold of the story, probably with the help of Rudy's adoring mother.

The headline read: 'HIGH PRAISE FOR MEDFORD BOY.' The story began:

> Mrs R. S. Scholz, 801 North Central, mother of Rudolph Scholz, received the following letter recently from Joseph A. Sullivan, vice-president and prefect of discipline, Reserve Officers Training Corps, Santa Clara, California:
>
> 'Dear Mrs Scholtz: I know that you will be glad to hear of Rudy. Our dear boy is now safely landed in Camp Fremont to win for himself and you a commission in the army. Yesterday he and twenty companions journeyed with me to the camp. At six o'clock we had solemn high mass for them, at which they and the entire student body received holy communion. Immediately after breakfast, the whole battalion…accompanied our boys to the station. What a sight! There was scarcely a dry eye amid that entire crowd.
>
> 'I myself never felt more proud, more gratified in all my life. Dear little Rudy is a gem. In every department of activity here at Santa Clara he excelled. But in all, he manifested a rare manhood, a sincerity, a wonderful spirit of loyalty and fidelity. This is what made him so deeply loved by us all. Your good boy had only one regret on leaving and that was that he didn't have an opportunity

to see you before he left. And this is the reason that Rudy was such a grand success – he loved his mother and never forgot the lessons she so carefully taught him. That he should always remain just Rudy and be your everlasting joy is the fervent wish of Your devoted friend,
FR SULLIVAN,
Vice-Pres and Prefect of Discipline,
ROTC
May 16, 1918.'

It was high praise indeed, though the 'herogram' might have earned Rudy some severe kidding from friends who read the paper and perhaps failed to see how a spoilt 'teacher's pet' with a doting mother was going to cut it in the tough world of the military. Rudy was to prove them wrong. 'He probably was spoiled,' admitted his son Dave much later, 'but he had more than enough positive qualities to outweigh that, and he loved the discipline of the army.'

Rudy knew that he had faults like everyone else. But he kept any faults well hidden, for in that year of 1918 he had been awarded Santa Clara's Senior Nobili Medal (so-called because the first President of Santa Clara College was named Father Jon Nobili). It was given 'To the Student who shall be deemed First in Morals, Obedience and Application to Study.'

None of this guaranteed Rudy's passage across the pond to the European theatre of war, however. He was stuck in Norfolk, Virginia, still on the conveyor belt which prepared American troops for shipment across the Atlantic.

At least Rudy – by now Lieutenant Scholz – had kept himself fit as he waited his turn to go to war. He had excelled in a variety of sports and had become Athletic Director of the First Battalion of the Twelfth Infantry at the Army Supply Base in Norfolk. And he received a glowing letter from J. Stanley Hoyt, Athletic Director for the War Camp Community Service, about his ability as a basketball player and manager.

It began: 'Dear Mr Scholz: I wish to commend you and your basketball team for the splendid performance at our Red Circle theater March 13th and 14th, contesting the championship basketball title of the service league, of which the St Helena team were declared winners. The work and spirit of the Army team in this tournament stood out as a feature, and too much praise cannot be given you as manager of the team, and the boys who played with you…'.

This letter provided early evidence of Rudy's ability as a sporting leader, and went some small way to explaining the hurt he would feel later, whenever those leadership qualities were overlooked. But for now Scholz just wanted the chance to show what he could do for his country in the trenches and beyond. All the sports commendations in the world were not going to ease his only fear – that of missing the boat to war.

Babe Slater was about to see that war in all its gory detail. Strangely, however, given that Babe was a naturally combative sportsman, he was assigned to the Medical Corps and trained for ambulance driver duties on the front line. 'I don't know why that was, but his strength would certainly have helped him to carry the wounded on his back when he needed to,' observed his nephew Norman later.

Babe would soon find out – if he didn't know it already – that the role of medic in the midst of the carnage would also prove to be extremely dangerous. It was never going to lead anywhere but right to the epicentre of the fighting in northern Europe. But Babe's job would be to help save lives instead of taking them. Not that the shells and bullets would make any distinction as they sought out their victims. It would take a brave man to focus on his duty as he dodged them.

Rudy Scholz would have suffered almost any hardship in order to get himself onto a ship and sail to the place where the bullets were flying. But the reality of reaching the ships to go to war wasn't much fun, never mind the ordeal that waited at the other end of the voyage. Babe Slater described the final stage of his coast-to-coast journey – across New York to his designated pier – in his diary, as the troops '…had to leave our packs on our backs – 2 hrs and never spent a more miserable period in my life.'

Scholz would still have been an envious man had he been forced to watch Slater's company set sail on 12 July 1918, aboard a ship called the *SS Olympic* – an interesting name given the way Babe's life would play out at the start of the next decade. Yet the cramped, dehumanising conditions on the *SS Olympic* were hardly enviable. Slater wrote: 'The men were forced to sleep in the dirtiest holes of the ship where a rat couldn't live.... The men are herded around by sentries and officers and the way they bathe with a big hose reminds me of a herd of hogs. . . .

'The crew and the soldiers do not get along very well – the crew are these English cockneys and they are cocky – they talk against the US and on several occasions so far the soldiers have layed out 4 or 5 of them for saying too much...'.

Slater might have allowed himself to think that the worst was over, at least temporarily, when they docked in Southampton, England, on 20 July, though deep down he probably knew that the worst had not even begun. Babe and his 'Liberty Boys' were sent straight across the English Channel to Cherbourg, where they were allowed to rest for five days. Nothing was very comforting about the cuisine though. He wrote: 'The grub here sure is the bunk – same thing every meal – hard tack-cold stew. Sanitation is never considered and we are just crowded in...'.

Life didn't get much better for the rest of July and August, when Babe was based in St Nazaire and Nogent in France. But at least he wasn't fearful for his life yet.

By September, however, all that had changed. Slater could hear and even see the enemy, though at least the Germans appeared to be getting the worst of it at that stage. In one diary entry he wrote: 'While we were waiting for orders in the evening we saw a German plane being fired on – shrapnel all around him but he escaped out of range and was attacked by our own plane who swooped down on him and kept his machine guns going but no hit – he finally left and each returned to their own lines.'

Babe was to feel little sympathy for the Germans after he discovered how they had forced Belgian citizens from their homes. He wrote: 'They killed lots of civilians for refusing to go. The people stayed in their homes during all the fighting and only evacuated when the Huns started to shell with gas. The Bosche do bombing every night but don't do much damage to the towns' houses.'

Babe's nephew Norman insisted later, 'Nothing could ever change him as a person, he wouldn't let it. Whatever he went through, he just wasn't the type to let anything affect him too deeply for very long, even if he was seeing a lot of terrible things, as was part of his job as an army ambulance driver.'

He certainly seemed to be clinging to normal thoughts and feelings to help him through the ordeal. So with his very next words in that 1918 war diary, Babe returned to his first love: 'This country is sure wonderful for farming – all flat as can be, maybe with a small hill here and there, and numerous Dutch windmills dot the landscape.'

This focus on positive images was a basic technique for self-preservation. Some men found it impossible to stay in touch with their former selves during World War One, and suffered terrible psychological consequences. Others like Babe somehow managed to retain an inner balance by staying true to their natural likes and dislikes, whatever else life threw at them.

Norman Slater added: 'Long after he came back he used to say what wonderful sheep they had over there, though he knew they wouldn't have survived in our climate.' It was almost as though Babe was shutting out the horrors of the front, even later in life.

But in September 1918, he confronted them head on by writing about them in his diary.

The Meuse-Argonne offensive had the Germans on the run that month at long last. In many ways, however, the instability spelt a new level of danger for Babe and his colleagues. For it was their job to follow the chaotic battles, and evacuate wounded soldiers from the killing zones into the comparative safety of the field hospitals.

Babe wrote: 'The big drive opened Sept 26th early in the A.M. That night we went about 3km [1 ¾ miles] the other side of Avocourt – the first town taken from the Germans – and the roads were a terrible mess – all shell holes and no bridges. Caught up all night in the traffic with wounded men and got to the hospital around 9am…'.

It isn't hard to imagine the anguish Babe must have felt. The sounds of suffering men would have filled his ears, yet he remained powerless to deliver them to doctors swiftly. But Slater's very worst First World War experiences were still to come. He went on:

> …That night went up to the sector near Epionville – slept in the office dugout on the floor. Next day we evacuated from the dressing stations near the support trench to the field hospital. Had to go over about three kilometers of country road and it sure was a rough one – coming back was good and smooth. After a

couple of days there the Deutsch started bombarding the place and kept it up nearly all night, but not many came close, only a few that wounded several men…all next day they kept it up. We stayed six nights at Epionville and the last two nights were sure terrible for shell fire and aeroplanes. The Bosche…bombed and shot from the planes and killed lots of men and wounded a bunch and killed several horses. One plane was shot down by our plane about 3am. October 4th we evacuated Epionville after a heavy barrage that was sure hell…'.

Those final 48 hours at Epionville could easily have been Babe Slater's last on earth. It is difficult to see how the images of mutilated men and animals could ever have left him entirely. No wonder he sounded keen to remind himself that normality still existed somewhere. Ironically, given what he would experience in the same city six years later, Babe seems to have found a train journey through some of the less picturesque parts of Paris strangely reassuring. Later in October he wrote: 'We arrived in the suburbs of Paris about 11am. The effects of the war are very little shown here. The train switched north about three kilometers from the center of Paris – on the north rail road here. We saw considerable of the business district – large buildings of five or six storeys… . The industrial section was the largest of any – many large factories…'.

He was destined for Amiens, 75 miles (120km) north of Paris. A battle had been raging just to the east of Amiens for most of the year, initially with significant gains for the Germans. August, however, had brought a big Allied advance and many Germans had surrendered. Though there was plenty of evidence that heavy fighting had taken place, Slater's journey soon became a source of some much-needed comfort. At first Babe scribbled: '…Near Amiens great trench systems cover the hills and the fields are shot full of holes. Below this point we passed some wonderful agricultural country – well-cultivated fields and everything pointing to prosperity – the scenery of the hills and valleys was more than gorgeous…'.

You could understand why he wanted to write about that picturesque scene while he could. A couple of pages later he told his diary about his latest surroundings, and a bridge with far more sombre associations.

Slater wrote: '…only a short way from here the Canadians and British buried 250,000 men and officers killed by the new German gas…'.

On 25 October 1918, while marching from Ypres to Roulers, Babe could see '…nothing but devastated country – worse than the imagination could ever stretch it – for miles and miles all that could be seen was torn-up ground that resembled a choppy sea with great tanglements of barbed wire and railroad tracks.'

Near a Belgian town called Oudenaarde on 3 November came Babe's most heroic moment, and perhaps his closest brush with death. Ironically, it came just days before the end of the war and Babe could easily have become one of the last Americans to die. He volunteered, with a colleague called Jim Gregory, to go into the town to find out whether the dressing station there was still intact. They effectively had to run the gauntlet of German fire down to a river. On their way the shelling began. Babe said he could also see 'a Bosche plane swooping down and firing' on troops 'who were evacuating across the fields'. He added, 'We could see the [German] shells hitting all over the town and especially on the big cathedral where American machine guns were located. We had to go there…where shells were hitting all along and we had several close calls…'.

Ironically when they reached the dressing station in the city hall they found that it was virtually immune to mortar bombardment, unlike the men who had risked their lives to check on its status. Slater wrote: 'It was a big six-storey building with walls six to eight feet (1 ¾–2 ½m) thick with great arches supporting the ceilings. Shells were hitting it but not doing much damage. The civilians were crowded in one end of it – they were all praying out loud. Many civilians had been shot by snipers during the day – even women and girls. The bridge across the [Schelde] river to the German line was only about 300 yards [275m] from where we were and things are sure lively. The French took over the sector and immediately sent all the civilians back out of town. The next morning the roads were just filled with civilians going back.'

That was their choice, though Babe wouldn't have wanted to hang around any longer than he had to. He and Gregory appear to have tended to the wounded and assessed the situation in the city hall, then made it back out to their company and the comparative safety of Roosebeke, Belgium. There Babe remained for the next few days, while momentous events took place. These developments would signal the end of the war and secure Slater's survival.

The Kaiser abdicated on 9 November, and two days later in the Forest of Compeigne the Germans signed the armistice that ended the fighting. Of course, few could have realised back then that the way the peace was handled would eventually prove disastrous. The severe oppression of the German nation and its people sowed the seeds for the Second World War. In some respects a new global conflict was already on its way – one that would bring Rudy Scholz into direct contact with the sort of butchery from which Slater had somehow just emerged. But in November 1918, peace seemed free from such dangers.

Within days, Oudenaarde felt like a place of celebration instead of tragedy, and to the Americans' dismay, no one even bothered to come to the fully manned dressing station that Slater's company had put up in order to take quick advantage of the end to the violence. There could be no denial of the mass slaughter though; there were reminders of it everywhere. And a trip to the battlefields around Paaschendaele gave Babe some of his most vivid memories of war.

He wrote:

'The whole country as far as the eye can reach is pot-marked with shell holes so thick they merge. We saw the most ghastly sights imaginable – of hundreds of men lying decaying in shell holes – their bones within remaining – men lying where they fell with guns in hands and skulls in helmets. In some places Germans and English would lie in the same shell-hole…Millions and millions of shells shower the battlefield…The most amazing sight was the huge number of tanks on the battlefield…We examined several aeroplanes all destroyed and got some souvenirs off a Bosche plane. We were the first sightseers to pass over that section for nothing was touched and no footprints were evidenced. We spent in all about eight hours traveling over the fields and hiked back to Ypres…'.

No photographs or 'souvenirs' could have captured the horror of what Slater saw better than the words he chose. But if you visit the Babe Slater Collection at the University of California at Davis, you can still find envelopes filled with the flimsy metal identification placards. On them are written words such as: 'Militar Flugzeug' – 'Military Aircraft' in German. Also the type and make of the plane: 'Albatros. Berlin-Johannisthal.' They seem harmless now, but they certainly represented something more sinister to Babe in the previous century. For he had taken those plates from the carcass of an Albatros D.Va bi-plane – a German fighter-plane used to wreak havoc on Allied troops before it was downed on that same Paaschendaele battlefield in 1918. Fortunately, Babe's writing is preserved just as carefully. The Davis University collection contains a small notebook; and just about legible in scrawled handwriting is Babe's haunting description of the Passchendaele battlefield.

Babe Slater must have felt truly lucky to have survived the war. There is a heartwarming picture of him playing in the snow that winter, as if just happy to be alive. That same snow caused him more pain during the war than the picture might have us believe, for it was not kind to his poorly protected feet.

His nephew Norman affectionately recalled: 'Babe never said his feet were too big for his army boots – he said the boots were too small. He had to wrap bandages, taken from his own ambulance, around his feet just to keep them warm. He also used pieces of cloth to keep away the frostbite. He often used to talk about that.'

Babe's physical suffering was alleviated in Brussels, where he was able to celebrate life, survival and the Christmas of 1918 with some of his fellow soldiers. They took a hotel room, enjoyed their best meal for months and accepted the acclaim rightly reserved for liberators. Babe wrote: 'Christmas Eve was sure being celebrated and everyone in good spirits – the Americans were quite a novelty and would bring cheers and applause in every joint.'

Rudy Scholz would have to wait a while before he saw Brussels, because he never made it to the First World War; he had lost his race against time. Later he put on a casual air about what had happened. 'When the Germans heard I was coming they quit', he joked. The quip hid the hurt he likely felt at missing out on the chance to prove himself in combat.

No longer was there any reason for Rudy to be in the east. A 1919 newspaper article from Norfolk, Virginia, recorded the departure of sporting star Scholz as he headed back west towards San Francisco. With a hint of sadness, Rudy tried to make the best of his situation.

The headline read: 'ARMY BASE LOSES STAR ATHLETE IN SCHOLZ.' The story went on:

> Lieut. A. R. Scholz of the Twelfth Infantry has been discharged from the service and will be on his way home tomorrow.
>
> Lieutenant Scholz has been stationed at the Army Supply base for some time, where he has been prominent in athletics, being the crack goal tosser of the basketball team and captain and shortstop of the nine. He also acted as timekeeper at the boxing bouts at the Monday night shows in the arena.
>
> Lieutenant Scholz's home is in San Francisco. He will return home by way of the Panama canal.
>
> 'Want to see something of the big ditch on my way home,' he explained, remembering to compliment rural Virginia before he left. 'Wonderful country,' said Lieutenant Scholz, 'and I'm sorry to leave here, but home is home, you know.'

Home was home, but the battlefields of northern Europe had been his preferred destination, and he was disappointed to have missed out. Given the carnage that Corporal Colby 'Babe' Slater witnessed there, perhaps it was just as well that Lieutenant Scholz wasn't granted his wish.

Babe wouldn't have seen too much glory in having to wrap his feet in bandages constantly, or being stuck in traffic jams with screaming wounded. The 'ghastly' sights he saw on the battlefields, and the stories he heard in the aftermath of the killing, didn't seem to lead Slater to believe that war was very glamorous.

Probably craving normality, Babe didn't get back to the US until April 1919. His military service ended in May, after a hero's welcome in San Francisco. By the time he settled back into farming California-style that summer, the city of Brussels must have represented nothing more than a memory, a feeling of relief at the end of a dark nightmare.

Astonishingly, Babe would be back in Brussels inside a year – this time with Rudy Scholz by his side.

chapter 3

FROM HAND GRENADES TO RUGBY BALLS

IN THE AFTERMATH OF THE FIRST WORLD WAR, THE FUTURE OF the Olympic Games hung in the balance. No meetings of the International Olympic Committee had taken place since June 1914. The minutes of a British Olympic Association Council Meeting, held on 31 January 1919, illustrated the fragility of the Olympic movement globally. Those minutes acknowledged that 'the question of future support to the Games was before the Meeting. If it were decided to continue, they [the Council Members] must be prepared to do everything possible for the encouragement of sport, and the participation in future Olympic Games. If they were not prepared to do this, it would be much better not to continue. A general discussion ensued, and it was generally agreed that the representatives of Associations should have the opportunity of placing the question before their Associations…'.

The same uncertainties were faced by national Olympic committees the world over. The Modern Games, it seemed, were no longer the priority. In the USA, for example, American football was all the rage again. It didn't look destined to become an Olympic sport, but no one seemed to care. You didn't judge a sport by its suitability for a global event that took place once every four years. Gridiron had returned with a vengeance to California and that meant rugby, like the Olympics, was soon in a grim battle for survival.

The conditions in which rugby had flourished no longer existed, mainly because American football had cleaned up its act. Besides, this seemed to be a good time to reinforce national identity. Given the massive loss of life during the war, no one wanted to be patronised about the risks they might be taking on a sports field. So the American west coast joined the rest of the country and embraced Gridiron, a football game unique to its own shores, packed with big hits, set plays and the recently introduced forward pass.

Though fun while it lasted and full of flowing grace, rugby had been on the decline since 1915. There were still some holdouts such as Stanford University, but even Stanford had lately become more dependent upon traditional west coast rugby outposts like British Columbia for opposition. Finally the University bowed to the inevitable and returned to the native game as its main contact sport in 1919.

It was goodbye rugby, though part of the swansong came in the form of a tour up the coast by a select side from Stanford and Cal-Berkeley. They faced teams from Vancouver, the University of British Columbia and Victoria, playing four matches in all. They won every single match, and returned home proud to have given their dear old game the chance to go out in a blaze of glory. But the unbeaten tour left one man in particular, Wilfred Harry Maloney, thinking some outlandish thoughts. Maloney wasn't ready to allow the sun to set on rugby just yet. The problem for Harry was that hardly anyone else seemed to be thinking along the same lines.

By the end of the decade, some of the finest exponents of rugby in California had moved with the times and forgotten all about it. Rudy Scholz, who was now back at the University of Santa Clara to do the final year of his law degree, hadn't played rugby for years. Instead he had been making a name for himself as a quarterback for their American football team, known as the Missionites. And the man who coached Scholz in 1919 was none other than Robert E. Harmon, the very same college tactician who had introduced Babe Slater to American football at Davis Farms in 1915.

The fact that Santa Clara lost four and won only two of their matches in that first season didn't seem to stop the rave reviews for Scholz and his displays. After a defeat to the 'Olympics' [Olympic Club of San Francisco], one 1919 newspaper article proclaimed: 'Rudy Scholz is one of the best signaling quarterbacks on the Pacific Coast. He is also one of the best field generals. His ability to handle his team on the field was the cause of much comment among the coaches who attended Sunday's game.'

Such glowing praise for Scholz's leadership skills might have been worth remembering when the time came for the US rugby team to choose its captain. He seemed annoyingly perfect in so many ways. One of Rudy's report cards from his 1919–20 year at Santa Clara University had separate sections for Application and Conduct, to be marked out of one hundred. Scholz scored a maximum one hundred in both categories.

Yet the American football team Rudy played on was far from perfect. A 13-0 Gridiron loss to Stanford introduced Scholz to the rival university's rising stars, men such as Robert 'Dink' Templeton and Jack Patrick, who would turn into future Olympic teammates for both Rudy and Babe. One newspaper described how Stanford always had players 'right there to smear whichever Santa Claran caught the ball. Usually it was Scholz, speediest back on the Mission eleven. But the Cards [Stanford] did not give Rudy a chance to get away.'

Despite the fact that Santa Clara were shut out entirely, the same report put Scholz at the head of a short list of 'the bright and shining lights for the Red and White aggregation.' In that year of 1919 there was an awards ceremony for the Santa Claran American football team. Another newspaper described how 'Rudy Scholz, who is president of the Big Letter society, gave a short address which was received with rounds of applause.'

Scholz the leader, the quarterback, the respected public speaker; whatever he tried, he was always in sparkling form. Like Babe, Rudy was blessed with such easy sporting versatility that there was no reason why he shouldn't just move with the times and embrace football. Rugby, their teenage sweetheart, was in her death throes. They might even have felt sorry for the eccentric old English game. But there wasn't much time for sentimentality when they had new sporting reputations to build in Gridiron. With a new crop of powerful young men coming through, hungry tough guys who had never even played rugby, it would have been dangerous for Rudy and Babe to cling to the past.

Like Scholz, Slater was living in a Gridiron hotbed now, and loving it. Farming and football, both physically demanding, went together just fine. Babe had teamed up with a friend called Bob Lockhart in Woodland, California, a quiet place not far from Davis, to pursue his love for farming. They managed a section of the Conaway Ranch in Woodland and raised sheep and pigs. One winter's day, such a sudden flood washed through their part of California that cars were swept away or deposited in ditches. A Model T Ford was stuck in a ditch near Babe's house during this flood, and there was no equipment available to get it out in a hurry. The elements had handed Slater a physical challenge and he wasn't about to walk away. So Babe and his colleague, Bob, lifted the car out with their bare hands; problem solved.

Slater's strength seemed to be growing by the year, and the demanding life of a farmer further honed his extraordinary physique. His next sporting adventure saw him play for the American Legion in Woodland, known specifically as 'Yolo Post No. 77'. He even coached the team too. As usual, Babe Slater proved to be a winner, and the Woodland Legion team romped to one victory after another on their way to the regional title. There is a photo of that Woodland team, with 'full-back' Slater sitting proudly at the centre of the front row, the ball at his feet. 'Their line crossed but once this season,' the caption read, 'Woodland's Legion footballers compare with any grid organization to be found anywhere in the interior.'

What is truly scary about this picture is that several of Slater's teammates looked even bigger and more fearsome than he did. The giant was back in his element, and living life the way he wanted. Emotional ties between the Legion's hard men had been established through common suffering in war. Yet the nightmare of that war in Europe was over, normal service had been resumed. Farming and sport dominated his days again, just as they had done before the war. As it was for Scholz, so Babe's rugby days were becoming a distant memory.

But that was about to change for the veteran of Belgium; and for Rudy, the man who had wanted to be there.

The 1920 US Olympic Committee needed the request from the California Rugby Union like a hole in the head. In every sport that is going out of fashion, there remain a few die-hard traditionalists who dig in their heels and dare to dream out-dated dreams. So it was ironic that W. Harry Maloney, President of the CRU, was actually a long-time soccer coach at Stanford University. He also loved rugby, as we have seen; and he had thought of a way to save it. Now his letter had arrived at the USOC office in New York, with an unlikely proposal: Maloney's CRU wanted to send a rugby team to represent the United States at the Antwerp Olympics of 1920.

To put this request into some sort of context, not even England's Rugby Football Union, the sport's home organisation, wanted to send a team to the Olympic Games. They had been warned by the French that there would be complications if they tried. In the late summer of 1919, when 'Throwing the Hand Grenade' was still under genuine consideration as a possible Olympic sport, the French Olympic Committee wrote to their British counterparts. On the agenda were not only those flying grenades, but also the proposed Antwerp rugby tournament, among other matters. The French warned that their Union des Societes Francaise de Sports Athletiques (USFSA), an influential organisation which oversaw all kinds of sports in their country, was seeking changes. They looked ready to press for British rugby to be restructured for involvement in the Antwerp Olympics. The report sent to the British by the French Olympic Committee included the following unsubtle hint at USFSA intent:

'...The Union has perhaps desired the innovation that in a tournament, say of Rugby Football, Great Britain should not be entitled to a team each for Scotland, Ireland, Wales and England. If this is the meaning it is perfectly justified, and it is to be supposed that this perfectly equitable request, although not in conformity with the constitution of the International Board with which the USFSA is connected, will be willingly accepted by the Antwerp Committe...'.

So there it was. The British would have to send one rugby team only if they were going to take part. It appeared that the Belgians had already been sounded out about the proposed amalgamation and had given the idea their full support.

If the English RFU had been lukewarm about the idea of sending a rugby team to the Olympics before, they were now firmly set against what they probably regarded as an attempted assault on their individual union's identity. In fact, there was about as much chance of a 'Great Britain' rugby team in Antwerp as there was of the British Olympic Association giving the green light to 'Throwing the Hand Grenade' as the latest sporting craze.

The French Olympic Committee's communication to the British did not specify whether anything or indeed anyone was supposed to be blown up as part of the proposed grenade-throwing tournament. Whether they were a test of accuracy, distance – or both – the idea of grenade throwing as a sport was not destined to make a big impact on Olympic history. Indeed a common desire to prevent grenade-throwing from taking its place alongside the discus and shot-putting events did at least offer respite from the sporting tensions that festered elsewhere. This particular item in the report from France's governing body was short and to the point: 'Throwing the Hand Grenade. There seems to be a general agreement that this (Bomb throwing) event should be suppressed.'

One might have said the same about the rugby event. By the start of the Olympic year, it seemed on the verge of cancellation due to lack of interest. The annual report of the British Olympic Council stated at that time that:

> …the Committee of the Rugby Football Union have decided to withdraw from representation to the Council on the grounds 'that Rugby Football is not suitable for inclusion in the syllabus of Olympic Games.'
>
> Your Council have endeavoured to persuade the Rugby Football Union to reconsider their decision, but without avail.
>
> The withdrawal of the Rugby Football Union is the more regretted in view of the work which lies before this Association in the future of promoting in the United Kingdom all forms of sport, a work in which the assistance of the Rugby Football Union, with its high ideal of the amateur, would be most valuable.

In most English-speaking countries, particularly those still attached to the Empire, the impact of the English RFU decision to pull out of the Olympics was significant and a domino effect followed. The sheer cost of sending entire rugby squads to Antwerp from far-flung places such as Australia, New Zealand and South Africa would also have been weighed against the possibility that they might remain something of a fleeting sideshow at the Olympics. Since the All Blacks and Waratahs were used to holding centre stage for months on end during their famed rugby tours to the northern hemisphere, it was easy to see why they preferred to follow the British lead and turn their backs on Olympic rugby.

In America, however, they either didn't know or didn't care what the Brits and their Empire were doing. W. Harry Maloney wanted Californian rugby players to live the Olympic dream, and he wouldn't rest until he had the support he needed.

It wasn't as though Maloney was stuck for a project, or that his sporting life would be left empty if rugby was allowed to rest in peace. The man with the big ears, neatly-parted blond hair and craggy, weathered face had been Stanford's first basketball coach from 1913 to 1915. He went on to coach six different sports over three whole decades. He ran soccer at Stanford for 29 years, fencing for 22, and boxing for 19 years. He served as head coach of athletics, and became director of minor sports. He coached wrestling and yes, he also coached rugby. And it was Maloney's versatility that probably gave him the broad mind and vision to see what a sensation a US rugby team might just cause in Belgium. But only if their country's Olympic Committee would give them the chance.

It is fair to say, however, that the USOC didn't share Harry's enthusiasm. Whatever strings he tried to pull among his contacts there, Maloney met with only limited success. You could see the other side of the argument. The Olympics were supposed to be about the promotion of international sport, not the self-indulgence of one State. How could the CRU have the audacity to put in a bid for the funding of a US rugby team at Antwerp, 1920, when nowhere else in the USA played the game?

The USOC might have felt differently had they considered the Californians capable of taking on the world's best rugby teams, but they clearly didn't believe there was much chance of gold at the end of the rainbow. Perhaps they went as far as asking a few questions, and found out that the USA had taken part in a round-robin rugby tournament at the Inter-Allied Games (a Services tournament) in Europe the previous year. Both France and the USA had beaten Romania to set up the decisive match; but on 29 June 1919, France had defeated the United States 8-3. The USOC probably didn't see how it could be any different this time around. They weren't aware that Babe Slater, one of the best American forwards, was already back home by the time his compatriots had played the French. Meanwhile Rudy Scholz, the influential scrum-half, hadn't even made it to war in the first place.

At any rate, the USOC were only prepared to meet the CRU halfway, and responded quite abruptly. They wrote back: 'Due to the fact that California is the only state playing rugby in the United States, the Committee has decided that, while its sanction will be given for a team to represent the US, the financial aid must come from the State of California itself, and by the men from whom the team will be chosen.'

The USOC probably believed that would kill off the whole crazy idea; for they must have known that rugby wasn't even popular in California any more. Who would want to spend money sending a rusty, ill-prepared team to the Olympic Games to compete in a sport that was virtually extinct back home? However respectably the Americans had performed against European rugby teams the previous year, a sound beating was the only likely outcome against any country which still played rugby with the required intensity and regularity.

But there were those in California who started to think that W. Harry Maloney might be right, and saw this situation as a challenge and an opportunity. The California Rugby Union had been created by men with a fond nostalgia for the rugby years, strong characters who dared to believe that the dream of Olympic gold could be turned into reality against the odds. Patiently, they built bridges with American Olympic officials, when it might have been more tempting to hit out at their refusal to give financial support.

The sanction to represent the US had at least been provided. So now the CRU needed to satisfy themselves that enough quality players would be interested in this proposed trip to turn it into something more than a humiliation. Men of true sporting talent had to be recruited to the cause if it was to gain the sort of momentum that might win over potential financial backers. Rudy Scholz was targeted early in the process and he would soon become a vital component in the 'dream machine'.

Rudy could have been forgiven for resisting a recruitment drive that was sure to place huge demands on his time and energy. After all, Scholz had plenty of good reasons for staying in California, where life had always been good to him. Not only was he just graduating in law, with a bright career ahead of him, but Rudy had also met a girl named Cecilia, and was becoming increasingly fond of her. Though she wasn't a beauty, she had a warm and thoughtful face, and possessed a depth and quirkiness of character that Rudy found appealing. He later likened another girl to Cecilia by saying she appeared 'modest and retiring', while in reality he was convinced that the facade was merely 'a cloak for a rather vivid personality.' We can only assume that Cecilia's true character was equally bubbly and alluring, once Rudy was given a look behind her public persona and beyond the more formal social conventions of the day.

A surviving photo of Cecilia raises some questions. Wearing a pretty white dress, white stockings and white shoes, Cecilia is a picture of innocence as she sits on some steps, her hands clasped around her knees. But there seems to be a hint of annoyance, perhaps even anger, in her face as she looks past the camera. Was she worrying about how to keep that dress from getting dirty, now that her photographer-friend had put her in a pose on those filthy steps? Or had Scholz just told her that he would soon be bound for the other side of the Atlantic without her? For it seems that neither romance nor professional ambition were enough to compete with the glory of sport. Nothing could prevent Rudy from falling back in love with rugby. The idea of an Olympic adventure in Europe was simply irresistible. So when the men who mattered came calling, there could only be one answer.

On 19 February 1920, a San Francisco newspaper ran the following story:

'Missionites' Wanted For Belgium.
Santa Clara Rugby Stars May Make The Trip to Belgium

A committee from the management of the Olympic games recently visited Santa Clara University in the hope of securing the services of the star rugby men who made the old Mission School so famous in the past. That some of these marvels will journey this year to Antwerp is hardly to be doubted. Most of the stars will receive their degree in law just at the time the athletes are supposed to take a ship from the US.

Rudy Scholz is being sought as the half-back for the big team. It will be remembered what a sensation he created in 1916, when this little wonder did so much to help Santa Clara tie that most humiliating defeat on Stanford. John O. Miller, himself one of the best rugby men this State ever produced, declared that Scholz was by far the greatest half-back the game ever saw in these parts. Rudy is fast on his feet and just as fast with his thinking apparatus. For him to think is to act and he seldom makes an error of judgement. Old Antwerp will see some speed if Scholz ever gets going on their turf…'.

The idea that Babe Slater could be persuaded to come on board seemed at first even more far-fetched than taking Scholz away from a potentially happy, lucrative life in San Francisco. Babe also had a sweetheart, a nurse from Davis hospital. And though romance had seemed less important than sport and farming in his life so far, a woman's touch must still have been a comfort after all the ugliness he had witnessed abroad. The notion of returning to Belgium so soon after seeing the worst of the war in that very same country would have struck fear and revulsion into the hearts of many lesser men.

Yet the 1920 Olympics had been taken away from Budapest and awarded to Antwerp precisely because Baron de Coubertin and his fellow committee members felt that the Games would help to heal war-scarred Belgium. The Austro-Hungarian Empire had supported the Germans during the war; therefore Budapest was one of the villains of the piece. Belgium was regarded as one of the true victims of the tragedy that had been the Great War. Therefore Antwerp was considered more deserving of the international support the Olympics would bring. The USA had been called upon to be part of that healing process. So the American athletes, in turn, were expected to answer their country's call as and when required. Babe was very patriotic and his love for sport was very strong. For those two reasons at least, he was prepared to listen.

However, for rugby players who agreed to become Olympians, it wasn't just a question of saying yes. That was when the hard work really began. Fundraising events had to be organised if the long journey to Belgium was to become a reality. Slater set about raising money in his own Woodland community, while Scholz helped to organise even more lucrative events in San Francisco. Rudy also began to help coordinate the organisation of the selection and training process, so that suddenly all his natural skills were coming into play around one sporting passion.

It would have come as no surprise to anyone when Scholz was later named as one of the five-man Executive Committee that essentially managed the trip to the Antwerp Olympics. He worked so tirelessly to make it happen that he clearly deserved a place at the table of the decision-makers. An example of his high-energy, hard-sell approach to fundraising came in a letter to the college of Santa Clara, where he had grown from boy to man. He was just a month away from graduating in law at one of the USA's finest colleges.

The *Santa Clara News* reported on Friday, 21 May 1920:

$300.00 ASKED FOR SUPPORT OF
S.C. RUGBY STARS.

The following communication from R. J. Scholz, chairman of the Santa Clara Olympic Games Rugby Track committee, sets forth the reasons why Santa Clara should raise $300 to help finance the All-American Rugby Team in its European trip:

'Chamber of Commerce,
Santa Clara, Calif.
Gentlemen:
For the first time in the history of Santa Clara there is an opportunity to send representatives from here to the Olympic Games, which will be held this year at Antwerp, Belgium. This representation will come through the University of Santa Clara and will consist of at least three men being selected on the All-American Rugby Team which will compete in the Olympic Games. The caliber of the team is not to be doubted and the only

hitch in the well formed plans of the committee in charge is that of finances. To obviate this difficulty certain men of great financial standing were approached and asked to contribute enough to finance the team and the answer of practically all of them were [sic] to the effect that they were more than willing to give their support but they wanted to know first, what was the attitude of the universities and the cities that contained the universities on the subject and what were they doing to support the project and to what extent. The result was that each university and city were [sic] given a quota of money to raise in order to demonstrate that they were heartily in accord with the movement.

Santa Clara's quota is $1,000.00 and I deem it a fair division to have the university raise $700.00 and the town of Santa Clara $300.00.

The advertisement that will accrue to the town is not hard to imagine but I may say in connection with this that it will make Santa Clara known not only through Europe but also throughout the United States and I base my assertion on the following reasons:

Sporting Writers from the Associated Press, the United Press, various syndicate writers, special writers, etc, will accompany the team and newspapers all over; the United States will be flooded with publicity in the shape of news, on the Olympic Games and their activity and, inasmuch as this is the first attempt to meet the Europeans in rugby, on their soil, and because of the fact that one state has taken unto itself the task of upholding the honor of the forty-eight states and furthermore that the chances are better than even that they will be victorious (based on the competition in the Inter-Allied Games held in Paris and the victorious trip of the Stanford-California team to British Columbia last Christmas) the rugby team will at least receive its share of the publicity.

The result will be that it will foster a more intimate knowledge of California and Santa Clara, from a worldly standpoint than any other one event. The people of the United States learned more about Australia as a direct result of the American tour of their rugby team than any other incident. Commercial relations were certainly stimulated by the trip. More, much more, could be said about the advantages that will fall to Santa Clara as a result of this trip, but your time is no doubt limited so I will hurry on to what we, in charge of Santa Clara's drive, wish from the Commercial Club.

First of all, the unqualified support and approval of the trip of the rugby team to the Olympic Games. Secondly, a pledge of financial support to the extent that you feel justified in giving. Said pledge to be null and void if in case the Rugby Team does not make the trip or that Santa Clara is not represented by at least three players.

In closing, I would like to say that Stanford has raised the sum of $3000 in the university alone and that surely we of Santa Clara can and should raise $1000. The spirit of the community and its reputation demands it.

Yours very truly

RJ SCHOLZ,

Chairman of the Santa Clara Olympic Games Rugby Funds Committee.'

This eloquent plea is understood to have been successful. However, the project would probably never have become credible without the support and patronage of richer and more powerful figures. James D. Phelan, for example, was a former Mayor of San Francisco, who had become a United States Senator for California. He was therefore unquestionably the right kind of man to have on your side. The son of an Irish immigrant who became wealthy during the California Gold Rush as a trader, merchant and banker, Phelan liked tough sport and pioneering Americans. This rugby idea sounded like his kind of adventure, and Rudy Scholz decided he was worth a try.

Rudy went to see Phelan to ask him face-to-face for help in making the Olympic dream become a reality. If this wasn't exactly a make-or-break meeting, it was close. Scholz doubtless prepared the same kind of arguments he had used in an attempt to persuade the Santa Clara committee to part with their cash: success at the Olympic Games would bring fresh fame to California, promote positive business relations between San Francisco and Europe and bring glory to all concerned.

To his credit, the 59-year-old Phelan found time in his busy schedule to listen carefully; and he clearly liked what he heard. The Senator dug deep into his pockets to give material assistance to the rugby hopefuls, at a time when the odds were still stacked against them. Phelan's moral support was almost as important as the money. With the senator now behind them, California's rugby men felt the tide turn in their favour. The serving Mayor of San Francisco at the time, Mayor Rolph, was quick to jump on the bandwagon. And William F. Humphrey, president of the Olympic Club of San Francisco, was a staunch ally. He had enthusiastically supported the founding of the rugby team at the Olympic Club back in 1908, so he was quick to warm to this exciting cause.

In general, the most talented players seemed to lead the fundraising. And one newspaper story explained why Rudy was rated so highly. Under the headline 'Santa Clara Rugby Stars Sought', one journalist had previously written,

> ...Scholz has played nearly every position in the backfield on the rugby team, but his best playing has been at the half back position. There are hundreds of fans in this locality who have attended games, rain or shine, for nothing more than to see this little whirlwind athlete in action. It has taken the biggest man on the team, yes, two or three or them, to stop Scholz on one of his runs. They have thrown him to the ground and before they can realize what had happened, Scholz had bounced up and was halfway down the field. Should Scholz make the team, even the Olympian spectators would have a treat in store when the sturdy little athlete got into action.

John 'Jack' Patrick, who would later become an important teammate of Slater and Scholz, was a Stanford American football star. He was persuaded to use his growing celebrity to become fundraising figurehead for Palo Alto, California. Early in the summer of 1920 he was appointed local chairman of the 'Antwerp Dance Committee' to organise a money-spinning event scheduled for 23 July. A band called the Six Stanford Syncopaters were to forgo their collective fee – more than

$45 – for playing at the party. Tickets would cost men $1 and, despite the fact that ladies were still 'to be complimentary', vital money came pouring in.

Pretty soon everyone wanted to chip in; and Patrick was deeply appreciative when a little restaurant donated $15. He explained, 'Operated by two self-supporting Stanford undergraduates, the Californian Restaurant personifies the spirit of real assistance and co-operation by a donation which, proportionately, is as large as has been received during the course of the campaign.'

A showdown between 'All-British' and 'All-American' teams at San Francisco's Ewing Field was due to help the squad selection process in mid-June. But Rudy Scholz didn't appear in either of the team line-ups advertised by one newspaper prior to that match. Maybe he was injured, or his selection was already considered a foregone conclusion; perhaps it was a mixture of the two. He may already have been clearing his head with a final get-away-from-it-all break in Pacific Grove, Monterey. He was certainly there prior to the start of the Olympic rugby squad's intensive training week in Stanford at the end of July.

Many other stars did play in the trial match in mid-June and one man in particular had rugby in his blood. Danny Carroll, who had won rugby gold at the 1908 Olympic games with Australia before touring the USA with the Waratahs in 1912, was still hungry for Olympic glory. He had been a US citizen since January, so there was no reason why he couldn't represent his adopted country later in 1920. He had certainly earned the right. Long before the First World War had reached its climax, Carroll had enlisted in the US Army. He had fought rather like he played rugby – with courage and a determination to prevail. Despite being wounded, Carroll survived the chaos and was awarded a Distinguished Service Cross for his valour.

Danny's injuries hadn't stopped him from playing in the post-war Kings Cup rugby tournament in 1919; and he had retained a passion for the game. Now Carroll felt he could give the USA's would-be Olympians the benefit of his experience. And everyone in the Californian rugby community realised that Danny was a man worth listening to when it came to squad selection.

No one knew better than Carroll what it would take to compete with the other Olympic rugby teams; and the mighty French in particular. There is some suggestion that he became the most important selector of all, though Maloney would also have wanted a strong say. And Danny's knowledge of how rugby's rules were interpreted in other parts of the world was sure to be vital. Carroll became the Olympic squad's 'playing coach.'

Most of his teammates had never played in a match outside North America; and some were almost entirely in the dark about the workings of the game. Danny would have his work cut out trying to turn these American rugby players into Olympic champions. Still, he wanted to give it a go; and the squad he coached would not be short of muscle or raw talent.

Another important candidate for that squad was Robert 'Dink' Templeton, who, at 23 years of age, was already deemed to be a peerless kicker in California. Rudy Scholz once said, 'Dink was the greatest kicker I ever saw. He could put 'em over four out of five from 50 yards [45m] out. And he could put 'em out of bounds – kick for touch – from 70 yards [63m] away.'

Templeton was also a track and field star well known for his jumping prowess. But he was disqualified from the Olympic high-jump trials because his 'Western Roll' style was ruled illegal. He made the long-jump team, but wanted a piece of the rugby action too. That trial match at Ewing Field in mid-June would hold the key.

One newspaper previewed it like this:

> ...Stars of college fifteens, from Stanford and California; high school rugby experts, and ruggers from the various clubs, especially the Olympics (the Olympic Club in San Francisco) will be represented on both sides in tomorrow's game.
>
> Danny Carroll, the flashy backfield man who wrote rugby history in Australia and later Stanford University when the 'scrum' game was the big intercollegiate business on the coast, will appear in the game. 'Dink' Templeton of Stanford, greatest kicker on the coast, will also be in action, as will (Jack) Patrick...'.

Babe Slater was down to play as 'Breakaway' for the All-British team alongside Templeton, Carroll and Patrick. And he appears to have been the only representative from Davis Farms to be called in for consideration. His talent was such that he scarcely needed to be familiar with his teammates in order to catch the eye. So it hardly mattered that his usual Davis sidekicks were absent. Babe didn't intend to let a chance to earn his place in the Olympic squad go begging.

Neither did one of Rudy Scholz's fellow Santa Clarans, John 'T' O'Neill. The wiry little hooker, whose job it had been to time his 'strike' in the scrum to coincide with Rudy's 'put-in' of the ball, was desperate to be part of the adventure. What further enhanced O'Neil's potential importance to the trip was the fact that he came from a fabulously wealthy family, and was therefore able to make a significant contribution to the financial cause. He drew upon his family's fortune and used their contacts to make his fundraising events an overwhelming success. But he wasn't just some spoilt little rich kid. His lion-hearted approach to big matches would become evident soon enough.

Charles Tilden, a former Cal student, was in the mix for a number of reasons, not just sporting. A natural leader and steady character, he also became hugely important in harnessing goodwill and funding for the project. His father was a Major and well connected; the family was influential. For an Olympic dream to become a reality, you had to think beyond the field of play.

A clever American Athletic Union representative called Sam Goodman – who would go on to manage the 1924 US rugby team – helped the Californian Rugby Union to oversee the various efforts being made on its behalf. Goodman, who was short and deceptively gritty, despite his comically large ears and shortage of hair, struck up a rapport with Scholz that would last for four years. The organisational abilities of both men were crucial to getting the show on the road in 1920. Like Carroll, Maloney and Tilden, Goodman was also on the selection committee. And after that final trial match, the 'All-British' v 'All-American' contest at Ewing Field, they quickly met to choose the Olympic team. The Associated Press agency, with a noticeable lack of precision, announced on 17 June:

STANFORD UNIVERSITY – Twenty athletes were named today for the rugby team that will represent the United States at the Olympic games by W. Harry Maloney, president of the

California Rugby Union. One week of intensive training before the team leaves Stanford on July 29 is planned. The players expect to sail from New York August 5. Several games with Belgian teams are being arranged to precede the Olympic game schedule, which is set for August 30 to September 5. A tentative schedule calls for the following games after the Olympic contest: September 8, Brussels, Belgium; September 10, French champions at Paris; September 15, Rugby-Football Union of England at London; September 18, Plymouth, England; September 20, Canborne [sic] at Cornwall, England.

Members of the American first fifteen are: R. L. Templeton, Mat Hazeltine, Danny Carroll, Les Wark, John Patrick and Charles S. Righter of Stanford; Richard Scholz and J. Muldoon, Santa Clara University; J. Winston, Charles Tildon [sic] and J. Meehan, University of California; H. S. Wrenn and G. Hunter, Beliston Club; J. 'Bab' [sic] Slater and Arthur Erb, Olympic Club.

Substitutes include David Wallace, George Davis and Charles Doe, Stanford; Fred Brookes, University of California; William Muldoon, Santa Clara University.

There were some glaring omissions, looking at the fledgling team-sheet printed here. John T. O'Neill would eventually make the side, despite his less than impressive physique. So would Morris Kirksey, who was so fast that he also made it onto the US sprint team for the 1920 Olympics. Teach him a few of the basic rules of rugby, point him in the right direction and above all remind him to put the ball down when he reached the try-line. That was all it would take.

The squad, when it did assemble in its final form, would be a collection of rusty rugby players and risky additions, who would have to be taught the game on the way to Europe. The classy Charles Tilden was made captain, and the boys were almost ready to go. But at the last moment the entire campaign was almost derailed by increased demands from the American Athletic Union (AAU). It was Sam Goodman who probably dropped the bombshell. Just when the rugby squad thought they had reached their funding targets, they were told to think again.

Rudy Scholz had already begun his 1920 Olympic diary. On

Tuesday, 27 July, he had to say farewell to his sweetheart Cecilia – or 'CJ.' He was given the bad financial news on the very same day. Since he had assumed a major fundraising role, it would largely be Rudy's responsibility to come up with the extra money at the eleventh hour.

He wrote: 'At work all morning, saying good-bye. Walked to car with C. J. – I couldn't contemplate it as a good-bye. I intended to go over in the afternoon to see her but – didn't. Left at 2.37 for S.F. Reported at Berkeley – found out AAU had increased the amount of money asked of us to $8,000.00 – means drive must be prolonged and hard work.'

By the following day, however, his concerns about the money had eased, largely because of the obvious generosity of the local community. Scholz wrote: 'Wednesday July 28. Berkeley – worked out in morning at football – solicit in afternoon – drive coming along fine . . .'.

And he was his usual chirpy self again 24 hours later. With typically self-deprecating humour Rudy scribbled: 'Practice football in morning – have as much speed as ever which ungrammatically speaking "ain't any." Finished drive in afternoon – a thousand dollars over...'.

Not only had Scholz done it – he had even earned the squad some spending money too. They began to head east on 30 July, and Rudy recorded the following thoughts:

'Good-by to Cal – big crowd of friends and relatives at station to say good-by. Sort of wished my mother or Cecilia was there. I must get away from those thoughts.' He tried to do so immediately, since his next words were: 'En Route – a splendid bunch of fellows. We held a "night-shirt" parade thru our Pullman...'.

The joking around no doubt had its uses as a bonding exercise. For Babe Slater, however, the start of this train journey across America must have brought back memories of a similar train ride two years earlier, the first stage on the road to hell.

In his diary, Rudy described going 'across the great breadth of sand as we came thru Utah,' and the 'Great Salt Lake – a pleasing antithesis to the white glue of the desert.' Later came 'Wyoming – a queer country – here and there barren fields – dotted with a few ranches a great distance apart.' From there he sent a card to Cecilia and was clearly missing her already.

On 1 August, Scholz and the squad reached one of mid-America's most spectacular sights, the great Missouri River, though it seems that

Rudy was too busy fulfilling his managerial role to enjoy it. He wrote: 'After leaving Omaha we crossed river Missouri into Iowa. Here various demands of the seventeen kept me busy until twelve. (midnight).'

But Rudy's appetite for fun suddenly returned, and the victims of his latest little joke were Bill and John Muldoon, teammates and friends from Santa Clara. Scholz explained: 'At twelve I went out on the observation car but it was hard to distinguish anything even tho' there was moonlight. The bunch became acquainted with two girls and on asking us where we were going we told them New York to take the Muldoon brothers to an Insane Asylum. They fell for it (pardon the slang).'

They finally reached New York on 3 August. 'NY looked as if well named – the Empire State' wrote Scholz, who was about to be reminded of his frustrating failure to be fast-tracked into a leadership role in time for the First World War. For he added starkly: 'Pass the camp of the West Point cadets into Albany and New York – arriving there at 4.30 in the evening.'

How he would have loved to have been a West Point cadet himself. But there wasn't much time for introspection. He explained: 'In the evening the executive committee had a long session – [John] Muldoon [his friend and teammate from Santa Clara], [Charles] Tilden [Captain], [Harry] Maloney [manager], [Harold] Von Schmidt [a teammate] and myself. After the meeting they went to a show excepting myself – I wrote to mother and Cecilia.'

On 4 August there was a warm-up match against a Metropolitan New York XV played in Newark, New Jersey. The Olympic squad won comfortably by 21-3, and Rudy's choice of company for his last night in the USA was interesting. Given that there were more than 20 companions to choose from, and it is normal practice on any tour for teammates to go out in big groups, what happened could be considered unusual. Rudy wrote: 'Immediately after game Babe Slater and myself went to N.Y. and after a hasty lunch went to the Lyceum to see Ina Claire in "The Gold Diggers." She is a great actress and the show was exceptionally fine.'

Though Avery Hopwood's comedy was doubtless witty and Ina Claire's acting as good as Scholz suggested, his verdict may also have been influenced by the fact that Ina Claire was also one of the most beautiful women ever to walk the Broadway stage.

Babe and Rudy continued to take in the sights and tastes of New York, though the match and the long journey across America was taking its toll. Rudy added, 'Babe and I were both tired so after wandering around for an hour, during which we went into a Chinese place and had some suey, we took elevated back to our hotel.'

The tallest and shortest guys on the team must have looked quite a sight as they strode through Manhattan together, their friendship already apparent. They were an odd couple on the face of it, Babe almost a foot taller than his teammate. But they wouldn't have cared about their physical differences, and the evening clearly seems to have been a success, despite their fatigue. Their rapport had been firmly established and would endure for the rest of the 1920 adventure.

From what we know of their respective characters, it was probably Rudy who did most of the talking on their night out together. On one particular subject, however, Scholz would have preferred to listen. It is likely that Rudy knew about Slater's involvement in the First World War by then. And if he knew Babe had experience of Belgium, Scholz would have wanted to hear all about it. With Rudy's natural love of the military, there can be little doubt he respected Babe for what he had been through. As they toured New York that night, did Rudy persuade Slater to tell him a few stories about his hellish close calls during the war? We will never know. Maybe they just talked about Ina Claire and how beautiful she was.

If he was smart – and Rudy was – he wouldn't have pressed too hard for war stories. He probably already understood the poignancy of their destination – the very country where Slater had suffered two years earlier. They were even due to sail there on a troop transport ship called the *Sherman*, of roughly the kind Babe had boarded on his journey to war in 1918. They would board the *Sherman* the following morning, from the North Side of Pier Four in Hoboken, New Jersey.

First there was a little media attention to court, though it is hard to imagine a shy young Babe Slater being attracted to the media spotlight. Scholz liked the limelight much more, and possessed the bubbly confidence of a born leader and front man. So he was the one who handled the press conference the next morning, just before the team's departure for Europe.

What Rudy could have said about the opposition that awaited the

Americans in Europe is a mystery. Beyond the French, who had agreed to field a team, only Czechoslovakia and Romania were believed to have accepted the Olympic rugby challenge at that point. Perhaps more countries would join the party nearer the time.

At any rate, a seemingly carefree Scholz couldn't resist one last joke and wrote: 'As publicity agent (I forgot to mention) I told reporters that Jim Winston [another teammate] is designated as the only living nephew of Sitting Bull.'

It is not known how closely Winston might have resembled the famous native American chief, General George Armstrong Custer's nemesis, but the frivolous description is an indication of Rudy's natural ability to hold centre stage and use that silver tongue to entertain. Babe Slater couldn't have been more different. His nephew, Norman Slater, explained in 2007: 'He was a quiet man and he didn't waste any words that didn't have good meaning in a conversation.'

One man had been to war, the other hadn't. One man had lived it, the other could only imagine. Such a gulf in life experience isn't easily bridged, though they seem to have liked each other well enough at this stage in their eventful lives. As the Manhattan skyline faded into the distance and the vast Atlantic beckoned, their thoughts turned to the Olympics. Babe and Rudy, their bond forged on Broadway, were united in a common cause. Together they prepared to do battle on the rugby fields of Belgium. It was a far cry from war, this 1920 challenge to their physical prowess and personal courage. However, at least one of them would be physically scarred by their foreign adventure. And neither man would ever forget the weeks to come.

chapter 4

THE 1920 OLYMPICS

THE SAN FRANCISCO NEWSPAPERS HAD ALREADY RECORDED HOW the crude, 'rat infested' accommodation on board the ship taking the US track and field team to Antwerp had almost sparked a mutiny. How would the rugby team fare? On the face of it, the signs looked ominous. As we have heard, the *SS Sherman* was built much like the *SS Olympic*, the ship that had taken Babe Slater to war. So the rugby boys might have feared conditions similar to those that Babe had suffered on his cramped, gruelling voyage to Europe two years earlier. Mercifully, however, it appears that the authorities had learned their lesson before the rugby players sailed the Atlantic.

For Babe, Rudy and the boys, the *SS Sherman* turned out to be far more comfortable. There was even space for the team to train, dance and kid each other as young men do. Indeed, Rudy Scholz was able to record, '...a word about the meals they are great – only they give too much... – variety, thy name is the Cook of the Good Ship Sherman'.

With the right kind of fuel in their bellies, the American rugby players were able to stay in reasonable shape. Early on the voyage, Rudy wrote, 'At ten, call came forth for practice and we put on our uniforms and tennis shoes. It started to rain so we confined our work-out to running around the promenade deck for half an hour and discussing football [rugby] for an hour after lunch...In the afternoon I saw a school of porpoises playing and sporting in the water. We are 3,250 miles [5,200km] from Antwerp today. Our average speed is 12 knots per hour...Had a workout from 5 to 6 under direction of Maloney. At dinner we kidded [Jack] Patrick so much that he spilled a whole plate of soup over his lap.'

After Scholz had attended Mass on the first Sunday on board, 8 August, he heard that the ship taking most of the athletes to the Olympics, the *Princess Matoka*, had arrived in Antwerp after an 11-day voyage. The track-and-field team wouldn't have much time to recover from their ordeal. The Olympic Games would already be under way in Belgium before the rugger boys arrived for their turn. In the mean time there was plenty of time for thinking.

Not unusually for him, Scholz was torn between love and war at times: love for his girlfriend Cecilia and a conflicting, nagging desire to test himself in mortal combat. Rudy's lingering fascination with the idea of going to war was not something that would have consumed Babe Slater any more.

Scholz wrote in his diary, 'Lieut Burke [a fellow passenger, probably British] and I got into [a] discussion relative to army affairs. He is going to Poland. He informs me that both Britain and France are going to send a division to fight the Bolsheviks. Wish I had a couple of lives to live. In the evening we had dancing but one dance was enough for me – it's too warm and besides I miss Cecilia.'

There was a comical moment when, having won 23 dollars from his colleagues in a dice game, Rudy entered into a fresh bout of gambling the following day. He wrote,

> I wanted to give the fellows a chance to win their money back so I played again. Result – won nine dollars more...In the evening Jim Winston asked me to play and as I am 32 ahead I couldn't refuse and lost $5 – all I had with me. I went back to the State room for more [money] and 'Swede' Righter, Stanford star center

on the football and basketball teams and my roommate, on being informed what I wanted it for, grabbed it from me and – the big lump of humanity – wouldn't give it to me – he said it wasn't my lucky night and tomorrow I could 'shoot' again. I told him I wanted to lose so I could quit but he couldn't see it that way.

Sometimes the friendly fights between teammates were even more comical. Scholz described one such encounter in his diary, saying, '[Jack] Patrick was in my room threatening to rough-house the room and Swede [Righter] when I arrived. I grabbed the water pitcher to force him to leave. He did so – but protesting…Patrick grabbed another pitcher and tried to douse me but I jumped behind Tilleth [Charles Tilden?] and Tilleth got all of it. The fight became more complex as it were, and before it was over, the whole row [of cabins] was in it.'

Rugby players down the ages have been involved in similar antics. It appears that teams from the early 20th century – including Babe and Rudy's team – were really no different.

A slightly more sobering distraction, particularly since the day was Friday 13 (of August) was a life boat trial. That same day came an indication of Rudy's executive role in helping to administer this Olympic adventure. He noted that he was 'working on tour of France and England.'

Often just a glance out to sea brought a remarkable sight and Scholz wrote of a school of flying fish that 'came out of the water like a flash for a distance of about ten feet [3m] then down into the sea again.'

There was no shortage of female company on board the boat, and a group of school teachers showed more than a passing interest in the fit Olympians. On Saturday, 14 August, Rudy's diary entry went like this: 'Wrote more on letter to Cecilia. One of the prettiest of the school-teachers asked me who I was writing to – I said Cecilia – She said "I thought you were in love when you were talking to me the other day but you will get over it."'

The young Americans wanted to retain their competitive edge too in the build-up to their Olympic adventure. So Scholz also stayed busy helping to design what he proudly called the 'First Mid-Ocean Olympic Games.' He added that they 'Started with a parade in which all the athletes dressed up in different costumes – Red Meehan as a harem girl won 1st prize. First event was a potato race in which Scholz won…'

This was followed by a match-and-cigarette race, an obstacle race (which Rudy regretted not entering), a boxing tournament between members of the crew and an egg race. Scholz was then triumphant again in the relay race alongside Joseph Hunter, Charlie Doe and Heaton Wrenn. Next came what Rudy described as 'an event in which two opponents were blindfolded and tried to hit the other on the forehead – the one doing so winning. Von Schmidt and Scholz defeated all-comers and in the finals Scholz won out.' Rudy didn't say whether part of the reason for his victory was the fact that he was so short. Any opponent aiming for the normal anticipated location of a forehead would simply have swiped mid-air.

It was a fitting climax to an enjoyable voyage, full of high jinks and frivolity. But one man is absent from Rudy's account of the outward journey – Babe Slater. Despite that absence, Babe probably took part in the fun and games on the 11-day voyage. One can't help thinking, however, that the First World War veteran would have found the sharp contrast between his first voyage to Europe and this second one somewhat strange. Two years earlier fighting men had been packed together like sardines and abused so badly that fights had broken out between troops and crew. What was awaiting them in Europe on that first occasion had been a nightmare beyond anyone's imagination. This time the atmosphere on board could hardly have been more different.

Babe was not one of those poor men whose souls had been all but destroyed by what they had seen on the battlefields of the First World War. He could still enjoy himself and light up an occasion with his goofy smile. Doubtless he would have played his part as he set out on his second odyssey to Belgium. But you get the feeling he would sometimes have been lost in his own thoughts, rather like Danny Carroll, their past experiences creating something of an emotional distance from the ridiculous fun had by the majority.

No one could have blamed Babe for keeping a lower profile than some of the others during the fancy dress parade, and what followed. He was a silent type anyway; and he might just have remained silent a little longer than usual on the summer voyage of 1920, as he remembered the men who had shared the first ship with him, so many of whom had been unable to return. It was a strange world. One year you could be sitting on a ship dressed in army uniform, ready to witness slaughter and its aftermath; another year you could be wearing fancy dress, ready to entertain, your destination the same country where so many young lives had ended. The weird and contradictory aspects of human nature really knew no boundaries.

Meanwhile Scholz was photographed on board wearing a cap and bright jumper, looking so boyish and innocent that it would have been hard to imagine him in a violent sporting battle among men, let alone a real battle. Rudy didn't look any more frightening when photographed in his sports gear while perched on one of the ship's large tie-down posts. Neither his toothy smile, nor his arms and legs, pressed together in a childlike pose, would have struck fear into opponents waiting in Europe. Appearances, of course, can be deceptive.

Babe Slater, it had to be said, looked more like the real deal in photographs, his muscles bulging as he tried out a rowing machine with some of his teammates. Even wearing a dapper suit and tie in another on-board photograph, Slater's awesome physique is perfectly evident. The pictures are another reminder of just how different Babe and Rudy were, in appearance at any rate. But then there is another photograph from the voyage, a team shot with each man proudly showing off his US shield on his jersey, primed for action. And there is something feisty about Scholz in this picture, as though the gritty side to his character has taken over. Slater, who had lost all innocence during the First World War, stands behind the seated Scholz, looking quietly confident. The team wouldn't have to wait very long before finding out whether their confidence was justified. They reached Europe on 16 August, and their contribution to the real Olympic Games was not far away.

Scholz noted in his diary the welcome sight of the 'St George Light House', though he probably meant Longships Lighthouse where the St George's Channel meets the English Channel. For Rudy the name wouldn't have mattered so much as the fact that this was 'our first sight of land for eleven days.' They were now able to make their way up the English Channel towards Dover. Then it was across to mainland Europe and up through Holland on the Scheldt River, past the dykes and windmills and into Belgium. Rudy added, 'Finally the city of Antwerp with its great port sheltering flags of very near every nation ...took a taxi and went to Olympic Headquarters where we are due to stay, about ten of us to a large room.'

The 'Olympic Village' consisted of accommodation in a military barracks and a school. It wasn't the sort of comfort the American athletes were looking for as they prepared for the biggest sporting challenge of their lives. The rugby players were put in the school; and one member of the team, Jack Patrick, hinted at his astonishment when he captioned a photograph with the words, 'Wrestlers practicing in school yard – where we LIVED!!!' Rudy Scholz had his own way of curing the claustrophobia. He wrote, 'Took in the city in the evening, its narrow streets and numerous cafes extending out on the sidewalks.'

The Antwerp stadium, with its classical arched entrance and sweeping stands, had been a fitting venue for the opening ceremony unlike any seen before. Baron de Coubertin had always seen the potential of the Olympic movement as an instrument for world peace. Never had the world needed such an instrument more than in 1920, as it struggled to recover from the Great War. So doves were released at the opening ceremony as a symbol of peace.

For the first time, the Olympic oath was taken by a host athlete. It was written by De Coubertin. The oath seemed a timely expression of how sport should be played between nations. After all, Belgium had been chosen as Olympic host because it had seen so much destruction during the First World War. The Games were a symbol of a new hope that men could behave towards each other in a civilised way, even when there was intense competition between them. The oath, first spoken by a Belgian fencer called Victor Boin, went like this: 'In the name of all competitors, I promise that we shall take part in these Olympic Games, respecting and abiding by the rules that govern them, in the true spirit of sportsmanship, for the glory of sport and the honour of our teams.'

The Olympic flag that Boin held while uttering those words was also new. And the spirit of global harmony found further expression in this powerful symbol. The blue, yellow, black, green and red circles, overlapping to convey friendship between the different parts and peoples of the world, created a unique identity for the Olympic Games, one that lasts to this day.

There was nothing ideal about the start of Rudy's own Olympic experience, though. On Thursday, 19 August – five days after that historic Opening Ceremony had taken place – he admitted, 'Got up at 10 – missed the truck taking the rugbyites to practice.' In the stadium, where he watched many of the races, things weren't going much better for the Americans either. He added, 'We lost the 1500 meters to an Englishman [Albert Hill] in the finals. He is a wonderful runner but it made me almost sick to see Joie Ray lose. It was a great race.'

Ray, also known as the Kankakee Kid or 'Chesty', was already a great national favourite and would later become an indoor mile world record holder. But in this race he only came in eighth, which led Rudy to come up with his own theory.

He wrote, 'All of our short distance men are coming thru but none of the long-distance men. I think it was because they had all the athletes down in the hold of the ship coming across and then the complete change of food, water, etc – which would not affect a short-distance man so much but would a long-distance one.'

The emergence of the Scandinavians, particularly the Finns, was another reason why the Americans were not as dominant as they might have hoped. Paavo Nurmi, who would become one of the great Olympians of all time, won the 10,000 and came in second to France's brilliant Joseph Guillemot in the 5,000.

Rudy was right about the impact the Americans were making in the sprints. One of the 'short-distance men' in action – Morris Kirksey, of Stanford – was also in the rugby squad. He was beaten to the gold medal in the 100 metres by just 18 inches (45cm). His fellow American and world record-holder Charley Paddock stole the glory. Throwing his arms in the air wildly as he broke the tape, Paddock took the title and with it the right to call himself the fastest man on earth. Kirksey bounced back with an amazing burst of speed in the last leg of the 4 x 100 relay to break the world record by two-fifths of a second. He had teamed up with Paddock, Loren Murchison and Rudy's cousin, Jackson Scholz, 'The New York Thunderbolt'. Kirksey therefore pocketed coveted gold and silver medals even before the rugby tournament began.

Meanwhile another of the rugby players, Dink Templeton, narrowly missed out on a medal by coming fourth in the long-jump. He would only have one more chance to come away with something tangible, and that would be in the rugby competition. The American rugby players at least had plenty of time to get into condition for the challenge ahead, because the rugby was scheduled towards the end of the Games.

Rudy's diary entry for Friday 20 August confirmed, 'Rain – but took a work-out just the same for an hour and a half. The army takes us to and from the stadium which is about three miles [5km] from here. Saw [Allen] Woodring beat the world in the 200 meters – "The Star-Spangled Banner" was played and it sure made you feel good you were an American. Saw Frank Foss break the world record in the pole vault – 13ft 5ins [4m].'

But according to Scholz some of the other sights were less pleasing on the eye. He added mischievously, 'As for the girls, the American Olympic Athletes state they haven't seen a good-looking girl yet – neither have I but I don't think we have an opportunity to see the best people.' Time and distance appear to have been leading Scholz to reflect carefully on his relationship with Cecilia back home, because he added intriguingly, 'Almost came to a decision about C.'

Meanwhile Babe Slater was keen to revisit Brussels, where he had washed death away during the Christmas of 1918 and rediscovered life in all its glory. Now, less than two years later, he invited Rudy along for company. Scholz, who had so wanted to be part of that war, was only too glad to visit the Belgian capital at last. And you can imagine Babe telling Rudy the significance of Brussels in his personal experience of the war; how reaching the city had felt like the end of the ugliness. Brussels had restored his faith in humanity, and now he was sharing the city with his new friend. While Rudy had reason to feel privileged that he had been chosen in such a way, it may not have been lost on Babe, either, that Rudy had lots of longstanding friends from Santa Clara on the tour, whose company he enjoyed. For all that he had chosen Slater, the man mountain, to spend time with away from the main party.

This new friendship was clearly something they enjoyed but you get the feeling that those images of 'men lying decaying where they fell, guns in hands and skulls in helmets', would not have been memories Babe would have wanted to share, at least not so graphically as he had described them in his extraordinary diary just two years earlier.

Norman Slater revealed: 'He never talked with us about picking up mortally wounded or terribly mangled men at all. I have read his war diary, so I know about some of the awful things he saw. But he didn't discuss it.'

Rudy only told his diary the basic details of what he and Slater had seen together. 'Saturday August 21…After dinner Babe and I went down to the Central Station and caught the train to Brussels, about an hour's ride. On arriving we wandered around for a while and then went to the Madrid Café – a three-storey café. The first floor resembled New York on New Year's Eve. The second floor was a little boisterous I thought – saw a bunch of sailors from Frederick in there. The third floor was the elite of the place.'

Babe was probably pleased that Brussels appeared to be timeless, still lost in wild celebration, just as it had been when last he visited.

Rudy revealed what happened next. 'We went into the Palace Hotel which is the best in Brussels – it reminded me a great deal of the Palace in San Francisco. We got one of their best rooms for 45 francs which is about $4 at the present rate of exchange.'

So there they were, rooming together, the world war veteran and the warrior wannabe; the quiet farmer and the silver-tongued city boy; teammates who respected their differences and looked forward to uniting in the quest for Olympic glory.

By 24 August Rudy was back at the Games because he wrote in his diary, '…went to the swimming meet – saw Duke K [the legendary Hawaiian swimmer and surfer, Duke Paoa Kahanamoku] break the world's record in the 100 yard dash…Heard "The Star-Spangled Banner" played and came back to quarters.'

And that, above all, was clearly what Scholz dreamed of – hearing 'The Star-Spangled Banner' played at the end of the rugby final. Yet the rugby tournament seemed no closer, and the waiting was driving the US players crazy. So there was time for a visit to neighbouring Holland, where Scholz saw horror and beauty in the Hague. He explained, 'Went to first Holland prison built in 1320 – still intact and saw all the instruments used during the Spanish Inquisition – the various cells where famous men of Holland died. Saw pictures drawn in blood. Saw the cell where they starved prisoners to death (kitchen nearby). Saw where the water was allowed to drop – drop by drop on the forehead of the prisoner until he became crazy. Saw lots of other things like that which time forbids telling. Saw the parliament, art galleries with Rembrandt, Rubens and other famous paintings…'.

It is unlikely that Babe Slater would have shown quite such a fascination for the horrors of the prison, given what he had seen with his own eyes less than two years earlier. Still, it is basic human nature that draws young men to such grim moments in history.

The rugby players saw the canals and cafes of Amsterdam too, before returning to Antwerp and the build-up to the Olympic challenge for which they had travelled so far. Yet the challenge was now to come in the form of a single, make-or-break game. Two of the four teams due to take part in the quest for rugby gold, Romania and Czechoslovakia, had pulled out of the tournament. That left the USA and France to play the Olympic final. The French considered themselves so superior that there was doubt at one stage as to whether they would even agree to play the underdogs from across the Atlantic. When the French relented at last and agreed to go ahead with the final against the upstarts of America, it was widely believed that the game would prove to be a one-sided embarrassment.

After all the track and field drama of the previous weeks, the American media that was gathered in Antwerp had completely overlooked the rugby players. Perhaps the US Olympic committee had been slow to draw attention to men almost certainly destined for defeat. Indeed it was only when reporters spotted a group of unknown Americans training outside the Antwerp stadium – and asked what they were doing – that the players were acknowledged at all. It seemed like a good omen, this chance meeting with the American media. Perhaps the people back home would hear about the rugby team now after all, whatever the outcome of the big final.

Not that the sports reporters would have been advising their editors across the Atlantic to devote too many column inches to the US rugby team. The French were practically playing at home and their rugby tradition was far more impressive than that of the USA. Though they had been edged out narrowly by most rivals in Europe's Five Nations Championship that year, they had beaten Ireland 15-7 in Dublin to remind everyone how good they could be.

Besides, the French had beaten the Americans 8-3 at the Inter-Allied Cup the previous year, as we have already heard. No one believed that the battle for Olympic gold would result in anything other than a victory for France. Their team consisted of seasoned players from Racing Club de France, Olympique Paris, Club Athletique des Sport Generaux and Sporting Club Universitaire de Paris. Based around the French capital, these players knew each other's game and knew how to work well together. A measure of their superior experience lay in the fact that France would field the oldest player to take part in the contest – Jacques Forestier, aged 30. The USA would field the youngest – Heaton Wrenn, just 20.

The Olympic Rugby Final took place on Sunday, 5 September. It would be one of the last Olympic events to take place in the Antwerp Stadium, with the closing Ceremony due to take place a week later on 12 September. If the Americans were nervous, it was understandable. Here was one chance for glory; one shot at winning a gold medal. Freeze and they would miss out. Babe, Rudy and most of their teammates had waited what must have seemed like an eternity for their opportunity to express themselves as Olympians. They had sailed stormy oceans, watched with mounting frustration as everyone else played a part in the sporting drama, while they were reduced to spectators. Now at last it was their turn. Within days the Olympic Games would be over. By then Babe and Rudy would either have seized their chance, after all that interminable waiting, or they would have blown it. The latter scenario didn't bear thinking about.

With the success of the trip in the balance, Rudy Scholz attended Mass on the morning of the match. It was his habit to do so every Sunday and he saw no reason to change now. His son Dave explained, 'My father loved the church, the army, the law and rugby.' Rudy probably didn't go so far as to pray for a win. Perhaps he prayed that morning to be allowed to do justice to the talent God had given him. Either way, the Americans would need all the help they could get against the skilful ball-handlers of the French team.

Kick-off was scheduled for 5.00pm. As the moment of truth neared, the weather took a turn for the worse. Scholz revealed later, 'At a council of war we decided that because the ground was wet and slippery and the ball likewise, we would make it a forward game. There was a crowd of about 20,000 present, despite the fact that it was raining.'

That was the second-largest crowd of the 1920 Olympic Games. The Americans didn't feel under any obligation to put on a spectacular show, though. They had come a long way and they wanted to win.

So the council of war, led by the player/coach Danny Carroll and the captain, Charles Tilden, had followed rugby's principles as identified by the father of the modern Olympics, Baron de Coubertin. The more flamboyant players were to respect 'the necessity for each man to think, anticipate, take a decision and at the same time subordinate one's reasoning, thoughts and decisions to those of the captain.'

Rudy Scholz would not be pumping his little legs like a whirlwind in his inimitable, trademark style, at least not in attack. Any speed he achieved would be designed to maximise the impact of a tackle on the opposing winger. This particular game wouldn't allow Rudy the joy of self-expression, ball in hand. Instead discipline would be the key to success, just as De Coubertin had always suggested.

Scholz, along with several teammates, had certainly been raised in the right educational environment to develop such discipline. Scholz added, 'Those from Santa Clara in the final line-up were [James] Fitzpatrick, [John Muldoon], [John] O'Neill and myself. Bill Muldoon and [James] Winston did not play.'

It might have required a certain discipline to watch the first half too, because it became a grim war of attrition, the rugby equivalent of trench warfare, with neither side gaining any significant ground. Rudy jotted down a statistic in his diary that you don't often find in rugby. 'Score end of first half 0-0.'

Keen to impress the crowd, some of whom were becoming increasingly restless at the lack of a spectacle, the European team began to gamble recklessly in the rain.

Rudy explained, 'The French tried a backfield game and although they were fast the slippery ball proved their undoing and the field was quite wet. Our forwards outweighed the French easily, and "Babe" Slater was a wonder in the line-outs, as were…Fish and Tilden.'

Despite the exploits of the other teammates, it is interesting that Rudy was anxious to describe his new friend Babe, first and foremost, as the star of those set pieces.

There are crystal-clear photographs of one melée forming, with Babe Slater momentarily aloof as he assessed where best to enter the fray.

His powerful physique was accentuated by his skin-tight shirt, which clung to his torso in the downpour. Meanwhile Scholz prowled behind the mass of bodies, directing teammates and waiting to intervene when the time was right. The photo summed up the match rather well, with plenty of thought going into how to break the deadlock.

Tactical discipline held among the Americans, with the outcome of the match still on a knife-edge. Rudy didn't see much of the ball, though he showed enough intelligence to be picked out later as one of the best US players on the day. Sometimes less is more. This was a match for the connoisseur rather than the thrill-seeker. The Americans began to frustrate the French, while holding back their own firepower.

Rudy recalled, 'We in the backfield didn't have one passing rush, but our defence was superb and Templeton [the last line of that defence at fullback] did not have one tackle to make.' Then came a partial breakthrough, though after the event Scholz sounded very matter-of-fact about what happened. He wrote, 'Middle of second half our forwards dribbled to the French ten yard line and then we marked a kick directly in front of the goal and ["Dink"] Templeton put it over 3-0.'

In his diary, Rudy made that kick sound easy, though it is worth remembering that in rugby the ten-yard line is near the halfway line. Therefore Rudy was closer to the mark when he wrote later, 'Templeton lifted a fifty-five yard [49m] drop-kick between the posts.' It was a wonderful reply from the man who had suffered high-jump heartbreak when his style had been outlawed; and then long-jump heartbreak when he had narrowly missed out on a medal. Rudy acknowledged 'Templeton – and Carroll at center three-quarter – were outstanding.'

The Americans had found the key to success at last. Kicking the ball forward through the mud as they advanced as a team seemed to spread more panic among the French than any other tactic. It was simple and less risky than keeping the ball in hand in wet conditions.

Scholz described the next big moments in the match. 'Latter part of second half we dribbled to their five yard line and when the French first five fumbled, Joseph Hunter picked it up and fell over the line. Converted.'

That try was an act of opportunism, the pressure created by clever tactics. It proved to be the climactic moment in an extraordinary first Olympic adventure. Templeton converted from a difficult angle. It must have been with a considerable sense of satisfaction that Scholz picked up his pen and wrote the following, simple conclusion to the match report in his diary. 'Final score 8-0.'

That was it. That was how Rudy described the glory. In that diary he had gone into detail about the fundraising, the pranks, the mock-Olympics on the boat and even the flying fish. He had talked of war and the prison in Holland. He had described his emotions while watching other American athletes compete. Yet when he and his teammates had finally secured their places in Olympic history, Rudy found just two words, two digits and a dash.

Perhaps he felt the score spoke for itself. The Olympic dream had come true against all odds. Babe, Rudy and their colleagues must have struggled with their emotions as they heard 'The Star-Spangled Banner' played in recognition of their achievement. It was a familiar sound in Belgium by then; the Americans topped the medal table with 41 gold medals. But when the band struck up the anthem for the rugby men, it must have sounded to them like the first time.

For the record, Sweden came an impressive second with 19 gold medals and Great Britain third with 16. But no one had come close to the USA's tally. Some of those gold medals had been more predictable than others; and few, if anyone, had predicted rugby gold.

Somehow a group of players who hadn't all known the rules of rugby when they left America had managed to pull off a stunning upset. And much of it was due to Babe and Rudy. The French critics heralded both American players as key match-winners, among the very best in the US team. Scholz had fought like a lion while sacrificing his own chance to shine in attack. Slater had starred in the forward set pieces, towering above his opponents as he jumped for the ball when it was thrown back into play from line-outs. The tallest and shortest men on the team had found the right formula and they had emerged triumphant.

Rudy recorded rather formally, 'In the evening we attended a banquet for the team.' That's probably where it all began to sink in. The Olympic journey that had seemed crazy when it was first plotted in a country where rugby had been dying a slow death for years. For daring to dream, the Americans had been given an unlikely reward. They might even have begun to look forward to a welcome home fit for Californian sporting heroes.

In reality, however, there was such a lamentable lack of coverage in the San Francisco newspapers that few heard about the victory by the 1920 US rugby team. The only mention of the big win seems to have been a tiny notation on page ten of the *San Jose Mercury Herald* for 13 September. The brief article was captioned 'American Rugby Team Is Title Winner.' Rudy sent the *Santa Clara Journal* a brief report from Lyons, France, which was published in the tiny newspaper on 9 October. That didn't exactly spark national celebrations. Being one of the last on the 1920 Olympic schedule seems to have counted against the rugby men when it came to press coverage.

There were far more shockwaves in France following the upset. Stunned, the French rugby authorities began to organise a playing tour of their country for the Olympic champions. It wasn't done out of the kindness of their hearts. The hosts were hoping to gain revenge before the Americans were allowed to go home. The US team agreed to the tour, though first they embarked on a trip they considered more poignant and important. The day after that extraordinary final, they headed out of Antwerp bound for the First World War battlefields where Slater had almost lost his life less than two years earlier. After an overnight stop in picturesque Bruges, Babe, Rudy and the boys reached bloody landmarks such as Ypres and the Hindenburg Line. Scholz wrote of how he saw many 'little towns all destroyed' along the way.

The players climbed over discarded tanks and took photos of huge, water-filled shell-holes and lonely, shattered pill-boxes in the muddy gloom. But at the ruins of the town of Ypres, there was a notice from the mayor in English, which read, 'THIS IS HOLY GROUND. NO STONE OF THIS FABRIC MAY BE TAKEN AWAY, IT IS A HERITAGE FOR ALL CIVILISED PEOPLES'.

Perhaps only Slater, Carroll and a few others understood the reality of what had happened at places such as this. Scholz and some of the others were pictured beaming in one location. However, Rudy looked more pensive as he studied part of what appears to have been an underground defensive network, still dressed in USA cap and blazer. Any members of the team who didn't fully comprehend the tragedy of these battlefields need only have asked Slater, for whom the images would still have been distressingly fresh. At no stage had he forgotten those less fortunate than himself. Perhaps the dead, whose muscles had been as strong as his less than two years earlier, were part of the reason why Babe had faced his demons to achieve Olympic glory in Belgium. He had refused to allow the venue to deter him. He had known all along that a return to Belgium would give him another chance to pay his respects to the fallen. Olympic victory had also been a good way to honour the comrades he had lost. It was pretty much all that had lain within his power, except perhaps to live life to the full. The American rugby boys would continue to do just that.

Some of the team, including Rudy Scholz, sailed down the Rhine and went to Berlin. They climbed mountains in Switzerland, then travelled back up to Paris. In the French capital, Rudy described the 'wonderful view' from the top of the Eiffel Tower and then, in a fit of moral indignation, professed himself to be 'disgusted' with what he saw as the seedier side of Paris nightlife. That fierce Catholic spirit was never more evident as he raged, 'I was disgusted with the show – the people evidently have little or no morals as the Folies Bergère are considered a first class show. I was glad to leave Paris the next morning.'

A more worldly-wise Rudy would return to the Folies Bergère four years later. For now there was a fresh sporting challenge to think about. The rugby tour of France was due to begin on Sunday, 19 September with a match against the South-East of France in Lyon. Those who had not already headed back to the USA boarded the train for Lyon on Thursday. Scholz noted, 'Talked finance with Charlie T en route.'

One can only speculate over how the conversation went; but US captain Charles Tilden seems to have been in agreement with other senior team members that they should be suitably reimbursed for their travel and living expenses before they played. The French had promised as much, but it was best to make sure. The game almost didn't happen at all. The French seemed reluctant to pay up front when it came to the crunch. Tilden refused to allow his team to leave the dressing room to play the match until the money was safely in their pockets. A stand-off developed. With a large crowd waiting, the Americans had the upper hand. Finally they were paid what they had been promised, and the contest could begin.

Scholz recorded, 'The game started at 3.00pm and 12,000 people were present as we dashed onto the field. A military band played "The

Star-Spangled Banner" and it sounded good. A minute later the French team came on and the Marseillaise was played.'

So the match had the feel of another international, and the pre-match controversy ensured plenty of edge. Scholz wrote, 'Our forwards per usual much heavier than the French. They put up desperate resistance but at the end of first half Videl [sic] and Patrick went over. Half time 8-0. Second half started again with rush and Scholz and Carroll went over. Later on Tilden, Patrick and Scholz scored again. Final score 26-0.'

That would teach the French to pay expenses more promptly on the rest of the tour. Rudy had run in two tries as the American back line cut loose in all their glory after the careful discipline of the Olympic final. It was another stunning result, and Scholz, the star of the match, was not short of admirers. He confided to his diary, 'I met a dandy little French girl called Emilie before the game and she congratulated me after the game and I asked her if I couldn't see her in the evening. She conferred with her mother and father and said yes. One of the Frenchmen said she came from a "tres bon" family....'.

But rugby hospitality in France is such that evening dates after matches cannot always be kept. Rudy explained, 'After the game the French and Americans gathered at a Brasserie, there was much good will and we drank to each other's good health in punch…and then went back to the hotel for breakfast! Found out that train left for Milan at 9.50am so only had time to try to explain to Emilie and leave.'

From Milan Rudy travelled to Rome, where he tried to see the Pope. Ultimately Rudy was denied an experience he would have cherished. Having consoled himself with the beauty of the Trevi Fountain and the majesty of the Colosseum, it was time to head north again. The next rugby match, against the South of France in Toulouse, was only days away.

Scholz had what he described as 'an altercation' with a big Italian businessman, who tried to take his teammate 'Swede' Righter's seat in the first class carriage when he wasn't there. Rudy wrote, 'He was for overruling my objection but when I shoved him back, although he weighed about 280lb [127kg], he changed his mind.' Anyone who picked on the little guy on the American team soon came to regret it.

After a stopover in Marseilles, the tourists arrived in Toulouse on the day of the match. It was Sunday 26 September, and they rolled in at 5.40am. Unfortunately they couldn't locate their hotel until 7.00am. Rudy slept until 10.30am but still insisted on attending Mass, having found a church that he said dated back to 800AD. With his spirit fortified he was ready for action.

Despite the fatigue they must have been feeling, the Americans were somehow still alert enough to strike first with a converted try. Then an emerging French talent called Adolphe Jaureguy drew in American defenders before passing to Bioussa for an unconverted reply.

There had been other victims of Jaureguy's blistering pace that year. He had already announced his arrival on the European rugby stage with two tries in Dublin during that 15-7 victory at Landsdowne Road. Now Jaureguy had put his side back in the match against the Americans at 5-3. However, the tourists' forward power began to tell and resulted in two more tries in less than three minutes. The physical force of men like Babe Slater proved the key and Rudy had enough tactical know-how to help maintain the momentum. Casually Scholz added in his diary, 'In the afternoon before a crowd of 15,000 we defeated Toulouse by a score of 11-3.' It was an extraordinary achievement after all the tourism and travelling.

The following day Rudy went to Lourdes, a moving religious experience for any devout Catholic, before going on to Bayonne and Biarritz in the Basque country. By Saturday Rudy was playing Roulette in Bordeaux and won 60 francs. On Sunday, 3 October, after High Mass in another beautiful church, it was down to business again, this time against the South West of France. The matches were becoming more difficult. Scholz wrote, 'We defeated Bordeaux 6-3 in a hard-fought game but we were clearly the superior team as the French admitted. We had lost "Pat" [Jack Patrick] and "Swede" [Righter] and that made a big difference.' The Stanford pair had begun their journey home to be part of the college American football season.

The French crowd had booed the lack of American enterprise, and their safety-first decision to rely on the strength of their big forwards. The honeymoon was over. Weary and depleted, the Americans headed back up to Paris for the final game, a full international against France. On this particular visit to the French capital, Rudy avoided the moral problems he had previously encountered at the Folies Bergère by enjoying a night at the opera, watching *William Tell*. The team had most of the week to prepare for the match and check out the city. Rudy's diary entry for Wednesday, 6 October included the following: 'In the evening Charles, Red, Babe, Doe and myself took in the Latin quarter including the Dead Rat.'

He was referring to the Dead Rat Café, a famous Bohemian Café of the 1920s in Montmartre. The original Café Rat-Mort, with its atmospheric stained glass, gas-lights and mirrors, had been a popular haunt for some of the most famous Parisian artists, such as Toulouse-Lautrec, Degas and Manet. However, much as Rudy enjoyed Babe's company and appreciated the artistic treasures of Paris, he was also prepared to explore other avenues that night and the next.

He set up a date for the following evening, and went to the Louvre, the famous Paris art museum, while he waited for the rendezvous. He wrote, 'In the evening I met a girl by appointment who I had seen the other night – she was small and pretty, and as she spoke fairly good English, and to get an insight into the life of a Parisian working girl, I made the date which she readily assented to.'

Eventually they went dancing and Rudy's escort, who was a sales girl, 'danced very good as all Parisians or French girls do. We left about 12 and I took her back to the Latin quarter and left her.' It seems that thoughts of Cecilia destroyed any chance of romance, because he wrote of his French date, 'She offered to kiss me goodbye but a thought of a sweet girl in America made the idea not to my liking so I said good night ("bon nuit") and left.' To ensure that his Catholic conscience was entirely clear, Rudy went on to insist, 'Even if I hadn't thought of the girl in America I wouldn't have because – well it wouldn't have been what I wanted, so altho' the girls of France are nice and very, very attractive, are good looking, love a good time etc, I never kissed one or even thought of doing so.'

It was another classic Scholz moment. But if anyone thought that he had gone soft with all the sightseeing, flirting and seemingly endless victories on rugby pitches in Belgium and France, they were clearly mistaken. The match against France on Sunday, 10 October turned into something of a war, and Scholz was one of the chief protagonists.

Rudy had stuck to his usual routine of going to Mass in the morning, before joining up with the team to travel to the Stade Colombes. As

Rudy put it, the Americans 'played the best team they could get together in France with a crippled line-up…in a mighty-hard-fought game.'

With 25,000 supporters demanding satisfaction, the French seemed to want a war. Many frustrations were let loose that day, including perhaps those that had built up in the aftermath of the real war. Sure, the French were out for revenge that day anyway, after their various teams had suffered four defeats in a month. Beyond that, however, the political tensions that still existed between France and the USA were never going to encourage smooth relations on the sporting battlefield. They could be traced back to 8 January 1918 and the moment the US president, Woodrow Wilson, had argued that Germany should not be brought to its knees. Wilson was anxious that the civilised world should not be motivated by base revenge for Germany's leading role in the slaughter of 16 million, and the wounding of 21 million more in the so-called Great War.

He had said, '. . . we have no jealousy of German greatness, and there is nothing in this programme that impairs it…We wish her only to accept a place of equality among the peoples of the world – the new world in which we now live – instead of a place of mastery.'

The French had lost 1,697,800 people while defending their country from German attack. So they were appalled by such a forgiving attitude towards 'the Bosch'. They demanded massive reparations for their losses; the sort of money that would ensure the Germans remained ruined for the foreseeable future.

So Wilson's 'Fourteen Points' had been largely ignored at the post-war Treaty of Versailles in 1919, which the USA failed to ratify. The Germans had been driven to their knees after all, both financially and territorially. This created the long-term bitterness that would provide a platform for Adolf Hitler's Nazis to rise to prominence in the 1930s. Although the League of Nations – the forerunner to the United Nations – was set up in 1919, the USA was barely involved because her views had been largely ignored. Therefore the fledgling organisation was weaker as a result.

So what did this have to do with the rugby match in Paris? Maybe nothing, but the political backdrop certainly didn't help. Largely due to their opposing views on how to deal with Germany, France and the USA were virtually political enemies when their two sides met in Paris in 1920. Their armies would never clash, of course; but that didn't stop war from breaking out on the rugby field that day. In all respects, the French were determined to put the supposedly domineering Americans firmly in their place. Perhaps, like that portly Italian businessman on the train, they thought that little Rudy would be an easy target. How wrong they were.

Though Scholz played on the wing, he made sure that he was very much in the thick of the action this time; so much so that he soon became the target for some highly cynical French foul play. Rudy refused to take this lying down, and wrote later, 'I was laid out with a big cut over my eye by a dirty kick but before the game was over I laid out two and helped lay out another. One I knocked out was trying to catch a short punch and I jumped at him with feet high and running as hard as I could. He came round in about five minutes. One of the "Frogs" swung at me and I ducked and swung back – we both missed.'

If seen in isolation by the referee, Rudy Scholz's violent conduct might well have earned him the dubious honour of becoming the first player ever to be sent off in a rugby international match. As it was, the match officials were dealing with widespread chaos. Perhaps mindful of the potential for a diplomatic incident, the referee singled out no one player for punishment.

The French were using every dirty trick in the book to try to restore their national pride with a victory. The Americans and Rudy in particular made the mistake of retaliating. And that was doing nothing for their chances of victory.

Baron de Coubertin had understood rugby's guiding principles, which seemed to have been forgotten by the tourists now. 'So many decisions require an agile mind and self-control…Discipline is the key to success,' he had written. Where there was no discipline, there could be no victory.

With their discipline all but destroyed in the Stade Colombes, the Americans failed to hold their line. Four times the French burst over for tries, including one from their majestic new superstar on the wing, Adolphe Jaureguy. It seemed that Jaureguy was a man who relished the big occasion. Though he hadn't played in the Olympic final, he was certainly making his presence felt now. And his punishing grace was proving the difference in the battle against the Californians.

The other try-scorers for the home side were the other winger, Raoul Got, the centre, Francois Borde, and the fly-half, Eugene Billac. Scrum-half Philippe Struxiano only managed one conversion, largely because many of their sweeping moves saw France score in the corners. The Americans' only reply came through a try scored by Harold Von Schmidt, converted by full-back G. W. Davis. The final score was 14-5. Rudy recorded in his diary how a French match reporter had attributed his violent outbursts to his German roots.

He explained, 'The paper the next day said Scholz played well but that he showed too much of the Bosche make-up in him.' The insult would have wounded Rudy on several levels, not least because he had been more than prepared to fight against the land of his German forefathers in the war. The newspaper critic didn't seem too anxious to point out that Rudy had been provoked by French thuggery either.

Rudy was left to defend himself in his diary when he added, 'But believe me I was sorely peeved to put it as mildly as I can for the dirty kick I received. It was the first game I ever saw red but I sure did that game. After the game I went to the doctor and had three stitches put in my eyebrow and had a shot of anti-tetanus, which cost 100 francs with the assistance of a French lad of 17…After that I went to the Louis 14 restaurant where the team was to eat dinner and invited the French lad to eat with me. The meal was very good and we all got up to make speeches.'

Diplomatic relations were apparently restored, though it had been a violent end to a wonderful adventure. The French had gained their revenge at last, though the Americans knew they would soon be leaving for home with what they had come for – Olympic gold medals. Babe and Rudy were intelligent enough to work out for themselves one of the most important differences between the two matches. The most significant quality that had won the US team that Olympic gold – their personal discipline – had been absent from the final match in Paris. If they didn't realise it, Baron de Coubertin could have told them.

Before the time came to say goodbye to Europe, there was one last opportunity for some sightseeing in beautiful Switzerland. As usual Rudy helped to organise the trip and obtain the appropriate stamps in passports. The boys saw Interlaken, Grindlewald and the Matterhorn mountain before heading back to Pairs and then Antwerp, scene of their

Olympic triumph. Finally it was time to set sail on the steamer again, docking first at Southampton, from where Scholz wanted to visit London. As it turned out there wasn't time.

Just as Slater had encountered some choice remarks from the English on the voyage to war in 1918, so Scholz noted that some of their sailors were keen to take all the credit for defeating the Germans. He wrote, 'These English are a cocky bunch and supercilious however – as we left the harbor or rather river after taking on oil the crew of an English ship yelled at us "Who won the war?"'

Babe Slater would have had the right to reply 'We all did.' The British were not the only ones to have risked their lives and suffered terribly a couple of years earlier. For Rudy, who had missed that war entirely, the English taunt would have hurt. One can only imagine how sore Rudy might still have been feeling about having been unable to serve his country militarily. At least he had done the USA proud on the rugby field at the Olympics. Now he had a scar from serving his country in France too, albeit a minor one. 'I took the patch off my eyebrow today,' he wrote on 20 October. Sailing away, he noted that 'the country of England looks nice and green with gentle rolling hills.' Four years later he and Babe would be back – and the English would create a much more favourable impression.

———

chapter 5

LOVE AT THE CROSSROADS

Rudy Scholz later explained why his first Olympic adventure should have marked the end of his love affair with rugby. Looking back in 1977 he wrote, 'We won the Olympic Games rugby gold medal in 1920, when Dink Templeton kicked a 55-yard [49m] drop-kick. That was the end of rugby as the Californian schools had gone back to American football in 1919.'

Between 1920 and 1923 the game of rugby was threatened with extinction in the United States. Competitive matches were rare, teams were dying out. Those who still loved the sport simply had no way to initiate its much-needed revival.

Babe Slater didn't seem to be too worried. He threw himself wholeheartedly into American football after his Olympic adventure. In fact he led the men of the Woodland American Legion to such dominance in northern California football that they only lost twice in three years between the two Olympic Games.

During the third year, however, an interesting communication from Paris reached the sports administrators of California. It wasn't about American football, but rugby football. The French were not prepared to allow the US players to change games so easily. Rudy explained, 'The French whom we defeated in 1920 demanded the US play in the 1924 Games. They insisted we come back. They asked our Olympic committee that we again get together a team, because it wasn't sportsmanlike for the defending champions not to return. California was asked to organise a team.'

Despite their victory over the Americans in the final international of the 1920 tour, the French craved a more complete and satisfying revenge over their Olympic conquerors. That could only be achieved in one way – to beat the USA to gold next time around.

Happily for the French, the 1924 Games were to be staged in Paris. For that honour they had Baron de Coubertin to thank. The aristocrat knew that the time had almost come for him to stand down as the President of the International Olympic Committee. He was haunted by the failure of the 1900 Olympics, which had also been held in Paris. Those Games, only the second of the modern era after Greece in 1896, had been held all summer in the French capital. Yet they were still somehow overshadowed by World Trade Fairs and other high-profile commercial occasions held in Paris to herald a new century.

To dampen the Olympic spirit further still, the Games had suffered from a lack of organisational foresight. Several events central to the Games had been scheduled on a Sunday, something that upset some of the American college boys as well as Christians from other countries. (Judging by what happened in 1924, the French never did learn from their previous mistake.)

The ethics of the organisers were further questioned when one athlete, a fencer, was even paid prize money. Other athletes were not paid when they won something; the problem was that they were not even awarded medals. In short, the Games had simply lacked identity, that special something to capture the world's imagination. In fact they had made such a poor impression that De Coubertin later reflected, 'It is a miracle that the Olympic movement survived those Games.'

These setbacks might not have created a compelling case for giving the French the Olympic Games again. But De Coubertin desperately wanted to leave the world a happy memory of France as Olympic host before he made way for his successor. He was in the perfect position to do something about it, and for the Netherlands his power was ominous. Though the Dutch had been due to host the 1924 Games, suddenly Amsterdam was told she would have to wait. Paris was to be given another go. Since the French had suffered so badly in the war, they deserved that second chance, or so the argument went.

The Olympics had to be a positive celebration in order to reflect well on France. The world waited patiently, with a degree of sympathy and understanding. The French had yet to completely recover their national pride after the horrors of the First World War. This could be the dawning of a new era for the country, a fresh source of respect.

This time, everything had to go smoothly from the start. Rugby provided the perfect opportunity. What better way for the Olympics to begin than for France to batter the USA in a one-sided curtain-raiser? They would shatter once and for all the notion that an American team could ever live with French elegance and excellence on the rugby field. This time they would not be caught cold, untrained and unfit. This time the match would be played earlier and the French would just be coming off their rugby season. Therefore they would be in great shape to settle an old Olympic score.

That's why in September 1923, the French Olympic Committee sent their official invitation across the Atlantic. 'They were looking for a punching bag', said Norman Cleaveland, one of the first to answer the call to try out for the 1924 team, even though he had never played rugby before. 'We were told to go to Paris and take our beatings like gentlemen.'

His future teammate, Dud De Groot, observed wryly, 'France, whom the United States defeated for the title in 1920, was very insistent that the title-holder enter a team so that she might be given the opportunity to remove the laurel wreath from the crown of her dear brothers from the USA.'

Three years after their 1920 Olympic triumph, even the gold medal winners were rugby-rusty. In fact most of them hadn't played the game since 'The Battle of Paris'. American football was king by now. Since Babe Slater had become a Gridiron prince, rugby was no more than a happy memory for him.

So it was for most of the 1920 heroes, though rugby die-hards were still scattered here and there. One of them was Rudy Scholz, who had become Secretary of the Pacific Coast Football Association. Keeping rugby alive was something akin to an impossible mission, though he had always loved a challenge. Even so Rudy's career had to come first, because by then he had his own legal practice in San Francisco. Rugby administration was a labour of love, though by then it was as though he were trying to hold back the sands of time. This was a new era; the best exponents of rugby had moved on. As Rudy put it later, 'We had rugby players who had not played for six or seven years and were older and in professions or business.'

That rugby still enjoyed a special place in Rudy's heart was partly down to the fact that a rival had disappeared from the scene. Cecilia, it turned out, was not the woman of his dreams after all. Rudy continued to harbour a dream, 'to meet a girl who has ideals and will sacrifice for those ideals – that is the ingredient to life.' Had Cecilia wanted to move their physical relationship on further than the fiercely Catholic Rudy had wanted to go? Had she grown weary of waiting to find out whether or not Rudy wanted to marry her?

We can only speculate as to why Cecilia, whom he had described as having a 'vivid personality', had fallen short of Scholz's ideal. Without doubt Rudy's standards were high, because he commented before very long, 'Perhaps it is a reflection of myself. An idealist maintained that all things are more or less a reflection of yourself.'

If there had been disappointment, even upset over the split, Rudy consoled himself with hopes for a happier romantic future. As his son, Dave, observed in 2009, 'Dad had an incredible image of the ideal woman and he didn't find her until later.' In the mean time, searching for such a woman would be fun. And now that Rudy no longer felt he would be leaving his heart in San Francisco, the second Olympic adventure might even be more enjoyable than the first.

For the trip to become a reality though, the US Olympic Committee had to allow the rugby team to participate in Paris. And even though Babe, Rudy and the boys were the reigning champions, the USOC met their overtures with the same pessimism and reluctance they had shown back in 1920. Once again it was made clear to the rugby men that they could only go to the Olympics if they found a way to fund themselves, 'for what would probably constitute a losing effort.'

This was no way to treat the Olympic title holders. And even if it was true that they were unlikely to win, what had happened to competing 'for the glory of sport'? De Coubertin's noble Olympic Oath didn't assert that it was only worth turning up if you were sure to win. To a feisty character like Rudy, such disrespect was only likely to inspire him to greater efforts. Scholz would just have to prove the USOC wrong. The question was: how many others felt like him? He couldn't do it alone.

Rudy needed to know at least some of the 1920 team were prepared to dust off their boots and defend their title. If Babe and the other old 'ruggers' had no appetite to turn back the clock, the project was probably already dead in the water. It wasn't as though Scholz could mount a nationwide search for ready-made talent. Rudy explained, 'We didn't have the love or money for try-outs all over the US or even California.'

But the recruitment drive did have that old Scholz determination behind it. So in that autumn of 1923, the Northern California Rugby Association was born, with Sam Goodman as chairman and Rudy Scholz as secretary. There was only one mission at its heart – to raise a team good enough to shock the world in Paris. Goodman and Scholz went straight to work. All the Boys of 1920 were contacted and a general advertisement was put in the press for rugby and American football players to come to the first practice.

One man whose imagination was captured by the prospect of an Olympic adventure was a dashing young San Franciscan sports star by the name of Ed Turkington. 'Turk' had the dark good looks of a film star, he was intelligent and witty, yet also armed with a toughness that was a product of the city in which he had been raised and the trauma it had suffered.

Though Ed had been just six years old when the San Francisco earthquake had struck, he remembered being evacuated amid the continued tremors and aftershocks. With the help of his family he escaped the fires, which raged all the more freely because the water mains pipes had cracked and there was little with which to combat the thunderous flames. The sense of helplessness many city folk felt as they watched large parts of San Francisco burn to the ground didn't last long. West Coast communities had been born because their people possessed a spirit of adventure and plenty of determination. No natural disaster was going to destroy that spirit; and the citizens of San Francisco rebuilt their lives just as quickly as they could.

By the age of seven Ed Turkington had settled into a new neighbourhood. There he developed a charming fascination for the new arrival in the Horton family, which lived below. Elaine Horton was tiny and sweet, and Ed used to creep downstairs and ask straight out if he could 'wash the baby'. More often than not his wish was granted, and both the Hortons and the Turkingtons marvelled at Ed's tenderness.

When the Hortons moved to a more prosperous area of San Francisco, the families lost touch. Ed missed the simple pleasures of bath time with Baby Elaine; but the Turkingtons also found a new home and that helped the young boy to look ahead. As fate would have it, however, the mothers of the growing children later met by chance on a downtown San Francisco street. Through that meeting, the children soon rediscovered each other too, though the age difference meant that romance didn't enter into the equation at this point. Elaine looked up to Ed, and would soon come to love him, though it would take time for those feelings to be reciprocated.

Ed was already a much-admired figure at the prestigious Lowell High School, where he became Senior Class President, 1916–17. It would have been difficult for him to resist the attentions of some of the prettiest girls on the social scene during those years. He didn't try too hard. In fact Ed broke more hearts than Elaine's during his teenage years, though somehow she always stayed close to him as a friend.

The dynamic between Ed and Elaine changed when she began to grow into a woman. Unsurprisingly, Ed began to look at her in a different way. As for Elaine, she had fallen deeply for this older boy who had first featured in her life so many years earlier. As far as Elaine was concerned, Ed was simply irresistible, with his dark hair, smouldering gaze and natural charm. The pair became sweethearts, just as it seemed that destiny had always demanded.

A lot of the time, however, Ed's mind was filled with sporting matters more than romance. He had the natural speed to excel on any sports field and had developed the physical maturity to match. They were still rebuilding the city when Turkington was a teenager, and during school vacations he spent many a long hour working on the building sites in the Marina district. Ed's reward for helping San Francisco to become glorious again was extra strength to go with some extra pocket money. 'Turk' remained lean and retained his blistering speed, but by now he had grit to go with his talent.

The art of sprinting requires a psychological edge and Ed was well equipped. While still in High School he won a city-wide track meet in two events – the 100 and 220 yard dash. No wonder he excelled at rugby when he first played the game at Lowell High School. But Turkington moved with the times as young people do; and American football soon became the dominant sport in Northern California. Before long, Ed became one of the rising stars of the game.

In fact when the time came in 1917 to plot his next step, Turkington was the only High School graduate to be offered three football athletic scholarships: to Santa Clara University, Rudy's old stomping ground; to the University of California, Berkeley, known to one and all as 'Cal'; and finally to Stanford University.

For the time being, Ed chose to develop his business skills instead. He became a Grain and Feed salesman for poultry and livestock all over Northern California. At the same time he stayed in shape and remained a highly rated sprinter with the famous San Francisco Olympic Club, an establishment which also had rugby at its heart. No wonder Stanford were prepared to leave the door open for Turkington, in case he ever decided that college life was something he might want to pursue at some point in the future.

One thing was for sure: Ed wanted to make the best possible use of this sporting prowess while still in his prime. Yet he wasn't quite fast enough to try out for the Olympic track team. So naturally he became receptive to rumours circulating in San Francisco that Rudy Scholz and Sam Goodman intended to advertise try-outs for the 1924 Olympic rugby team. He also knew that the pursuit of his dream was likely to create complications in his personal life, for he and Elaine were still very much an 'item'. That didn't stop him from wanting to go to Paris.

By 1923 they had been together for a good few years and some of the excitement seemed to have gone. Many a tearful scene saw them on the verge of breaking up, only for both to draw back from the brink and declare their love for each other. Elaine was not prepared to give up her long-term dreams of marriage, just because Ed sometimes felt a passing attraction towards another girl.

So they had stayed together through thick and thin; and slowly but surely Elaine appeared to be reaping her reward for her determination. The dashing Ed finally seemed to be showing signs of settling down with her; and the next natural step might even have been the announcement of their engagement. Perhaps that was part of the problem, because Ed seemed to be having second thoughts about their relationship and its comforts. These were make-or-break times.

The prospect of a rugby adventure at the Olympic Games in Paris, with all the freedom and excitement it offered, was as appealing as the most beautiful woman Ed could imagine. So the Olympics became his goal. And the way he saw it, the Games would also decide his personal future and the direction it would take. A foreign adventure would reveal what his true feelings were for the long-suffering Elaine. If he really loved her enough to want to spend the rest of his life with her, he would know by the time he returned.

On 16 December an advisory board was formed to oversee the US rugby team's efforts to reach the 1924 Olympic Games. Rudy Scholz was on that board and played a leading role. On 20 December the *San Francisco Chronicle* announced, 'Rugby Tryouts Slated Sunday.' It added, 'All amateur rugby players are eligible to try for the team.'

Within three days, some 85 players had expressed an interest in the first practice session, which was due to take place on 23 December. No one was more delighted than Rudy Scholz and Sam Goodman. When the day came, as 200 curious spectators gathered in the stands to watch the spectacle, Rudy and Sam waited to see how many players would actually turn up. The initial numbers would determine just how ruthless they would need to be towards the end of the selection process.

Local reporter Harry M. Hayward wrote, 'Rudy Scholz, former Santa Clara captain and now secretary of the Northern California Rugby Association, announced yesterday that, following the first and second practices, the squad would probably be cut down to about thirty men. These will be the ones showing the best condition and proving the fact that they are still fast enough to play the game.' Perhaps Hayward would be proved right for also having written, 'Although rugby has been supposedly dead for three or four years, the love for the game has been smouldering in the hearts of everybody who ever played it.'

Scholz would already have been hoping that a little of that love was still smouldering in the heart of Babe Slater, his friend from 1920. Babe was potentially a very important member of the 1924 team. After all, Slater had been 'a wonder in the line-outs' during the 1920 final, according to Rudy. The man was a colossus, his courage beyond question. Like Rudy, he was someone you could trust when the going got tough. Smooth-talking Rudy was Babe's opposite in so many other ways, yet Scholz still admired the quiet farmer, whose actions seemed to speak louder than words. So Rudy waited to see if Babe Slater would turn up at Ewing Field for that first practice. And no one would have been more disappointed when he didn't.

Was it just too close to Christmas for Babe, who was devoted to his mother, twice widowed? Moving to Woodland meant he was now a considerable journey from the bright lights of San Francisco, and you got the feeling he liked it that way. Perhaps he had fallen out of love with rugby forever, or maybe the stress and strain of another European adventure was something he just didn't feel he needed any more. Few could have blamed him had he felt that way. After all, what else did he really have to prove, as a sportsman or a man? Whatever the reason, Babe stayed away.

Fifty-five others turned up though, including Ed Turkington. One look at his rivals told 'Turk' that competition would be tough. Norman Cleaveland was a talented sportsman who had never even played rugby before, but was obviously a naturally powerful runner. George Dixon was an American footballer from the Olympic Club, blessed with speed and a strong physique.

The question was, were these men smart enough to grasp rugby's rules? Could these guys be taught to exert downward pressure on the ball in the endzone? All they really had to do was fall over, with ball in hand, once they crossed the line. That was a try. But for American footballers this was easier said than done, because their instinct was to celebrate prematurely before the ball was down. Suddenly they would find they had been bundled out before they could secure three points.

The clash of games doubtless provided some comical moments in that first practice. At least it would have been funny if they weren't supposed to be acting like potential Olympians. The players didn't know what they were doing just yet, so patience was required. Rudy wasn't the most patient man in the world, so he hoped the newcomers would learn rugby's peculiarities sooner rather than later.

There would be others to help teach the 'rugby virgins', because a wealth of experience turned up too. The Muldoon brothers, John and Bill, were there, reunited with Scholz, their old friend from the days of the Santa Clara rugby team. Harold Von Schmidt also tried to make his presence felt, though he wasn't quite the force he used to be.

It was a measure of the organised tone of the day that Charles Tilden, captain of the 1920 stars, and Dud De Groot, a former Stanford American football captain, were left on the sidelines because neither arrived in time to 'suit up' in their sports kit. Perhaps it was best that De Groot watched this session, so that he could learn something of this strange game he had never played. The idea that he was about to commit himself wholeheartedly to a sport that he didn't even know or understand sounds outrageous in the modern era. However these were pioneering, experimental times when anything was deemed possible if a Californian put his mind to it.

Tilden's appearance, albeit belated, cast further doubt on Babe's interest in the project. The former leader had made the trip from Woodland, where Babe was based. He didn't bring any news of the big man. Scholz would have been disappointed at Slater's absence, yet he still had a great turn out. Besides, a no-show for this first get-together didn't automatically mean exclusion from the squad. Neither did attendance guarantee a place. 'Swede' Righter was there along with Dixie Fish from the 1920 squad, yet neither man would make the final cut.

On the other hand, John O'Neill had moved to Montana and couldn't make the first try-out; while Jack Patrick was another noticeable absentee. Both men would be automatic choices once they showed willing. Some American footballers looked like lost causes, though there were noticeable exceptions. Dick Hyland was a freshman at Stanford and another of the 'rugby virgins'. He shone out in the crowd when he demonstrated an amazing ability to change direction at pace with a body-swerve. Since he was built for battle too, he promised to be quite an asset to the group.

A newcomer called Bob Devereux showed potential at fly-half, a key position in rugby. As soon as he receives possession, the fly-half has to make an instant tactical decision whether to kick, run with the ball or pass along the line. Make the right decision often enough and your team generally wins. Make the wrong decision and your team loses. Devereux made mistakes like any novice, but there were glimmers of hope that he might just have the makings of a rugby brain in that tough skull of his, given the right kind of tuition. Teach Devereux to pass backwards and release the ball when tackled, and you never knew what good things might happen in the long run.

Rudy and Sam would have known by the end of that first practice that they had the makings of some sort of a team. Whether or not it was a rugby team remained to be seen. And if it was, whether it would ever be good enough to chase the Olympic dream was another question entirely. For a first practice it was as much as they could have hoped for, even if Slater's no-show had been something of a blow. 'So we picked about 50 rugby and American football players located around the San Francisco Bay area', recalled Rudy later. Scholz and Goodman were in business; a little worried about how to turn this squad into champions, but in business all the same.

As a potential squad member, Rudy would not be involved in the final selections. That would be down to the coach and a few other very senior rugby men. The identity of the coach was still to be decided. Under consideration were Steve Guerin of the Olympic Club and Jim Wylie, the New Zealander who had stayed in California after the 1913 All Blacks tour. Wylie had helped to turn Stanford into an impressive rugby force, and what he didn't know about the game probably wasn't worth knowing. Then there was Charlie Austin, Stanford's assistant coach, who had played against Wylie in 1913. Pete Flanagan from the Barbarians was also in the running. Meanwhile Harry Maloney of Stanford was already earmarked as trainer. These were all good men with shrewd rugby brains. The signs were positive in San Francisco; the project had at least found some momentum. In terms of producing a cohesive rugby team there was only one way – and that was up. But they had some raw talent to work with; and that in itself was something.

Yet the signs elsewhere were not so encouraging. For all the hard work that Rudy Scholz and the others had put in, the French Olympic Committee still appeared to be receiving negative signals from their US counterparts. It seemed that rugby was the last sport in the world the

USOC wanted to endorse as the build-up to the Paris Games began. Why else would the French have felt compelled to urge the American committee to put its weight behind the adventure? The Secretary General of the Executive Committee for Paris 1924 was almost begging as he wrote, '…We will be eternally grateful to you for inviting the United States team to the Olympic Rugby tournament…the committee is requesting your support for the Olympic Rugby tournament…It is the most precious and powerful school for developing the individual and for teaching him to remain within the bounds of the loyal and generous mastery of self.'

The letter sounded as though it could well have been written by Baron de Coubertin himself. It certainly seemed to be inspired by his thinking. And the French were so keen to win the USOC's support for the Olympic rugby tournament that they ended with some unashamed emotional blackmail. 'The entire French community is awaiting your response, which, if negative, will result in deep disappointment and sadness.'

If there was still doubt over whether or not they would be allowed to compete, no one seems to have told the Californians, who were already preparing for the challenge. All were making personal sacrifices, some more substantial than others. Ed Turkington, for example, didn't consider it fair to expect his long-term girlfriend, Elaine Horton, to sit around waiting for him while he trained obsessively for selection. He intended to secure a place in the Olympic squad at all costs, and that meant total dedication. The squad was due to leave for France in the spring; and if he secured his place he would be gone for months. This wasn't the time to be reinforcing personal commitments back home. So one day soon after Christmas Ed suddenly turned Elaine's world upside down. He suggested a six-month trial separation. Stunned, she agreed to his request because it seemed her only hope for keeping her man in the long run. When the dust settled, however, there was no guarantee that she would accept the arrangement so dutifully. Neither did Ed count on her to be waiting for him like a love-sick puppy six months down the line. Human nature suggested that anything could happen in half a year. Feeling wounded and at least partially rejected, Elaine might meet someone else on the rebound. Everyone had their limits and she had been through plenty to keep them together already.

Ed didn't know how he would feel after a long trip abroad either. If he was experiencing doubts about Elaine now, what would the many temptations of Paris do to him? His relationship with his long-standing girlfriend suddenly looked weak and vulnerable. Cracks caused by sporting ambition were likely to widen under the strain of separation. The 1924 Olympics had left the couple's future in the balance – and it wasn't even 1924 yet.

New Year came soon enough, and with it the realisation among the rugby hopefuls that competition was about to intensify. When the second training session began on the morning of 6 January 1924, Wylie coached the forwards while Austin handled the backs. There was a practice match lasting half an hour at the end of the get-together, during which Harry Maloney and Steve Guerin moved players on and off the field as they saw fit, tinkering with positions as they went along. A banquet was held at the St Germain restaurant that lunchtime, where selectors decided it was time to start to separate the men from the boys.

A practice match on 27 January would provide some answers. Rudy told reporters that this game would also give the public a chance to see the Olympic team in action in a real contest, because it would consist of the first and second-string teams. The selection process hadn't actually reached such an advanced stage, though you had to admire Rudy's gift for public relations. And the pursuit of excellence was genuinely intense in the run-up to that contest. The next training session came just three days later, on 9 January, and was run by Rudy on ground opposite San Francisco's Civic Centre. Meanwhile Goodman learned that he was to be officially nominated as team manager. The application was to be processed by the Olympic Games Committee as soon as possible, making Big Sam the first certainty for the trip.

There were further practices for the players on the following two Sundays, 13 and 20 January. At one of these, Scholz was treated to a sight he must have been hoping to see for some time. The man-mountain, Babe Slater, arrived to join the party. Not only did Babe turn up for action, he brought his elder brother Norman with him too. Both men made enough of an impact to be chosen for the exhibition game, Reds against Blues, at the end of the month. The Slaters were placed with the Reds, which seemed on the face of it to have the stronger team. Jack Patrick and the new flare player, Dick Hyland, were sure to show the opposition a clean pair of heels given the chance. They were joined by another Woodlander man, Linn Farish. The Stanford University graduate was shaping up to be an impressive player. A geologist, Farish was highly intelligent and applied his analytical brain to events on a sports field too. He already spotted gaps and anticipated play to great effect in American football. Now he just had to learn to read rugby matches the same way.

Meanwhile the novice strong man, Dud De Groot, who had been forced to sit out the very first practice session, was from the same seat of learning as Farish. If anything he looked more frightening, his huge head and sky-scraper frame towering above most of his rivals. But he too would need to grasp rugby's fundamentals quickly if all that brain power was to be put to good use.

The 'Blue' line-up boasted greater experience, but looked thin on spectacular talent. At least Rudy Scholz would provide a threat on the wing. Even so, he might have been a little worried to feature in what he had personally categorised as 'the second string'. Rudy's consolation lay in the fact that he had his old friends Bill and John Muldoon for company, and that gave the Blues a distinctive Santa Claran flavour. Also picked for Rudy's side was Ed Turkington, though his position as a wing forward was perhaps unlikely to bring out the best in him. 'Turk' might have been better off among the backs, where he could have shown off his searing speed more easily during passing rushes.

It is not known whether Elaine Horton was among the 100 spectators at a rain-soaked Ewing Field for the trial match that would effectively decide her ex-boyfriend's fate. She would probably have been torn between wanting the man she loved to fulfil his sporting ambition to star overseas, and wanting him to stay in San Francisco so that she could persuade him that their future lay together after all. If she did show up to watch Ed in action that day, she would not have seen him shine. Others seized the day better, most of them on the opposing team.

Dick Hyland began to fulfil his promise with two tries for the Reds, and Morris Kirksey, the 1920 sprint king, also went over for an impressive score. Patrick nailed three conversions and the Blues were well beaten. That didn't stop one journal with a distinct Santa Claran bias from running the headline: 'Scholz Shines at Wing.' The single paragraph describing the game read, 'Rudy Scholz, wing on the 1920 fifteen, was exhibiting his fine old game in the second half yesterday, his defensive play featuring strongly. Tilden at breakaway was another Blue mainstay, while the Muldoon brothers, John in the thick of the scrums, and Bill in the line-outs, did their best to stem the Red tide.'

Turkington at least did well enough not to be substituted, though he was left sweating on whether or not he would be included in the final Olympic squad. The game asked more questions than it answered. And the main question for rugby veterans like Scholz and Slater was how on earth they were going to mould some of the Gridiron giants into rugby players. Rudy explained later, 'The American football players were young, big, strong and fast but knew very little of rugby and our try-out games left a great deal to be desired.' You could just imagine the newcomers passing forward, blocking each other and doing all the things rugby players aren't allowed to do, while Rudy tried not to tear his hair out.

February brought more hard practice – with Charlie Tilden still shining just as brightly as he had back in 1920. Meanwhile a busy Sam Goodman had already arranged two matches in England prior to the great Olympic challenge in France. The Americans would play Blackheath and Harlequins in the second half of April. Two of England's very best clubs would now be helping to knock the Americans into shape. That's if they didn't knock all the confidence out of the US team first.

To help finance the trip, a fundraising luncheon had been organised for 6 March. But squad members were still expected to raise enough cash to meet the daily living expenses incurred on any tour abroad. Therefore the sooner everyone knew whether they had been selected or not, the better.

A second match between Reds and Blues took place on Friday 22 February, George Washington's Birthday. It was notable for two incidents. Babe Slater scored a try, confirming his standing as one of the squad's most likely selections…and Rudy Scholz was injured. The precise nature of that second-half injury remains unclear, though it appears to have left Rudy's place in the squad in jeopardy. The list of lucky names was due to be finalised on 28 February. Time was running out for injured men to recover; and if Rudy wasn't fit, it wouldn't matter how much organisational work he had done. Then fate played a hand, causing delays in the announcement of the squad. Former All Black

Wylie didn't make it to San Francisco on the 28th to lend his experience to the selection process, so decisions were put on hold. Coach Austin missed the next practice on 2 March because he was sick. Time stood still for a few days more.

By 4 March, it was felt that 11 men could safely be named as certainties for the Olympic adventure. The very first man on the team sheet was Babe Slater. He may not have been present for that first practice, but he had shown his commitment to the cause since, and appeared to be even more formidable than before. Among the other players named were the most talented runners with ball in hand. Dick Hyland and Jack Patrick could turn a moment's hesitation among the opposition into a seemingly effortless try, thanks to a sudden change in pace and direction. As long as they remembered to touch the ball down it was felt that all would be well.

John O'Neill, Rudy's tough little teammate from Santa Clara, was on the list. What O'Neill hadn't told Rudy or anyone else was that he intended to undergo an operation to remove his appendix before the ship sailed for Europe. He thought he could mend in time to keep playing once he reached the other side of the Atlantic. A gambler by nature, O'Neill calculated that it was more of a risk not to have the operation. He seriously thought he could get away with the operation, as long as he didn't receive a direct blow on the wound.

Meanwhile 'Red' Meehan, Charles Tilden, Charles Doe and Joseph Hunter from the 1920 gold-medal-winning team were all selected early. Also safely on the trip was the rugby novice George Dixon, chosen for the wing; and the similarly inexperienced Al Williams, a former captain of the Olympic Club Gridiron team, recruited for the forwards. Norm Cleaveland was also given the good news, despite never having played the game. If the French had seen how many 'rugby virgins' were included in this initial list of 11, they would have been astounded.

Two days later the fledgling American team's fundraising luncheon was held at the St Francis Hotel. The event was run by William F. Humphrey, president of the Olympic Club, with the rugby team's manager, Sam Goodman, in attendance to impress upon the money men the importance of their contributions. In the space of just 20 minutes, some $25,000 was pledged by some of San Francisco's most respected businessmen. Now there could be no doubt. The squad would travel.

On 9 March, after another practice at Ewing Field, more novices were added. Dud De Groot and 'Lefty' Rogers, better known for American football and basketball, were given the green light. Norman Slater, Babe's elder brother, also secured his place. At least 'Nor' knew what rugby was all about. Ed 'Mush' Graff knew less, but was picked just the same; and so was H. P. 'Pete' Cunningham, for his versatility and guts. Yet there was still no confirmation that Rudy Scholz would be making the trip to Europe.

One more agonising week passed, at the end of which there was another practice at Ewing Field. Four more names were added: Linn Farish, Phil Clark and Bob Devereux were a formidable Stanford trio. The fourth man came from Santa Clara…and his name was Rudy Scholz. In the nick of time, Rudy had won his fitness battle and proved he was ready to go.

The squad suffered a blow when 'Red' Meehan was forced to hand in his resignation due to business commitments. So a stocky college American footballer from Santa Clara called Caesar Manelli took his berth in the front row of the forwards. And Manelli was to prove quite an asset.

By the time the last practice took place at Ewing on 25 March, there were just two places available. Ed Turkington would have been a desperate man by now, since it appeared that only two more forwards were required. More suited to using his pace among the backs, Turkington would nevertheless have given his all during that practice. Then he waited for the news…only to be hit by a sickening feeling of disappointment. The last two names were William Muldoon and John Cashel. Turkington was out and everything about his life – even his trial separation from Elaine – was suddenly thrown into chaos. They say what goes around comes around. Just as Ed had all but broken Elaine's heart, so his own heart was all but broken.

There were always going to be winners and losers when the final cut was made. Rudy felt the selectors had done what they had to do, despite the green look to the squad. He admitted, 'Our final team was composed of about half American footballers and half old rugby players.' No wonder the selectors were so keen to make room for Alan Valentine after it came to their attention that he was studying at Oxford University and was playing the game regularly.

Largely, however, Ed had lost out to men who had never played the game before and that must have hurt. At least he hadn't jumped the gun by launching a personal fundraising campaign for his Olympic adventure. So he didn't have to tell donors that their generous pledges were no longer necessary, because it had turned out that he wasn't good enough to be an Olympian. That would have been excruciating. It was bad enough having to face family and friends to give them the bad news.

Two days after Turkington had been handed one of the greatest disappointments of his life, something extraordinary happened. Charles Tilden, the captain of the 1920 team, was forced to withdraw from the squad due to ill health. Not only did this raise the question of who would be captain for 1924: but one more name was needed to complete the squad. The captaincy issue could wait, the selectors decided. For now it was more important to come up with a replacement name. After careful consideration, they reached a decision. This player could play wing forward or wing. His versatility might just provide a silver lining to the cloud cast over the trip by Tilden's withdrawal. The man the selectors chose was Ed Turkington.

The thrill of being named in the squad must have been even more ecstatic for 'Turk' than for the others selected, because Ed's good news came when his morale was at such an all-time low. He had risen from the ashes, just like the city he had been helping to rebuild. An ecstatic Turkington was all set to go…until he realised that he had no money to join the party. It was 25 March 1924 and the train was due to leave for the east coast on 2 April. Ed had just days to find the necessary funds.

Never shy, he hatched an extraordinary plan. He singled out a tower block in downtown San Francisco where the richest movers and shakers went about their daily business. It was called the Merchants Exchange Building on Montgomery Street and California Street in San Francisco's Financial District. As he burst through the building's front doors and took the elevator to the top floor, Ed realised that he would need to summon all his natural charm and energy for the task ahead. The race was on and it must have felt like an Olympic qualifier. In the next two hours, he moved like a whirlwind down 11 floors of the high-powered office block, asking men he didn't know to finance his Olympic dream. By the time he left through those same front doors, exhausted and elated, he had raised an incredible $4,800 dollars to see him to Paris and back.

Meanwhile Rudy Scholz was also involved in some frantic last-minute activity – to leave his legal practice in such fine order that it could run itself without him for the next couple of months. 'I think I average about twelve hours a day and I'm all in,' he wrote in his diary at the time. In comparison to all this office work, Rudy probably thought his Olympic adventure would feel refreshing.

When the Overland Limited train rolled out of San Francisco on 2 April to signal the start of the 6,000 miles (9,600km) journey to Paris, the rugby team was given a special car. Even in the opening stages of the journey, there was important business to be done, because the squad had not yet chosen their captain and vice-captain. The issue of who would lead the team from the front during the sporting battle in Europe might have been more important to some than others. There were seven men who had played in the 1920 Olympics, and the leaders surely had to come from those. Apart from Babe and Rudy, there were Stanford's Charlie Doe and Jack Patrick, Joseph Hunter of San Mateo, and John O'Neill and Bill Muldoon, old teammates of Scholz at Santa Clara.

Deep down, Scholz might have felt that he was a logical choice for captain. He had experience in just about everything, right down to solving logistical problems and processing passports. He had proved his worth as an assistant manager on the 1920 trip, while showing that he could still be one of the star players. Now Rudy was 28 and one of the oldest players in the 1924 group. He had natural authority and he was a respected lawyer with his own San Francisco practice. His silver tongue could handle any press conference the squad might have to call in England or France. He could promote their cause with consummate ease. In truth, Scholz had always led, as he had shown at Santa Clara and various military academies. His efficiency had improved year on year. Who had helped to keep US rugby alive between the Olympics, as Secretary of the Pacific Coast Football Association? Scholz had. Who had helped to organise the try-outs for this latest Olympic adventure, and had run at least one of the sessions personally? Scholz had.

So it would have been reasonable for Rudy to believe that his teammates would recognise his energy, his leadership qualities and his track record in the game. Sure enough, by the time the train came down off the Sierras and reached Truckee on that first day of travelling, the squad had come to a decision. Their captain for the 1924 Olympics was to be…Babe Slater. Yes, Babe, who hadn't shown for the initial practice a few months earlier; Babe, who had apparently turned his back on rugby in the years between the Olympics; gentle, silent Babe, who seemed to struggle to string a sentence together sometimes, even though behind closed doors he was a writer of some quality. What was Babe likely to be able to say to the players in order to inspire them? What was going on?

We cannot attribute such thoughts to Rudy Scholz, and he certainly wouldn't have voiced them, even if he might have been thinking something similar deep down. Instead Rudy would have been expected to congratulate Slater, and no doubt he did so. But he would have asked himself why he had been overlooked. One reason for the decision was probably simple enough; Babe was more popular than Rudy among the team, precisely because he was not as demanding as Scholz. Slater was more relaxed, less imposing. It appeared that the squad was trying to give themselves an easy ride, since Slater was a silent giant off the pitch, with a relatively soft nature. His nephew Norman said later: 'He didn't raise hell if people didn't do it his way. He was gentle, led by example.'

Yet there may have been another factor at work here – the vivid memories of those in the squad who had taken part in the post-Olympic French tour of 1920. Babe Slater, for one, would have remembered how Scholz had lost all self-control in the Stade Colombes. As the French employed dirty tactics during the last international between the two countries, Rudy had retaliated. He had knocked an opponent clean out with a flying kick; and he had punched a few more senseless. He had shown he was tough but to what end? France had beaten the USA 14-5. All discipline had been lost and, as Baron De Coubertin had explained quite clearly, 'discipline is the key to success.' Was Scholz the right sort of character to lead the US team into battle against the French four years down the line? Slater and the others probably thought not. All we know for sure is that Babe was chosen as captain and not Rudy. And most of the squad would have been pleased with the outcome.

So Babe had effortlessly taken centre stage again, without even seeking the starring role. It may have occurred to Rudy that Babe was achieving many of his own ambitions, either military or sporting, even though Scholz surely felt at least as well suited to the roles and challenges that Slater had been given in life.

To add insult to injury, Rudy wasn't even elected as Babe's number two. That honour went to Charlie Doe, a star full-back for the rugby team of Lowell High, Ed's old school, and half-back for Stanford University. Doe was a San Francisco boy through and through; and like Rudy he had been part of the 1920 glory. Scholz couldn't complain about the choice. But it wouldn't necessarily have made him happy either. Looking at Rudy's diary for this part of the adventure, you get the feeling that he might be trying to hide his hurt even from himself. 'Damn tired because of getting career into shape to leave country… Private car, fellows in high spirits…'. He already sounded slightly detached from the general mood of the group. That process was to continue for the rest of the trip.

Indeed from this moment on, it seems that Babe and Rudy's relationship became strained. There were no more diary notes of nights out together, or bonding of the kind we had seen on several separate occasions during the 1920 adventure. The big guy and the little guy, always opposites on the face of it, had been close friends back then. They had not grown up together, of course, but rugby had created a wonderful rapport between two men in their prime. Now rugby was pulling them apart. They appeared to inhabit different worlds, and the distance between them seemed to grow by the day.

Rudy's spirits did improve briefly, once he had enjoyed a good night's sleep and thought about what he could achieve within the group. The next day, 3 April, he wrote, 'Up late – feel better. Was rather all in from hard work during past two weeks…This trip promises to be much easier than the 1920 trip because we have a manager who handles the whole affair and does it exceedingly well – i.e. Sam Goodman.'

Scholz could at least console himself with the thought that his previous experience as an administrator and assistant tour manager might allow him to help organise various aspects of the trip alongside Goodman. Little did Rudy know that his relationship with Big Sam was soon to be tested to the limit as well.

chapter 6

TEETHING TROUBLES

Babe, Rudy and the gang reached New York after a six-day trip that did at least include a stop-off in Chicago and a run-out at the Illinois Athletic Club. There had been a visit to Niagara Falls too, though for Rudy it only brought back memories of his trip across the USA as a younger man, at which point he thought he had been preparing for war. He doesn't seem to have wanted to recapture that so-near-yet-so-far feeling.

'The first time I was here since 1918, when I came here with my company,' he wrote. 'It is a nice sight but after seeing it once you have no desire to see it again. The fellows got off here for two hours with the exception of myself and I went on into Buffalo…'.

Perhaps Rudy's feeling of detachment from the other players was noted by team manager Sam Goodman. Scholz may have felt at liberty to carve his own path because he still saw himself in some sort of executive role on the trip. He intended to act as an assistant to manager Goodman, helping with logistical arrangements. If no such arrangements had been made, as appeared to be the case on their arrival in New York City, Rudy figured he might come in particularly useful.

Dud De Groot, the giant whose newspaper columns cast him in the role of narrator for the trip, didn't hold back as he described the tensions in the Big Apple. He wrote later,

> We arrived at the Grand Central Station in New York at 6.00am [on 7 April]. Although none of the members of the Olympic Committee were present to meet us, one of the representatives of Spaldings [probably the A. J. Spalding Company, a well-known US manufacturer of sports equipment since 1876] happened along. He very kindly escorted us to the Park Avenue Hotel, where we were housed during our three-day stay prior to sailing.
>
> Our stay in New York, brief as it was, due to the negligence, the lack of hospitality, the oversight or whatever one may choose to call it of the Olympic Committee, was a nightmare. Valuable time, which should have been spent in practicing, was wasted in looking for a place to practice, in arranging passports, in trying to get appropriate equipment and in doing many other things which should have been arranged prior to our arrival. As a result not one work-out of real consequence was held during the entire three days spent in New York...the lack of attention and consideration which we received was decidedly 'felt'.

It was in this context that Rudy Scholz offered his assistance to the manager, Sam Goodman. Rudy didn't complain in his diary, as De Groot did later, about the team's grievances. So it seems unlikely that he complained to Goodman either. By offering his help, he was simply trying to be positive and improve a bad situation. But the team manager was a tough guy with a tendency to come out fighting when the chips were down. By now he looked like a slightly younger version of the coach, Charlie Austin, and had lost almost as much hair. If anything, Goodman was more confrontational than Austin. Perhaps feeling sensitive about the oversights that were causing unrest among the players, Big Sam apparently decided to put Scholz firmly in his place and instructed him to behave as a squad player and nothing else.

Feisty Rudy didn't take this lying down, and described the clash like this: 'Had a row with Sam Goodman over certain matters. Why cannot people be fair and why must I always try to help people out who instead of appreciating it seem to hold it against you?...Received a telegram regarding my business and felt tempted to return to San Francisco immediately.'

Scholz was burning with a sense of injustice; and that feeling wasn't likely to go away in a hurry. He believed the rugby squad had undervalued his talents considerably. In sharp contrast, his colleagues back home seemed to be in desperate need of his help. Why should he stay with those who didn't seem to want him? After due reflection, however, Rudy decided to board the United States Line ship *SS America* two days later with the rest of the Olympic rugby team. Perhaps relations would improve on the voyage to Plymouth, England.

Some 700 feet (200m) long and weighing in at 22,640 tons (285,000kg), the ship was big enough to become something of a playground to those who wished to use it as such. And since neither the rugby team nor its management seemed to value his services particularly, Rudy responded by showing a lesser sense of responsibility than usual. He consoled himself with some mischievous fun on the Atlantic Ocean. There was no shortage of desirable women on the ship who might appreciate an attentive man with a keen sense of humour.

On the very first morning of the eight-day voyage, therefore, he was able to report, '...saw a package of flowers being delivered to Miss Margaret Alliott and gave the porter a quarter to insert my card in the box. We shall see what comes of it. At lunch saw a girl who I think had a great deal to her because, while appearing only very modest and retiring – still it seemed a cloak for a rather vivid personality. Something like Cecilia. Cecilia – ah! A name to conjure with...'.

Thoughts of Miss Alliott and his old flame didn't last, however, because by that very evening, Rudy had his eyes on another girl – Miss Elfreida Cranz. He wrote later, 'She walked out on deck, I walked out too and asked her why she didn't dance. We talked until 11 o'clock and [coach Charlie] Austin was muchly peeved.'

The reason for Austin's annoyance was the fact that Scholz, like the rest of the squad, was supposed to be in bed by 10.30pm and ready for an early start. At 6.45am, in De Groot's words, 'every man was to hit the deck, put on his suit and go up to the boat deck for setting up exercises. These were to last for one hour and were to be followed by several laps around the deck, which was a good 220 yards [200m] per lap.'

It is not hard to imagine some of the young women on the trip straining for a view of this highly athletic group of young American men, Olympic glory their goal, showing off their muscles as they stretched and dashed around the ship. There was plenty of time for such women to be noticed by the team, too.

De Groot explained, 'A cold shower followed by a big breakfast at 8:30 put all of those who were not affected by seasickness in great shape ... The remainder of the day until 4 o'clock in the afternoon was at the disposal of each man.'

The day after he had been caught out late, Rudy and Elfreida talked for two more hours. Scholz didn't need to be too concerned about what coach Austin or his teammates thought about his behaviour outside training hours. Even so, the second deadline had to be met promptly. De Groot added, 'At 4 o'clock practice was held, lasting until about 5.30. For the forwards scrum work, hooking and passing the ball and picking it up in the open received particular attention, while the backs were thoroughly drilled in passing and catching the ball...After the afternoon workout, the big meal of the day took place, followed by moving pictures or a dance or both...'.

When it came to dancing, however, Rudy broke his own rules. It seems that Elfreida, with whom he talked 'all morning', according to his diary entry of 11 April, was dominating his thoughts. Scholz wrote later, 'In the evening we had a dance and I danced a bit and I had forgotten I swore off dancing during Lent. However I will not dance any more. It was the fact that I had forgotten.'

He was unable to keep his new vow, as we shall see. First, however, Scholz was in trouble with coach Austin yet again, having been drawn into a game of 'shuffle board' by an acquaintance of Elfreida, an Austrian aviator nicknamed 'Willie'. He confessed to his diary, 'We played all afternoon until I was called by the coach for not being ready at 4pm for a work out.'

For a military man with a natural respect for punctuality, this sort of behaviour seems out of character. We can only assume that Scholz was showing a certain contempt for the way he had been treated. For coach Austin, this represented a headache. He had played front five for Stanford as a younger man and wasn't short of grit. It was the transformation in Rudy that must have surprised him at first. Austin had thought he knew how to keep Scholz in line; they had always worked well together way back in their Santa Clara days. But this was a new Rudy Scholz and one who would need careful handling. Charlie knew that Sam Goodman and the squad had effectively denied Rudy any responsibilities on the trip. He could also see that Scholz was not taking this well. Perhaps time would calm the situation down. Yet it wasn't just Austin's rules that Rudy was bending, it was his own.

Scholz's diary entry of 14 April included the following rambling sequence, which sounds funny when you read it, but probably constitutes a genuine wrestling match between Rudy and his Catholic conscience. 'They had a dance and I don't know whether I should dance or not in that I did make a reservation not to dance which was not to apply in Europe if it interfered with my seeing Europe and by Europe I mean anything not American and we are not in America now and not dancing interferes with my observing first handed (sic) the different methods that certain young females have of dancing.' This was Rudy Scholz in all his glory, a complex individual whose sense of fun and duty seemed to be in constant conflict. Usually his sense of duty held sway, though on the boat to England the distractions were particularly tempting.

De Groot confirmed, 'Fortunately, although coach and players could not seem to agree on this point, there were several very charming young ladies aboard the ship who made the evenings, and, in fact, the whole trip, much more enjoyable than it might otherwise have been.'

And Rudy was clearly enjoying this state of affairs as much as anyone. He seems to have found the women better company than many of his teammates at this point. For Babe Slater's rugby squad left much to be desired as a unit, or at least that was how Scholz saw it. Although he was team captain, Slater appeared to have allowed a bossy clique to assume a certain amount of power. Yet the clique didn't possess a shred of official authority. An angry Rudy wasn't having any of it, though ironically he seems to have been worried that coach Austin's authority was already being undermined by the mounting tensions. He vented some of his frustrations in his diary.

On Tuesday, 15 April he wrote, 'Dissension has broken out on the team due to the fact that four of the fellows try to dictate to other fellows what to wear – how to act, etc. They have quite enough to look after themselves and if they could only see themselves as others see them. It is of course not hard to pick out faults of others and it is easy for most people to believe what they want to believe. Charlie Austin is trying his best to run things smoothly but he hasn't the power. With a good bunch Charlie would have a wonderful team.'

These remarks do not reflect well on Babe's early captaincy. Either Slater had turned into the sort of character who told other grown men what to wear and how to behave on the boat, which seems unlikely; or he had let the clique go unchecked until it felt important enough to start laying down the law. Either way, it was down to Babe to remind any upstarts which player was really in charge, and quick. Experienced captains usually try to eradicate any emerging clique at an early stage of a tour, so that team spirit isn't harmed. So if Babe wasn't part of this clique, why wasn't he doing anything?

You get the feeling that Rudy probably thought he could have done a better job of unifying the group – if only he had been given the authority to do so. Yet he was forced to accept that it was Babe, his old friend from the 1920 Games, who was now in charge. As far as Scholz could see, however, Slater wasn't doing much to remind people who was captain.

So Rudy appears to have taken up the fight against the tin-pot dictators among the group instead. You can just imagine the feisty Scholz telling the bullies that he would wear whatever he damn well pleased, as long as it looked reasonably smart. The clue to this clash lies in the subject that Scholz was asked to speak about during a team reunion four years later: 'What is the correct wardrobe for an athlete travelling abroad?' Since each player was given a topic that would allow him to be as humorous and as ironic as possible, relating to a memorable incident from 1924, it seems that Rudy had made a name for himself on this particular issue. And although people clearly found the 'difference of opinion' funny a few years later, the in-fighting and the tension it caused at the time was no laughing matter.

As a last-minute selection, Ed Turkington probably didn't concern himself too much with the political undercurrents of the voyage.

Besides, he was too busy getting to know some of the finer looking women on board, and found plenty of time to be photographed with many a young beauty. With his hair slicked back, wearing a US team cardigan and tie, Ed cut a dashing figure as he was snapped cuddling Miss Francesca Distinti, an Italian beauty. On another day he was pictured in dapper suit and bow-tie cuddling up to an even prettier girl, nicknamed 'Pete'. These pictures show that Ed was determined to enjoy his freedom. After so many years with Elaine Horton, Ed was a single man again and still only 25. He was not about to spend these precious weeks of freedom worrying about what Elaine might think, not when this trip abroad seemed to be handing him so many opportunities already. The whole idea was to forget Elaine for a while and do what he wanted, because only that way would he ever really gain the perspective he needed. To reach a point of insight, he would embark on as many romantic adventures as he liked. It was a tough way to test a relationship, but someone had to do it. Ed, who had always possessed a keen eye for the ladies, braced himself for action.

The voyage reached a climax with the Masquerade Ball on Wednesday, 16 April. Scholz described how ten team members came up with ingenious costumes, with 'O'Neill and Cunningham the best.' Rudy added, 'I wasn't going to costume myself until I thought that I had my army uniform with me and no one knows me in it and with a mask...'.

Even in 1924 Rudy was keen to show his love for the army. He may not have seen action in the war but he could still use that uniform to impress the opposite sex. His favourite companion on the boat, Elfreida, seems to have seen through the 'disguise' soon enough though. It wouldn't have been hard. Rudy was the shortest player on the boat and unless he wore stilts he was never going to hide it. So Scholz was able to write, 'Spent the evening talking to Elfreida. The weather was wonderful and if the fellows – that is about six of them – would play the game right it would be a most enjoyable trip.'

So even in this, what should have been a moment of pure happiness, it seems that Rudy still felt bitter about the threat to team spirit. Though he fell short of pointing the finger at anyone in particular, he seemed to be crying out for Babe Slater to get a grip, remove the unpleasant undercurrents and put the tour back on track before they reached England.

Rugby novices: a 17-year-old Rudy Scholz (left) had to play the mighty New Zealand All Blacks within six weeks of first picking up a rugby ball in 1913. Back in 1910, as a 14-year-old, Babe Slater (right) hadn't yet developed rugby muscles – but he soon would.

Born leader: sword in hand, Cadet Major Rudy Scholz leads Santa Clara's student Army Corps down a San José main street during a parade in 1918. But World War I finished before he could fight. 'When the Germans heard I was coming they quit', he joked later.

A snowball's chance in hell: Babe Slater somehow survived World War I and by December 1918 he could relax at last. His feet were too big for army boots and he often wrapped them in bandages to keep out the worst of the European winter.

Proud mum: Babe (left) and Norman (right) were towers of strength after their father died and their mother Louise's second husband killed himself. She could always depend on her rugby-playing sons for support.

Prowling on the periphery: Babe Slater (second from the right) waits to one side of the melee during the 1920 Olympic rugby final between USA and France, played in heavy Antwerp rain.

Sullen sweetheart: Cecilia was often on Rudy's mind during the 1920 Olympics. By the time this photograph was taken, perhaps the girl with the vivid personality had realised that the young couple were not destined to spend their lives together.

Boyish charm: a chuckling Rudy may be wearing his US rugby uniform but he still adopts a childlike pose as he sails to the 1920 Olympics. He looked innocent but he never backed down in a fight, as the French were about to find out.

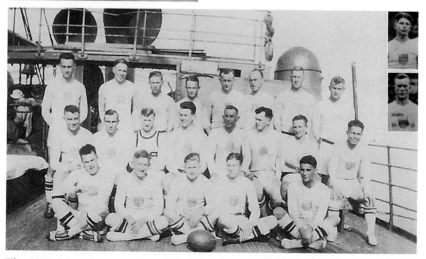

The 1920 US rugby team: (L-R, BACK) Wallace, Patrick, O'Neill, Fish, J. Muldoon, Fitzpatrick, Slater, Righter; (MIDDLE) Meehan, Hazeltine, Maloney (trainer), Tilden (captain), Carroll (coach), W. Muldoon, von Schmidt, Scholz; (FRONT) Wrenn, Doe, Hunter, Davis, Winston; (INSETS) Templeton, Kirksey.

Eccentric English: Babe Slater (sitting down, fourth from right) was shocked to discover when playing against Blackheath that London-based rugby players sucked lemons or even drank beer at half-time instead of refreshing themselves with a bucket of water. Communal baths were also a surprise.

Three cheers! Babe Slater receives an African doll called 'Cali' from American opera singer Luella Melius just days before the 1924 final. Note the difference in height between Babe and Rudy, who is fourth from the right.

The hunched body-shapes of the American forwards caused Rudy and Babe to come up with a drastic new plan for their scrum.

Dud De Groot (top, centre) climbs highest to win a vital lineout during the 1924 Olympic final while Rudy Scholz (far left) looks on.

The 1924 US rugby team: (L-R, BACK) Goodman (manager), Valentine, Cashel, Williams, Babe Slater (captain), Farish, Clark, Patrick, N. Slater, De Groot, Austin (coach); (MIDDLE) Graff, Turkington, Deveraux, Manelli, Doe, Cunningham, Dixon; (FRONT) Rogers, Hyland, Hunter, O'Neill, Cleaveland, Muldoon, Rudy Scholz.

Tough veterans: a pre-match shot of Babe and French captain Felix 'Rene' Lasserre, a World War I fighter pilot. Welsh referee Albert Freethy (middle) tried to send Lasserre off for punching Slater less than two hours later but Slater persuaded the official to show mercy.

Ready to pounce: Slater (centre) and Scholz (second from left) in the thick of the action during the Olympic final of 1924. Their experience was vital when cool heads were necessary to counter fierce French provocation.

Into the limelight: Rudy makes a break with Norman Slater to his left, keeping the Romanians at bay, and Ed Turkington to his right, ready to support. Ed was sent off soon afterwards for retaliation while Scholz emerged unscathed to fight another day.

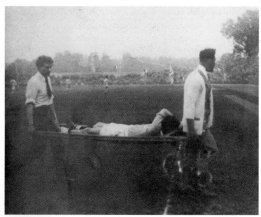

Stretcher bearers! There were many casualties during the bloody Olympic final of 1924. But the most controversial was French star Adolphe Jaureguy, who was 'carted off like a sack of potatoes', according to American vice-captain Charlie Doe.

Medals and wedding bells: Ed Turkington suffered more than a few setbacks at the 1924 Olympics, but he went home determined to marry his childhood sweetheart Elaine. They enjoyed 69 years of happy marriage – worth more than gold itself.

The soldier-husband: a 49-year-old Rudy Scholz is pictured here shortly before the battle of Okinawa. He had fallen in love with Mildred Sophey when he heard her sing in church in 1927. But marriage and the arrival of a young family couldn't keep him away from war.

Love and pride: Babe Slater married Virginia Cave from Clarksburg in 1932 and learned how to cradle a baby when their only child Marilyn arrived a year later. Babe and Virginia saw the world together until he died of a heart attack in 1965.

Play on! Rudy Scholz was still gracing rugby fields aged 83 – leaving men half his age in his wake such as here on the veterans' circuit in North America. Rudy's rugby career spanned some 66 years. Scholz died aged 85.

The *SS America* dropped anchor off Plymouth at 5.20am on Friday, 18 April. The place was significant for every American on board, because the Pilgrim Fathers had set sail from Plymouth for a new life across the Atlantic so many centuries earlier. Within a few hours, the rugby team had said goodbye to the friends they had made on the voyage, some of whom promised to travel to Paris for the big games a few weeks later. Then the players disembarked and headed for Plymouth's Albion hotel. Thoughts turned to their first match in England, home of rugby, against Devonport Services. It had been scheduled for the coming Monday.

There were plenty of other sporting events to take in before then. De Groot observed: 'The British people are sports lovers from start to finish. To my knowledge there were three soccer matches, a rugby match and a card of prize fights scheduled for [the weekend in Plymouth] alone.'

The Americans attended a boxing event on the Friday night and a rugby match between Plymouth Albion and Merchant Taylors the next day. A crowd of 5,000 gave the American team a big hand as they found their seats in the stands and the band even played 'The Star-Spangled Banner'. The US boys marvelled at how fair the crowd was to the opposing team and how little dirty play there was on the field. The referee was also afforded total respect, something that contrasted sharply with the general attitude to officials in the States. Meanwhile there was little talking between teammates apart from the occasional 'well collared, old boy' for a good tackle and 'well done my lad' for a try. Rudy Scholz claimed that Taylors 'took on the style of the All Blacks' and won 28-3. But even their supporters were remarkably self-contained, leaving the Americans as the surprising stars of the stands. De Groot explained, 'Our American college yells, the few times that we gave them, created quite a sensation and we were always called upon for an encore.'

What the Americans learned most of all, however, centred around the game of rugby itself. De Groot, still a rugby virgin in competitive terms, revealed, 'We learned many things from this first match, particularly the English interpretation of many of the technicalities of the game – little points which seem perfectly clear in the rule book, but which may be interpreted in any one of a dozen different ways.'

The Americans also marvelled at the level of sporting organisation in England, where national leagues had been created so that rugby and soccer teams played every Saturday, all over the country, between September and April. Yet the rugby players didn't even get paid for meeting their gruelling schedule. De Groot observed, 'The English people play the game for the love of it, no matter what it may be, good sportsmanship being the keynote of every match. They go at their sports from an entirely different angle than we do in America. Healthful exercise, good fellowship and good sportsmanship seem to be the ideals which they strive for in all their matches rather than any insatiable desire to win or to make a few dollars as is so often the case here at home... The members of the American rugby team soon agreed that we could learn a whole lot from the British about real sportsmanship.'

Not that the English were all sweetness and light, as Rudy found out when he became separated from his teammates and then lost his way back from a 'vaudeville show' at the Palace Theatre on that first Saturday night. He explained how he asked 'a very nice girl by the name of Elsie Squires, who directed me back to my hotel. She was quite a frank girl with not too good an opinion of Americans.'

Rudy's latest detachment from the group raised questions about how much he was trying to contribute to the team spirit he had already criticised. It seems that he needed to keep his distance from certain elements in order to avoid saying what he was thinking about their attitude. Tourism was a good way to divert his thoughts, and he told his diary how the boys saw the Hoe where Sir Francis Drake first sighted the Spanish Armada in 1538, and visited the more sobering location of Dartmoor Prison – 'a well-kept place.' It was also the place where many American prisoners had been held captive during the war of 1812.

By Sunday evening the countdown to the team's first-ever competitive match was well under way. But that was also the moment when Scholz fell for the charms of yet another woman. He wrote, 'In the evening went to Hotel Royal and saw the prettiest looking girl in England by far sitting with a young man sipping a whisky and soda. She looked at me and I looked at her for a moment when I couldn't help smiling and she smiled by return. I drank her health and subsequently we were introduced.'

It appears that Rudy had made a deep impression in those moments, because his diary for the day of the match began, 'Came down to breakfast and was surprised to find a letter from Katherine Gabes-Ryder – the young lady I was introduced to last night, saying she wanted to see me.' Monday was a Bank Holiday in England and the game was due to kick off at the unusual time of 11.00am. This didn't deter Rudy, who seems to have put his romantic inclinations before pre-match preparations. He wrote, 'I went to her house but missed her as she had gone to the game.' That indicated just how fine Rudy was cutting it in the countdown to kick-off. The crowds began to gather at 10.30am, and Rudy got lucky when his task might have been something akin to looking for a needle in a haystack. He revealed, 'Returned to the ground and saw her first thing – arranged to see her after the game.'

What coach Austin thought of this distraction on such an important day is anyone's guess, though Rudy seemed to be beyond caring by now. The same could not be said of the curious English crowds, who were prepared to pay 9 pence for standing room (about 18 American cents at the time) and up to 3 shillings (66 cents) for the best seated view at this novelty match. The Americans were given 'traveling expenses and incidentals' from the gate money. But the result would be more important than the cash because success or failure here could set the tone for the entire European adventure.

This game would determine whether Babe's new team could start to go about its business with true confidence, or be sent back to the drawing board instead. It was the first time that an American rugby team had ever played in the British Isles and no one quite knew what to expect. The way the American captain handled his men before the match would be significant. Babe didn't need to say very much – he never did. His huge physical presence and inner calm were reassuring. This man, they knew, had experienced the horror of war and the thrill of Olympic glory. On the face of it, neither had changed Babe much – except to confirm that he was ready for anything. His teammates would have fed off his mood as their first big rugby test approached in Plymouth that day. They would have looked for any signs of fear or nervousness in Babe. There were none, just a quiet determination in Babe to make the long trip worthwhile – and win for his country in the warm Plymouth sunshine.

On the stroke of 11.00am, Babe led his team out onto the field to a loud ovation from somewhere between 8,000 and 10,000 people jammed in around the Rectory Field. When the band struck up 'The Star-Spangled Banner', the English crowd sportingly removed their hats. Then Devonport came out and the British national anthem was played. As if the game wasn't already important enough, it had taken on the feel of an international too.

The Americans' biggest problem came in the scrum – ironically Babe's key area. They had opted for a 2-3-3 formation, the one the New Zealanders employed to great effect. Slater and Ed Turkington were the wing forwards, but the combination didn't seem to work well. The Devonport pack used a 3-2-3 formation and looked more compact. The English had the better of the set pieces. A newspaper report claimed, '...the Americans' scrum work was feeble and weak [and] the services pack heeled with greater frequency than the Americans. There were only one or two occasions when the American backs got into action from heeling by the pack...'.

From line-outs, however, Babe and his big forwards began to run riot. They also generally reached the ball first in the loose. Their tough tackling and superior physical shape stunned their hosts. The backs added some flare with some fine solo runs. Pretty soon it became clear there was only going to be one winner, though Rudy Scholz was less than impressed by his team's emphatic victory. He wrote, 'We played Devonport Services and in a game completed with brilliant individual efforts but not so much teamwork. We won by the score of 25 to 3.'

Later Scholz described the Devonport team as 'ordinary'. The Americans scored seven tries under the old scoring system of three points for a try. Dick Hyland led the way with a hat-trick to confirm his prowess in the centre. Al Williams went over twice, Lefty Rogers and George Dixon once, while Jack Patrick used his power from long-range to convert two scores from full-back. The only English reply was a penalty kick. Team manager Sam Goodman concluded, 'We put out a strong team and completely outplayed our opponents in spite of what was to us a great many new interpretations of the rules on the part of the English referee... The most impressive thing about our victory was the magnificent sportsmanship which the English team, as well as the English spectators, accorded us.'

The tourists were cheered off the field by the crowd and players alike.

Even if they had been short of teamwork, as Scholz had suggested, their baptism of fire had been a resounding success overall. Rudy, however, seemed more concerned about Katherine Gabes-Ryder than what the USA rugby team had just achieved. He wrote, 'Saw Kathy after game and drove downtown for lunch then met the rest of the team at the North Parade depot [train station] and Kathy edified some of the lads by kissing me goodbye. Arrived in London about 7.00pm…'. That was the last Rudy spoke about Kathy, 'the prettiest girl in England', though she seems to have helped to take his mind off his feelings of disillusionment regarding the way the trip was going.

London offered the players a full day's relaxation, with some sight-seeing at Westminster and Trafalgar Square, and some shopping in Piccadilly. However, the US team was just hours from what would prove to be a far greater test than Devonport had given them. A match against the oldest rugby club in the world, Blackheath, had been scheduled for late Wednesday afternoon, at the Old Merchant Taylor's Ground in Teddington, just a few miles southwest of the English capital.

Scholz told his diary, 'Coach Austin has asked me to play tomorrow.' But somewhere along the line that decision was reversed; and it might have had something to do with tensions that surfaced between Rudy and the vice-captain, Charlie Doe, on the day of the match itself.

Scholz explained, 'I walked over to the Tower of London which I saw thoroughly. I went with Charlie Doe but all he wanted was to look at it and then go back. So it is with all the fellows – they will simply go to a place, look at it and return and do not know anything more about it than they did before. Anyway Charlie left me and I joined a party and learnt a great deal of the History of England. Saw the mount guard also. Returned to hotel at 2pm, had dinner.'

But the match was due to kick off just outside London at 5.15pm, so by the time Rudy had finished eating – presumably alone – there were probably little more than two hours before kick-off. Perhaps that was why Doe had wanted Rudy to return with him, in good time for the build-up to the second match. Not for the first time, coach Austin was less than impressed with Scholz's time-keeping. Rudy wrote in his diary, 'Did not play.' It appears that Austin had finally lost patience. Perhaps his old friend Babe Slater had too.

The Blackheath team was, in Rudy's words, 'composed of graduates of Oxford and Cambridge', experienced and confident rugby men who were not prepared to submit to the physical might of the Americans quite so easily as the men of Plymouth had done. Pete Cunningham cracked two ribs during the match and suddenly looked doubtful for the Olympic Games. John O'Neil, still recovering from his appendix operation, was photographed examining himself at a distance from his teammates, as though hiding some new damage to his wound. What undid the tourists most of all, however, was a referee they claimed to be 'super-technical', who awarded no less than 18 mystifying penalties to the home side. When Babe Slater tried to request an explanation, so that he might better understand the local interpretation of the rules, he was simply waved away, as though his queries were a sign of dissent or disrespect. Even though Dud De Groot claimed that his side had 'completely outplayed our opponents throughout', the match ended in a 13-11 victory for Blackheath.

Rudy had another explanation for the defeat. 'We nearly won', said Scholz later on behalf of the men who did play. 'Individually we were better but not as a team.' It was Rudy's favourite theme, this need for solid teamwork to go with individual flare. Though Scholz believed that the lack of a team ethic had cost the USA on this occasion, he didn't seem so critical of his own failure to contribute to that team spirit.

The Londoners managed to kick two of the many penalties they were awarded, and enjoyed plenty of territorial respite as a result of the other decisions which went their way. One of their tries, claimed De Groot, 'was so questionable that after the game their own captain admitted that he thought the referee's ruling had been in error.' Ever positive, however, De Groot maintained that the Americans had learned a great deal from the experience, 'particularly about the rules of the game.'

Even now it seems incredible that the Americans were playing against some of the biggest and best teams in English rugby and holding their own, when some of their number had never played the game before. No wonder Scholz finally echoed De Groot's sentiments when he reflected later, 'We did pick up valuable playing time in practice games in England before going to Paris.'

Sam Goodman, the team manager, observed, 'We did some experimenting with the line-up…[and] met our first set-back, not, I can fairly say, at the hands of a superior team, but rather at the hands of a super-technical referee who accounted for three of the Blackheath scores and…robbed us of two fair tries. However we toured England to gain playing experience and to accustom ourselves to English referees and for those two reasons the game was a valuable one to us.'

The experience was an eye-opener in other ways too. Particularly surprising to the Americans was the English custom of sucking on lemons at half-time instead of refreshing themselves with a bucket of water. They also relied on tea and beer to further boost morale during the interval. After the match Babe and the boys were amazed to be faced with 'mini swimming pools', into which they were expected to jump ten at a time, effectively bathing in each other's mud and grime instead of having individual showers. As always, however, the hospitality and sportsmanship of the English shone through. Even the disgruntled Rudy Scholz sounded pleased with the way the Blackheath club 'gave us dinner at a famous restaurant with wine and everything in the evening.'

With Prohibition still very much in operation in the USA, such delights would have been well appreciated. Even so, the wine could not disguise the bitter taste of a first defeat. With the biggest games of all awaiting the Americans at the Olympics in France, the English press was not optimistic. De Groot wrote, 'Considerable comment about our team, and particularly about our chances in the Olympic matches was made in the sporting columns of the London papers and although all of the reporters openly admired our pluck in attempting such a feat they held out little hope for an American victory.'

As we have seen, there was another worrying defeat – plus more superb hospitality – at the hands of the Harlequins. Despite the lessons they could claim to have learned from the experience and the advice generously offered by the supportive English, American confidence had taken a knock. Coach Austin and captain Slater would need to do some repair work.

In the mean time, Babe attended the Harlequins dinner along with most of his teammates. But the increasingly aloof Rudy Scholz and his friend John O'Neill missed the camaraderie because they had other plans. Rudy wrote in his diary, 'Went to a dinner given by the Harlequins and present were a couple of Lords…We [John and Rudy] left early, in fact just as it started, because we had to catch the train for Ireland via Holyhead, which left Euston Station.'

How much this decision to leave the dinner impressed Babe and the management is very much open to question. Still, Oxford-based Rhodes scholar Alan Valentine and a few others had also arranged to make the voyage to Paris a few days later than the main party; so Rudy's trip to Ireland cannot in itself be seen as another rebellious act.

Scholz and O'Neill certainly missed a good night as guests of the Harlequins in Piccadilly. It was a measure of their wonderful hospitality and warmth of spirit that the Harlequins were still trying to trace Scholz in 1930, so that he could receive a medal. Either the London club had given each of the American players a souvenir on the night of that dinner back in 1924; or else Rudy had lost a personal possession in the changing rooms. Whatever the truth, Rudy hadn't been forgotten in London six years later.

Captain Stoop, the Harlequins executive after whom the modern Quins' stadium was named, wrote to Rudy from his Hampshire home to find out how the long-lost medal might best be sent to him. The simple letter, dated 5 September 1930, read:

> Dear Scholz,
> The little medal, which has been missing since you played against the Harlequins, has now come to light. Please let me know if this reaches you. If it does I will send the medal on to you.
> Yours truly,
> AK Stoop.

Back in April of 1924, while Scholz and O'Neill began a tour of Dublin, Kilkenny, Limerick and Cork, the rest of the USA rugby party continued to be feted in London. The following night it was the British Olympic Committee's turn to play host to the Americans and they did so in style.

Indeed it may not have escaped the Americans' attention, reflecting upon their recent experience in New York, that the British Olympic Committee seemed to be more solidly behind their efforts than their own US Olympic Committee. And the British good wishes were also in stark contrast to what the Americans were soon to face just over the water. The US rugby team was about to walk into a storm, and not just in the English Channel. Rudy Scholz, still in Ireland, could count himself lucky to miss what happened next.

chapter 7

———

INSULTS

THE 90-MINUTE VOYAGE FROM FOLKESTONE TO BOULOGNE ON 28 April 1924, was a nightmare. De Groot claimed 'the swells were so gigantic that they seemed to engulf the whole ship.'

Life became no more comfortable when they reached port. Team manager Sam Goodman echoed, '[It] was extremely rough and we were in no mood for the unpleasant reception we received at the hands of the officials of the country who was supposedly entertaining the world's athletes. There was no one to meet us; our baggage was seized and for a time we were not even allowed to land on French soil, simply because the French Olympic Committee had not taken care of our visas.'

Significantly there was no Rudy Scholz to help smooth over the problem. So many times when there had been passport complications at the last Olympic Games, Rudy had come to the rescue of the squad. But this time Goodman had taken away all Scholz's previous administrative authority and let him go sightseeing in Ireland. Those decisions had just come back to haunt him.

There is confusion about what happened next, because some accounts claim that the players took matters into their own hands. Did Babe, usually the gentle giant, finally lose his temper in defence of his team, many of whom had been sea-sick on the crossing and were suffering still? Whether or not Slater personally led the charge, it seems that the Californians formed a rugby-style scrum to take on the immigration officials blocking their way. Once that happened there was only going to be one winner, whatever the technical problems Babe and the boys had recently experienced on the field of play.

The Americans forced their way onto dry land, though that wasn't the end of it. They still hadn't received official clearance to continue their journey on French soil, and had to watch the Paris-bound train they were booked on leave the railway station without them. Perhaps understandably, many of the American players cursed the French loudly at this point.

Their hosts responded with some name-calling of their own – in print. When French journalists heard rumours of the physical confrontation that had taken place, they branded the Americans as 'streetfighters and saloon brawlers' – hardly the sort of public relations a sports team hopes for on arrival in a host country. In fact these labels gave the Americans such a bad name that further trouble was almost sure to follow sooner or later. A newspaper report explained, 'The bitter feeling...developed first when French newspapers attacked the American players, most of whom are college men from the Pacific Coast, as sluggers and streetfighters; not withstanding that the Americans had at that time not played a game...'.

One newspaper tried to liken the 'Battle of Boulogne' to a rugby match. 'The first obstacle encountered by the American Olympic rugby football team coming from England was the French passport authorities at Boulogne and they had a comparatively easy time in vanquishing the American team. The Americans, the first contingent to arrive in France to participate in the summer Olympics, registered several long kicks against the passport officers, but it was not until the referee, the American Vice-Consul at the port, Mr William Corcoran, interceded that the squad was allowed to continue its journey to Paris.'

After a three-and-a-half-hour train journey, the US rugby team reached the French capital at 9.30pm. They were underwhelmed by the welcoming party waiting for them in Paris, which consisted of an American newspaper reporter and no one else. Though the French Olympic Committee had been wired about the Americans' late arrival, its representatives had still somehow managed to wait at the wrong train station at the wrong time before giving up on their guests for the evening. This brought more loud condemnation of the French organisers from the US rugby players. On a diplomatic level, the trip had not started well.

At least the American journalist helped his country's squad to find their way to the Exelmans Hotel in the quiet Parisian suburb of Point du Jour. It appears that Sam Goodman, the team manager, had stayed in Boulogne to ensure that immigration would issue the correct visas to Scholz, O'Neill and five others when they arrived from the British Isles a few days later. At any rate, Goodman didn't reach Paris until 1 May.

For now coach Austin and Babe Slater were running the show; and they were doubtless relieved to see that the team hotel on the Boulevard Exelmans was a pleasant enough place. It was brand new and ideally situated for rides down the nearby River Seine. Meanwhile a gap between two arches on the Boulevard afforded a stunning view of the wooded hills of St Cloud in the distance. Though Point du Jour was picturesque, the hotel was conveniently located just 20 minutes by subway from the 'Opera' district, in the heart of Paris. The Exelmans would become an important refuge from the madness that was to follow, especially since the Olympic village in Colombes wasn't yet ready for athletes.

Babe, for one, would probably have counted his blessings as he finally hit the sack that night. The trials and tribulations of a difficult day's travel were nothing compared to what he had been through before in this part of the world. Yet the ordeal Babe had undergone during wartime just made the latest French welcome – or lack of it – all the more annoying. Having seen so many Americans lose their lives in 1918, partly to protect the freedom of the French, he was appalled by how shabbily the host nation for the 1924 Olympics had dared to treat his young players. They had been invited to these Games, indeed their presence had been virtually demanded. They were reigning rugby champions and deserved a little respect, just as they had respected the tournament by travelling so many thousands of miles to defend their crown. In truth, the attitude of the French bothered Babe more than the hours of waiting around. Still, as captain he knew he would be expected to help avoid what had almost turned into a diplomatic incident already.

By the time a French reporter turned up at the hotel the next morning, the French Olympic Committee had already prepared a complaint to the Ministry of the Interior over the treatment of the American team by the passport officials in Boulogne. Babe and his players knew it was important to make a good impression while the fuss died down. They didn't have to say much, because their awesome physiques were enough to impress the local journalist. Even so, acting manager Charles Austin and the French-speaking Ed Turkington made the introductions.

The reporter wrote,

> The American team were waiting for the Olympic Committee to designate them a field on which to train. The manager of the team and the forward, Finkington [sic] presented the players to me, all with the solid, strapping builds of great athletes...Impressive sets of shoulders, such as those belonging to C. Slater, captain of the team, the best American forward, who played against France four years ago; the brown-skinned Italian-American Manelli, massive and powerful, the enormous De Groot, a descendant of the Saxons with enormous muscles, the immense Patrick, who will play at the back. The front row of the forwards must average no more than 86 to 88 kilos [190lb], but there isn't an ounce of fat on these athletes well practiced in every sport.

The reporter then recalled the words Turkington used to introduced him to O'Neill. Ed seemed to admire John's wealth and love of gambling as much as his sporting pedigree. 'He has already played in an Olympic tournament, four years ago. He has a large personal fortune, and on the first day [of our trip] he played under the mark of his own name. He won 30,000 Francs and we drank champagne. O'Neill is also involved in boxing promotions and he was one of the organisers of the Jack Dempsey-Tom Gibbons match-up.'

Rounding off his article, the journalist explained how he was presented to 'the best players in the team. Here is the famous Slater who, four years ago, made the biggest impression; the best American half-back, Charlie Doe, and the fastest three-quarters, Hyland and Cunningham…Time passes and the Americans are still waiting for transport to a playing field. So they begin their training on the Boulevard Exelmans, throwing long, hard passes of around 40 meters [130ft], men such as Cleaveland and Hunter, as if challenging the best throwing arms in France.'

The team's transport did finally arrive, because an Associated Press dispatch later explained at length,

> Paris, April 29 – Members of the Olympic rugby football team, refreshed after a good night's sleep, soon forgot all the troubles of yesterday's journey from London to Paris…Finding the Colombes Olympic stadium unavailable for practice this morning, they crossed the Auteuil racetrack and began kicking the football around, putting the famous track to use as a football field for the first time. They will hold their first uniform practice at the stadium this afternoon.
>
> The French Olympic Committee, desirous of holding the official reception which miscarried yesterday owing to the late arrival of the athletes, invited the boys to headquarters this noon where they were welcomed by Frantz Reichel, general secretary; Alan Kuhr, international secretary, and Count Clary, a member of the international committee.
>
> Colby ('Babe') Slater, captain of the team, and Charles Austin, acting manager, both agreed with the French choice of Admiral Percy Royds of the British Navy, vice-president of the International Rugby Union, as referee of the France-United States rugby match May 18. Sam Goodman, manager of the Americans, when he arrives Thursday will be offered the job of refereeing the Franco-Romanian match next Sunday.
>
> The Americans seemed in the pink of form and their husky appearance made a fine impression in French Olympic circles, where they are regarded as having an even chance of winning the championship. They are brimful of confidence and say that hard tackling will cause them to repeat their Antwerp victory, in which they defeated the French 8 to 0.

So Babe and coach Austin had agreed to a very senior British referee for their key match, in spite of the problems they had encountered with referees in England a few days earlier. This initial acceptance of 'the French choice', Admiral Royds, was interesting, given the storm that was to break a few days later. Babe and Charlie seemed keen to rebuild a few diplomatic bridges after the two sides had come so close to outright hostility the previous day. In fact their acceptance of Royds would only make matters worse in the long run.

Meanwhile the Americans were about to get their first look at the Stade Colombes, the Olympic Stadium. Forty-four countries were due to take part in the Eighth Olympiad, which would be the biggest yet, and preparations were well underway for the main events later that summer. A 400 metre dirt track surrounded the central turf where the rugby teams would do battle. Already taking shape were jumping pits, shot, discus, hammer and other rings.

There was still plenty of room for the clear markings of a full-sized rugby field, and the stadium itself was spectacular. It could take 60,000 to 70,000 spectators, with open standing areas at each end. Two grandstands ran along the sides, covered with sheet metal roofing and supported by immense steel girders. These provided seating for around 20,000 people.

Surrounded by the Colombes Olympic village, the grounds of the Racing Club of France and several football fields, the Stade Colombes was around 15 miles (24km) from central Paris. Trains, buses or cars could reach it easily enough. And Babe's squad couldn't wait to take advantage and get a feel for the place.

Another Associated Press dispatch, later on 29 April, was headlined, 'US RUGBY PLAYERS DRILL IN STADIUM – Hold First Practice at Scene of Olympic Competition in Driving Rain. TEAM IMPRESSES CRITICS – Men Appear to Be in Top Form – French Ministry to investigate Boulogne Delay.' The report said that the Americans devoted most of their time to kicking and passing.

> It was raining hard and the boys went to the stadium not intending to do anything more than to take possession of the dressing room, but could not resist the temptation of the greensward and went out for an hour under the direction of

captain Colby (Babe) Slater and acting manager Charles Austin. The team greatly impressed spectators at the stadium, John O'Neill and William Muldoon, veterans of the Antwerp Olympic championship team, Caesar Manelli and Dudley De Groot (Groot particularly) giving indications of great strength and speed.

The Olympic Village, specially constructed to house entrants in the various events, will not be ready to receive the team for eight or ten days, and in the mean time the Americans will practice each morning in the Parc des Prince's Velodrome, a ten-minute walk from their hotel, and in the afternoons will turn out at the Colombes Stadium to get acquainted with its wind and sun peculiarities.

Private Ceremonies Today.

Acting manager Austin has been invited to attend the ceremony tomorrow morning at which the stadium will be officially turned over to the French Olympic Committee by the contractors. The function will be strictly private and even the press will be excluded.

The French rugby clubs of Paris are getting their men together to give our men a practice match on Saturday, to be played behind closed gates, as the French Olympic Committee does not desire that any admission be charged until the real Olympic competition begins.

All seemed well – except that the Americans felt that their hotel had put them on starvation rations. De Groot explained, 'The food was typically French with plenty of French bread and the tiniest dabs of this and that and the other thing, with not enough meat served to the entire team to adequately satisfy one member. And worst of all it took them about an hour and a half to serve us both the noon and the evening meal, which for men who were practicing football was an ordeal which was almost unbearable…'.

Coach Charlie Austin wasn't about to stand for the lack of meat and a confrontation with the hotel staff wasn't long in coming. The French chef argued that the players were more likely to starve on the 'Austin Diet.' The food controversy even made a story for a newspaper back home in California, under the headline, 'Local Rugbyites Rout French Chef.' The report read, 'Paris – May 1 – The American Olympic rugby team has scored one victory in France already – entirely upsetting the well-ordered regime in the kitchen of their hotel. Manager [sic] Austin, who is a stickler for discipline, ordered a training table diet, including bran and California prunes, steaks done just right and the ever-present toast. Chef Jean Baptiste protested in gesticulatory fashion that the American athletes would pine away on such Spartan diet, but Austin had his way...'.

So the players got their meat, though their meals didn't reach their tables any more quickly. De Groot admitted, 'The food improved as time went on...although the speed with which they served it remained as slow as ever.' After a few days, Babe Slater was able to write, 'We are getting better food here now – at first they served regular French meals served French style which would hardly keep a canary bird alive. Now they are coming round to our way of serving which isn't bad at all...'.

Rudy Scholz may have been unaware of this clash of culinary wills because he didn't spend much time at the hotel on his first evening in Paris, that of 1 May. Having dumped his kit there late in the afternoon, he took O'Neill downtown to the Folies Bergère, which may have been the venue for a general team night out. This, presumably, was the same Folies Bergère that Rudy had described as 'disgusting' in 1920. It seems that four years' extra experience of the world had broadened his mind a little. Or perhaps he wanted to see whether his school friend John would be as outraged as he was when he first saw the degree to which young ladies were prepared to expose themselves in public at the famous nightspot.

Babe's elder brother Norman also liked to behave like a tourist whenever he could, though the sights he saw generally appear to have been less controversial. When Babe wrote home at around this time, he said, 'Nor is getting quite a kick out of the trip – he is the first one up in the a.m. and hikes around all day taking in the sights, etc. He has picked up considerable weight and looks fine.' But Norman Slater didn't forget what the boys were there for. Even if he had wanted to, his brother Babe would not have let him.

Pretty soon the USA rugby team, with the possible exception of Rudy Scholz, started to concentrate on their sporting mission to the exclusion of virtually everything else. They were so focused that the squad's sheer intensity began to strike fear into any Frenchman who came into close contact with it. Babe, who had seemed to Rudy unable to unify a disparate group, was steadily growing as a leader.

At this point a perceptive French journalist called C. A. Gonnet visited the Hotel Exelmans to take a look at the men who had already been written off in many minds as serious contenders for the rugby crown. He would soon write an article under the headline 'A visit to General Yankee's District' – with Babe Slater very much cast in the role of General Yankee. The piece was even accompanied by a cartoon caricature, a profile of Slater sketched by an artist, presumably while the interview took place. First Gonnet was greeted by the hotel's manager and invited to cast an eye on the American players already emerging from their exercise room. '…Five or six young people with the shoulders of grizzly bears, about 1m 90 [6ft 2in] in height, with the clear bright eyes of young athletes in peak condition.'

An increasingly worried Gonnet was told how the American preparations for the Olympics are regulated down to the finest detail. One hour a day of physical workout in the hotel gym, an open-air work-out in a Parisian stadium each afternoon; and rugby theory for an hour each evening with the help of a blackboard. The rest of the time, smiled the hotelier, four or five of them are always out in the street with a ball, amusing themselves. Their host declared himself to be 'stupefied by their strength, whether lifting weights or throwing the ball, and by the precision of their kicks. Oh, they're going to be tough opposition, really tough,' he warned.

The reporter asked about diet and was told by the hotel manager,

It's special. Grilled steaks, lots of them. To drink, water. For dessert, with each meal, they have two enormous chocolate drinks with ten or twelve cubes of sugar in them. No alcohol, no cigarettes…naturally. They are locked in here at ten o'clock in the evening.

Neither dancing nor theatre leads to what you might guess. They were driven off to the Folies-Bergère one evening, and on another to the Empire. But as soon as the shows are over, they are brought back to the hotel in double-quick time. There will be compensations after the final, no doubt, but until then they are consumed by only one desire – to win.

The hotel manager was mostly right, though even the US rugby team was human. Chasing women was kept to a minimum in Paris, although four years later Muldoon was required to speak to the reunited squad on 'How I kept the team pure by taking care of the ladies myself.' And coach Charlie Austin's subject was 'The dangers surrounding a rugby team or how to keep out of the divorce courts.'

With a gold medal to fight for, the general rule seemed to be that you could look at the beautiful French girls but you were not supposed to touch; although even captain Babe Slater later confided in a letter that 'the girls were a good treat for sore eyes.' And when Ed Turkington was interviewed about those weeks in France some 50 years later, he seemed upset that one aspect of his Parisian experience had not been covered by the journalist's line of questioning. 'You didn't ask me about the girls over there', he said with a chuckle.

Only one thing really mattered to these young men at this particular point in their lives, though – rugby. The hotelier had received that message loud and clear, and added, 'I shouldn't hide from you the fact that they have also promised to kill themselves if they don't beat France. They intend to play a very brutal type of rugby, in the style of their own American game. They don't want to be condemned by the French press, or cast the United States in a poor sporting light. But they are going to put all their passion, their science and their perfect physiques into this. And hell, that is going to tip the balance.'

French journalist Gonnet knew that these Americans hadn't exactly played like supermen in London a week earlier. 'What do they say about their defeats in London?' he asked.

'Why don't you question their captain, Colby Slater, on this subject?' replied the hotelier.

Gonnet described what he saw and felt next: 'I see a tough-looking giant, with a strong, cordial handshake, who weighs 110 kilos [240lb]. He is the best forward in the Olympic team.'

Babe didn't waste any time before answering the question. He said, 'We were beaten in England because we didn't understand certain interpretations by the referee, because we took great care to learn our lesson, to play the role of conscientious pupils from start to finish, from one end to the other during our matches. For all that, we could easily have won over there: and I wouldn't judge us on that per-formance. You'll see us at work soon enough.'

These were strong answers, humble yet confident. Maybe Rudy Scholz wasn't the only one who could deal effectively with the press after all. Asked to describe his players, Babe said, 'Pure Californians, students most of them, who have for the last three months abandoned American football to learn your game of rugby exclusively.'

Given the way they had run the cream of English rugby so close, it was easy to forget that Slater's team was full of novices, many of whom were only just coming to understand the intricacies of rugby. Most coaches use blackboards or their modern-day equivalents to run technical sessions in training camps. But how many Olympic coaches have used these get-togethers around a blackboard to teach their team the fundamental rules of a game?

Even Babe, the experienced captain, had been guilty of drifting back into an American football mindset in the big match against Harlequins at Twickenham. He had often been penalised for passing the ball forward carelessly. If Slater had looked naïve at times, it wasn't hard to imagine how the true newcomers to rugby must have appeared.

Back in the Hotel Exelmans, however, Babe turned his players' varied sporting backgrounds into a positive for the press man to consider. He added, 'There are baseball aces, runners, rowers and swimmers. It's the best group of all-round sportsmen the United States could have brought together. And when it was a question of calling them up for this long trip to Europe, not one failed to accept. There wasn't one who didn't consider it an honour to represent their country. Some of them have even interrupted their studies to come to France.'

Babe was warming to his theme now, and he was beginning to attract the attention of his teammates in the hotel. Slater, the quiet man, who could go hours without opening his mouth at all, was speaking. Not only that; his words were inspirational. Slater was finally beginning to sound as he played – like a true leader. He went on, 'We hope to win. And we will do everything possible to achieve that, because the spirit of the Olympic preparations back home was dominated by one expression: that of America, alone, against the world. In the field of athletics, what you might call a hopeless, misplaced pride exists to achieve our ambitions. And our victory, even in rugby, will be welcomed over there with an enthusiasm of which you could have no idea.'

Babe's notion of one country against the world wasn't quite why De Coubertin had revived the Olympic movement. In fact Slater's vision sounded like the perfect opposite of the Olympic ideal in that respect. No matter. Babe's patriotism was welling up inside him along with something else – a contempt for the apparent lack of patriotism and enthusiasm among his French hosts and competitors, especially those in the French rugby community. The biggest rugby star in France, Adolphe Jaureguy, had so far failed to guarantee that he would represent his country in the Olympics. The French Championship had only finished the previous Sunday and there was little enthusiasm among the nation's top players for a fresh round of matches, even with Olympic gold at stake.

Jaureguy wasn't in Paris yet for the latest challenge – and it seemed that he might not bother to turn up at all. He appeared to consider an Olympic rugby tournament against weak opposition almost beneath him. This prima donna attitude was somehow in keeping with his profile as a sporting god.

The speedy winger's celebrity had reached cult status the previous April, when two more touchdowns against Ireland, this time in the Stade Colombes, had seen Adolphe chaired back to the locker-room on the shoulders of his adoring public. By December, Jaureguy was dominating the front cover of France's satirical magazine, *Le Rire*. A witty cartoon showed him in full flow, leaving countless would-be tacklers in his wake. His trademark, pencil-thin moustache gave him an aura of untouchable class in that picture, as he raced beyond despairing opponents with nonchalant ease. He lived up to that image on New Year's Day, 1924, with another brilliant score in France's 12-10 win over Scotland at the Stade Pershing. It seemed the man could do no wrong. After such heroics, it appeared that he regarded the Olympic matches as contests unworthy of his credentials.

As a true sportsman, Babe could admire Jaureguy's talent, and even respect his starring role in the 14-5 defeat of the USA in Paris four years earlier. What he wouldn't tolerate was this lack of respect in return, and Babe was about to put Jaureguy and the entire French rugby community firmly in its place. With more and more people stopping to listen in the lobby of the Hotel Exelmans, Slater added, 'Our first surprise, on arriving here, was the curious indifference you seem to have towards the tournament, and for a sport which is virtually national here. Stemming from the fact that only three nations responded to your call, it seems that you have lost interest in this competition. We have been through your sports newspapers with a fine toothcomb and we never see the training results of your fifteen, or news of their definitive competition for selection.'

Only three teams – France, Romania and the United States – had entered the Olympic rugby competition and, according to most of the French and British papers, it was a foregone conclusion that France would win the title, hands down. France was scheduled to play Romania first on Sunday, 4 May; the United States was due to meet Romania the following Sunday and the final game was to be played on the third Sunday, 18 May, between France and the United States.

Yet with the first match only days away, Slater virtually accused the French of being slovenly and disrespectful to their own Olympics. 'You don't seem to be preparing yourselves. Your players don't even seem to be gathered in Paris yet. In short, you don't seem to understand, as we do, that an Olympic triumph is a national triumph; or know enough to care too much about preparations. Finally, we are astonished to see athletes in your country pull out, without any valid motive. Isn't it a joy, an extreme honour, to wear the colours of your country?'

By attacking an apparent lack of national pride in the host country – and pointing an accusing finger at her superstar winger Adolphe Jaureguy – Babe risked lighting the touch paper for a diplomatic incident. Perhaps this was why, when it came to the hilarious US rugby team reunion four years later, Babe was asked to speak on 'The responsibilities of an international delegate.'

If Babe's preference for diplomacy in public had gone out of the window, he didn't seem to care. He had risked his life in France and Belgium a few years earlier and he expected better from the host country now. His powerful speech had another effect. By voicing the thoughts and frustrations of the entire American team, Babe was arousing an even more intense patriotism among them.

French journalist Gonnet noted, 'While the Yankee spoke, other "ruggers" made a circle. I suddenly have the impression of being small, scrawny in this mass of chests and shoulders all bulging with muscles. What a painful feeling!'

At first, Slater's teammates would have been astonished that he was speaking at all. So many sentences all at once from their quiet captain! This was unlikely to have been a phenomenon with which they were familiar. Then there was the explosive content to consider; every phrase seemed to contain an incendiary device designed to blow up in French faces and release at last the anger that had built up among the Americans. It was controversial and it was brilliant. Babe Slater had suddenly come of age as a captain.

In a similar position, would Rudy Scholz have condemned the French team, media, virtually the entire country to a local reporter? Rudy was a natural risk-taker, but would he have said such things had he been the team's leader? Even for the fast-talking Scholz, this tirade would probably have represented a step too far. Yet the effect of Slater's extraordinary speech was immediate. Suddenly there was a unity of purpose among his players, and a passion even more tangible than before. Babe and the boys spilled out onto the street to show how good they were with a rugby ball.

Gonnet wrote: 'Now the Americans from across the Atlantic, on the given command, juggle with the ball. Their passes are prodigious in their speed. A flick of the wrist, and the oval is sent, like a shell, some forty metres [44 yards] straight, without trajectory. The receiving back, very powerful, collects the ball with his finger-tips and sends it back without effort. Little or no clumsiness and what vigour, in all their movements; what cat-like agility in those big, relaxed bodies where sparks fly.'

Gonnet departed having seen ominous signs that the French will face a far greater challenge in that Olympic showdown with the USA than they could ever have imagined.

I take my leave, having shaken the extended hands, a little sad. A little sad to see that, while the so-called sports press perseveres by trotting out 'we must win easily', like blind, stubborn sheep, the Yankees say nothing and work. While our fifteen doesn't even manage a get-together, or training, doesn't have a manager or equipment, or a ground or a communal day-to-day existence, our adversaries have already made formidable progress; they have created the ambiance they had to, they have pursued faultlessly a methodical organisation where nothing is left to chance.

I don't know, I cannot affirm that France will be beaten – but in all conscience these men scared me. And twenty minutes among them taught me more about the reasons behind their athletic supremacy than all the articles or brochures in the land. Ah! If we had known, wanted, created similar organisation! If, regardless of our internationals and the constraints of their affairs, we had just put together a fifteen of military men, students or people of independent means, assembled at some point far away from Paris, and subjected them to a fortnight of the same specialisation! If the France team that will play Romania would just stay at Colombes until May 18!

But this is the voice of a cry in the desert. And an article that more or less changes nothing!

It may have had some impact upon Parisians, though. They would not have been pleased to read of the US captain criticising their nation. Feelings in France were still raw after the First World War. Just a few years earlier, France had needed a power from across the Atlantic to come to her rescue. That did not make France feel good about herself. So the Americans were not regarded as heroes for bringing France her liberty. They were a reminder of recent French weakness. The foreign forces had created something of an inferiority complex in France. Only by rejecting the Americans collectively could the French regain their own post-war identity.

A new sense of national pride would not be achieved by pandering to the greater power. It would be achieved by showing Americans that they were no longer needed and no longer necessarily even welcome.

Why should the Americans feel entitled to call the shots on any European matter? They had come into the First World War late in the eyes of many Europeans – then tried to take most of the credit for winning it. Furthermore, the USA seemed to have done its best to prevent Germany from being subjected to financial ruin and territorial penalties – the severe punishment the French had called for in the light of so many millions of First World War casualties. The French didn't see it as America's place to influence such matters.

The bigger nation had not suffered like the French during the war. The French had suffered 1,397,800 military deaths and 300,000 civilian deaths. The total number of wounded, 4,256,000, was staggering and tragic for a country of her size with a total population of fewer than 40 million at the time. Only the Russian Empire, with a population of closer to 100 million, sustained greater casualties during the war. Terrible as each individual casualty was, the suffering of the Americans was not on the same scale. The US had sustained 116,708 military deaths and 757 civilian deaths; their total number of wounded came to 205,690. That amount of misery didn't compare to the ordeal of the French people, at least not in the minds of Parisians. As far as they were concerned, the Americans had never earned the right to forgive the Germans and their allies for what they had done to France.

The USA was therefore cast in the role of villain almost as much as Germany. Never mind that Woodrow Wilson's 'Fourteen Points' – set out while the war was still being fought – had shown extraordinary wisdom and foresight. Never mind that he had been awarded the Nobel Peace Prize for his efforts. The French believed that the Americans had been interfering in European affairs they didn't understand.

By 1924, the French probably had reason to feel they had won this argument against the meddling Americans. The Germans were indeed on their knees, so much so that their suffering would open the door for Adolf Hitler's Nazis to rise to power during the following decade. As far as the French were concerned in 1924, however, justice had been done. That didn't make them feel any friendlier towards the USA – not when the Americans had, in French eyes, so recently tried to pervert the course of international justice. The Parisians would take no lectures from an American pulpit, thank you very much, especially not from a rugby player.

Such resentment may have been hard for Babe Slater to understand. Babe knew how he had suffered in France and Belgium towards the end of the Great War. He knew that Americans had also made many personal sacrifices and even laid down their lives to free France. No political complexities could change that. If the Americans weren't going to be shown eternal gratitude for what they had done, they at least deserved respect and some basic hospitality. Moreover, he felt the Olympic movement deserved French respect too. The Americans, he had claimed, were totally committed to their Olympic mission.

Of course Rudy Scholz and his diary painted a rather different picture. Babe probably didn't know how Rudy felt, such was the distance that seems to have grown between them at this point; and he certainly wouldn't have been impressed had he read those diary pages alleging that it was 'each man for himself' within the US team. However, Slater was clearly more representative of the general mood. So Scholz would have to stop sulking and start showing the same commitment if he was to stay involved in this particular Olympic mission. Otherwise he risked being discarded entirely.

chapter 8

ED'S DATE WITH RUGBY HISTORY

THE AMERICANS COULDN'T WAIT TO GET A GOOD LOOK AT THEIR opposition, and the opportunity came on Sunday 4 May. The match between France and Romania effectively opened the Olympic Games of Paris, 1924, though the official Opening Ceremony would not take place until two months later, on 5 July.

The problem for the Romanians was that they had only arrived in Paris the night before, having spent five days and nights in a third-class train carriage. They stepped out onto the field like lambs to the slaughter, in no physical or mental condition to compete. This, of course, was just how the French wanted to begin their Olympics. The hosts took the chance to send out a message to the world. On this first day, at the very least, no one was going to doubt their sporting superiority.

Rudy wrote in his diary later, 'Romania acted as if they didn't know what it was all about.' De Groot agreed. 'It was clearly evident from the start of that sad contest that the much smaller and really pusillanimous group of athletes from the Balkan state were no match for their hardier and more experienced antagonists...The Romanians had nothing but fight; the French had one of the finest teams any of us had ever seen...Particularly were they well fortified in the backfield...Never had we seen such beautiful passing, such clever swerving and so much speed on one team before.'

France ran in 13 tries and the star of the show was Adolphe Jaureguy, the danger man singled out by the English a week earlier. Perhaps riled by Babe Slater's attack in the French press, he had turned up at the last moment to remind the world just how devastating he was. The message seemed to be that masters of their craft didn't need to train for exhibition matches against apprentices. As if to prove his point, Jaureguy of the Stade Francais club scored four tries in a virtuoso display. The Americans knew immediately that they had to find a way to keep Jaureguy quiet or suffer the same fate. If the French winger's confidence was allowed to remain intact, he had so much talent that he would destroy the Americans almost single-handedly.

Jaureguy apart, there was one glimmer of hope for Babe, Rudy and the others. De Groot observed,

> The French forwards were only mediocre, although quite clever in the scrum, where they hooked the ball almost every time...We left the stadium fully realising just what we were up against, a decidedly sober bunch of Americans, trying to figure out just how we were going to stop that French backfield. And we decided right there and then that the only chance we had to win against such a team would be to keep the ball to ourselves and never let it get out to their backfield. But how we were going to accomplish that against a scrum which was so clever in hooking the ball, for admittedly our weakest point in the games we played in England was our inability to hook. That was our problem, and but two weeks remained in which to solve it.

There seemed no obvious solution. Two of the wisest old heads, Rudy Scholz and Babe Slater, barely seemed to be communicating with each other anymore. It appeared they only had one thing in common – a firmly held belief that France would probably beat them in the big game. In the aftermath of that fearsome French victory over Romania, both Babe and Rudy wrote privately of their pessimism.

On 5 May, Rudy noted in his diary, 'Practice – things look pretty bad for us to win versus France. We have no team work – no real spirit – due to the attitude of the fellows. They want me to play half back [just behind the scrum] now that they know what they are up against...'.

Scholz had been played out on the wing in England. It was a position which could earn you the glorious role of running in a few tries in a rout; but it could also leave you isolated and virtually redundant when your team was struggling in a match. Now that the Americans had realised just how formidable the French were, keeping possession would be the key. Rudy was therefore being thrown into a more pivotal role in the heat of the action, where there would be most pressure and only a split second in which to make the right decision if the ball reached him from the scrum. No wonder Scholz felt he could now afford a wry smile. He had been moved into a minor, peripheral role in this Olympic adventure from the moment Slater and Doe had been voted captain and vice-captain. Even the team manager, Sam Goodman, had failed to recognise Rudy's seniority within the squad. He had almost felt as though he had been stripped of his rank. Now they had suddenly realised they might require his talents and experience when it mattered after all. What a pity they hadn't done so earlier, when he might have been able to get the entire squad working as one.

Rudy's latest criticism of team spirit came at such a critical time, just days before their first Olympic match, that it could only be seen as yet another damning indictment of what he saw as a failure of leadership. The team captain was responsible for unity, the coach for tactics, the manager for administration and executive decisions. Therefore team spirit was down to Babe – and Rudy stubbornly continued to insist there wasn't any. Could this really have been true, in spite of the French reporter's impressions of the fearsome American unit? Or had Rudy's bitterness got the better of him? Whether there was team spirit or not, Rudy couldn't change anything, so he grew cynical. Rather than confront his old friend Babe Slater about his feelings, it seems that Scholz had chosen to withdraw from the core of the group.

Though he was keen to make his contribution against Romania that Sunday, Rudy felt sure he could see where this ill-conceived journey was going to end. It would all finish with a humiliating defeat against the French the following weekend. Scholz had felt powerless to create the united front so essential to any effort to compete with the might of France. Therefore in his mind it didn't exist; and he didn't much want to be part of the day when the USA rugby team's apparent lack of unity would be cruelly exposed. Shocking as the confession still sounds today, Rudy confided to his diary, 'I am really training hard for the game Sunday but hope I won't have to play the next Sunday.'

Had Babe and the management realised quite how disillusioned Scholz was, they might even have sent him home early. Though many of Rudy's teammates probably agreed that their audacious bid for Olympic gold was beginning to look like an impossible dream, no one else would have allowed his morale to sink so low as to admit to himself that he didn't even want to play in the biggest game of all, having travelled so far. Besides, others felt there was more spirit within the group than Rudy suggested; enough at least to play with pride and emerge with credit from a battle with the French, whatever the outcome.

Though Babe Slater had strained a tendon, which was probably playing on his mind, he was upbeat due to what he perceived as excellent team spirit. On 6 May Babe wrote to his mother. '...This trip is considerable improvement over the last one in that we have a better bunch of fellows and it is better managed...'.

Could this remark be interpreted as a criticism of Scholz and his attempts to act as assistant manager at the 1920 Olympics? As for the 1924 trip, Babe's claim was certainly at odds with Rudy's assertion that players hadn't really formed a unified group at all. It appears that Babe and Rudy could hardly have felt more differently about most of their colleagues.

Even so, Slater did have one gripe, about the financial sacrifices they were making in order to play for their country. Babe added,

> Financially it is the bunk. We anticipated that we'd make plenty expense-money in England but quite the reverse, we had to dig in our own pockets for the train fare to France. We played in England just at the close of their season and they had lost interest

in the game and besides our games were poorly advertised and at the final game there was a soccer match going on that same time at Wembley which drew about 100 thousand people. However, even if we haven't any money we are having a splendid time.

We are staying in a nice hotel about half an hour from the center of Paris right on the Seine River. We go to Colombes every afternoon in a big bus that is provided and practice for a couple of hours.

Living through a world war had made Babe a realist if nothing else, and he wasn't going to pretend the Americans were favourites for the gold medal. 'Last Sunday we saw the French play the Romanians, the frogs won easily 61 to 3. They have a very strong team and I frankly believe our chances of beating them are slim although we are sure going to let them know they have been in a battle. We play Romania on the 11th and France on the 18th.'

So there it was – the bombshell. Even Babe Slater, the captain, the figurehead, the symbol of American strength, thought he was going to lead a losing team. The man every member of that team looked towards for positive thinking and inspiration had all but written off his team's chances. In this, at least, Babe and Rudy were in agreement, even if Slater seemed to possess so much more fighting spirit than Scholz.

The immediate concern for coach Austin was not the French, but getting his player selection right for the match against the Romanians. In consultation with Babe Slater, he decided that it would be prudent to rest injured players, experiment a little and make sure that everyone on the trip had a chance to play at least one Olympic match, thus ensuring a medal for each man. Babe Slater was still nursing a nagging tendon strain; and although he was captain he was going to sit the first match out. Lefty Rogers didn't need more punishment inflicted on his broken nose than was entirely necessary either. Meanwhile Linn Farish and Dud De Groot had already been so impressive among the forwards that they had virtually secured their places against the French. They could watch the first match too – and make sure they understood every aspect of the rules as interpreted in mainland Europe.

The vice-captain, Charlie Doe, would lead the team in Babe's absence. Doe was shifted to full-back so that Scholz could be tried at scrum-half. Bob Devereux played fly-half, with Norman Cleaveland and Dick Hyland in the centre. Coach Austin and Babe opted for an eight-man, 3-2-3 scrum formation, much like the one used in rugby today. Cesar Manelli, John O'Neill and Mush Graff occupied their usual front row places. Alan Valentine (the Rhodes scholar who had joined the team in England) and Jack Patrick were placed in the middle row, with Al Williams central in the back row while Norm Slater and Phil Clark acted as flankers. Incredibly, the Americans were still trying out new tactics going into the Olympic competition itself. Meanwhile two more players made up the XV. George Dixon was on one wing, and on the other was…Ed Turkington.

The dashing young San Franciscan, who had gambled so much in his personal life to cut free and follow his dream, had now found a place in the USA Olympic rugby team's starting line-up. He was no longer the 'fastest forward', a position which didn't entirely suit his slim build, despite his sinuous muscularity. Now he could use his pace to fly down the wing. Perhaps he could even score the tries that would set up the last match against France as the real final. Would Elaine Horton, the long-term girlfriend he had left for rugby and romantic adventure, be pleased for him? It didn't matter because he wasn't in France to think about Elaine. He would seize his opportunities as they came – and this was one hell of an opportunity.

Ed's sporting ambitions were coming to fruition, until they were suddenly placed in jeopardy by events off the field. Attention suddenly switched to the identity of the referee for the USA v France showdown the following week. A row broke out that became so serious it threatened to destroy the Olympic experience for Turkington and every other American rugby player. The British Admiral, Percy Royds, had already been chosen to officiate in the big game, and both Babe Slater and Charlie Austin had approved his appointment. But Sam Goodman refused to accept 'the French choice'. We can only speculate on how this difference of opinion between senior members of the American party was handled. Goodman would not have been happy with Austin and Slater for playing into French hands so easily on this important issue. There may well have been some tense exchanges between Goodman and Austin in particular.

As vice-chairman of the International Rugby Board, Admiral Royds was a rugby fanatic and in favour of the sport's inclusion in the Olympic Games. Yet he was a stickler for the rules, and perhaps Goodman feared that a military man's interpretation of the game would prove to be too rigid for the Americans. Maybe the chosen man's naval connections rang alarm bells with Goodman, after some indifferent officiating had robbed the tourists of an even bigger win in their opening match in Plymouth against Devonport Services. More likely, wily old Sam worked on the maxim that if the French wanted a particular referee, there was probably a good reason why the Americans should make sure they didn't get him. At any rate Goodman ruffled more than a few feathers by telling the French to forget Admiral Royds.

An Associated Press report had kept initial news of the row short and sweet. Under the headline: 'Goodman Protests Referee Suggested', it read:

> Paris. May 5. Samuel Goodman, manager of the United States Olympic rugby football team, has refused to accept Admiral Percy Royds of the British navy as referee of the France-United States Olympic rugby match May 18.
>
> In place of Admiral Royds he has proposed the names of John Jeffries of England, who refereed the match at Antwerp in 1920, and James Wyle…'.

The French had lost in Antwerp and undoubtedly felt that Goodman was seeking a referee who would be lenient if the Americans attempted rough-house tactics. So they weren't keen to accept Goodman's suggestions either. A newspaper report dated 6 May carried the headline, 'GOODMAN FIGHTS RUGBY REFEREE, DEMANDS SQUARE DEAL FOR US.' It read, 'The deadlock between Samuel Goodman, manager of the American Olympic rugby football team, and Alan H. Muhr, representing the French Olympic Committee, over the question of a referee for the France-United States match, May 18, continues, the Americans absolutely refusing to accept Admiral Percy Royds, of the British Navy, whom they feel Muhr is trying to impose upon them.'

As the argument escalated through the week, Goodman threatened to pull the American team out of the Games entirely. He was on the warpath about another issue too, as the same newspaper report explained:

> In addition, the relations between the Americans and Muhr are somewhat strained owing to Muhr's refusal to allow the Americans a real rugby practice match before the game with Romania next Sunday. Manager Goodman feels that the efforts made in America to send the rugby team to France at great expense, $8,000 being subscribed in California alone, should be taken into account and members of the team afforded kinder treatment. Muhr personally favors allowing the Americans a practice match, but has been placed in an unsatisfactory position as buffer between the American players and the French executive committee.

The Olympic hosts had also retaliated by taking away the right of the Americans to train on the practice fields around the Stade Colombes. It didn't seem to dampen US passions, since the newspaper report added, 'Meanwhile the Americans are practicing with a vengeance and tackling one another as hard as they would their opponents in the Olympic competition. Assistant manager Austin this afternoon had to curtail the energy of Rogers, O'Neill, Manelli, Cunningham and Muldoon who were tackling too earnestly. Cunningham injured two newly mended ribs which were broken in one of the English matches.'

The latest crack to Cunningham's ribs was to put him out of the Olympics, a bitter blow. The players were clearly taking out their frustrations on each other after so many days of poor treatment at the hands of the French. Perhaps that was why Goodman was so desperate for them to find someone else to play before the tournament started.

Goodman later commented, 'Without going into details about our stay…it is only necessary to remark that we were accorded anything but hospitable treatment; in fact, many times we were treated with open hostility. The authorities, through control of all playing fields, would not allow us to engage in any of the previously arranged games with local clubs.'

The ongoing arguments soon saw relations deteriorate further still. Pretty soon there was a fresh controversy over which to do battle.

Perhaps it was Goodman's mention of the money that had been spent in getting the American team to Paris in the first place; or maybe stories were still doing the rounds about how the Americans had refused to play a match in their 1920 post-Olympic tour of France until they had received adequate expenses. But as a 7 May newspaper article explained, 'City Counsellor Armand Massard, sporting authority of La Liberte… in an article yesterday hinted that [the American Olympic rugby football team's] amateurism was considerably tainted.'

The Americans had demanded that their expenses be paid before they were prepared to step out onto the field during their post-Olympic tour of France in 1920. That was only fair, since it had cost money to travel to the south of the country. But had this demand since been taken out of context and distorted to make it sound as though the tourists were professionals masquerading as amateurs?

An unnamed member of the American rugby team gave the press his reply to the latest allegation. His provocative words acknowledged the fact that Massard was an expert swordsman who was often given to settling his disputes in dramatic duels. Given that lawyer Scholz had experience of dealing with the media, and was usually both feisty and witty during these exchanges, there is every chance that the following riposte, under the headline 'US Rugbyites Are Wrathful – Duels May Be in Order Next' – was from Rudy himself:

'Just let him come down here, choose his own weapons, footballs or foils, and we'll soon show him whether we are amateurs or professionals. We haven't had the pleasure of a visit from him and wish that before writing again he would investigate.'

The demand that Massard confine himself to the facts also smacked of legal training, and the tone seems to have the Scholz stamp all over it. The facts, as later revealed by Babe Slater in his letter home, were that the Americans were losing money – not making it – on this Olympic adventure. Due to the poor turn-out at Twickenham for the Harlequins match, the American players were by now having to dip into their own pockets to help finance the all-important Parisian leg of the adventure. Of course, the French public didn't know that. They would simply have read what sounded like an invitation to a violent confrontation. Perhaps this would stay in their minds as the big matches approached.

As if this dispute wasn't enough to turn the pre-match tension up to scarcely bearable levels, another argument broke out, with Sam Goodman once again at its epicentre. The 1924 Olympics were the first to be filmed by moving picture cameras. The question was: who would be doing the filming? That same 7 May newspaper report explained what was happening:

> Another hitch in the hitherto friendly Franco-American sporting relations has arisen over the determination of the American players to take their own photographs of the match with Romania, Sunday, for documentary and training purposes, despite the insistence of the French Olympic committee that exclusive contracts had already been let to French firms for all photographic work in connection with the Olympic Games. It is expected that the difference will be smoothed out at a conference tomorrow, in view of the determination of the Americans to take photographs whether or no. The team had a good workout of two hours this afternoon and all are in fine fettle.

Of this particular dispute, team manager Sam Goodman was quoted as saying,

> I feel that our photographers should be allowed to photograph our men in the rugby matches, for it is planned to use these pictures in the States for educational purposes. The American photographers know better than any others the pictures that will interest the people back home who are following the work of their representatives with the keenest interest. We do not think that we are asking too much. It is merely a demand for something justly due us. Everything ought to be settled without any misunderstanding. Our men will take the field Sunday determined to live up to the reputation for fair play – a reputation for which our men are noted and deservedly so.

Behind the scenes, however, there was no guarantee that the belligerent Goodman would even allow the US rugby team to take to the field unless he got his own way. And in an atmosphere of acute tension bordering on open hostility, the US team's workouts were now restricted to scrubland near the Hotel Exelmans. It was on a grim little field, overlooked by grey apartment blocks. This was hardly the sort of stage upon which Olympic champions were used to being put through their paces. For now, however, the Americans made do with what they had. They practised for two hours in the morning and one hour in the afternoon. Yet all the time they were seething over the way the French had suddenly denied them access to the Stade Colombes until all disputes were settled. It was not a suspension the Californians intended to respect for very long.

Unwilling to be brushed aside by their hosts, Babe Slater led his team down to the Colombes Stadium the very next day. It was Thursday, 8 May, and a photograph survives to show what an unstoppable mood the Americans were in. Finding a ladder to overcome the high fence topped with barbed-wire, Babe and his players scaled the perimeter and dropped down into the stadium. Pretty soon they were working out on the hallowed turf, a vast improvement on the scrubland near their hotel. It was an important session too, because this was a trial game to decide the line-up for the first big match against Romania that Sunday. They wanted to conduct that decisive workout in stadium conditions and they were not about to be told by their hosts that they were barred.

Norman Cleaveland admitted many years later, 'It wasn't the best way to conduct international affairs.' But Charlie Doe, the vice-captain, remained defiant, 'If they wanted to push us around then we damn well pushed back.'

Unfortunately there was a price to pay for breaking the stadium ban and it was exacted swiftly. In his diary entry, Rudy Scholz explained, 'Thieves entered the dressing rooms and robbed all the fellows except four or five. I left my money and watch at home and thus saved it.'

Although they had paid an attendant well to guard their clothes, most of the Americans returned to the stadium dressing rooms to find that they had been robbed of cash and personal possessions. It amounted to more than $1,000 of losses. One player who came off the field for an early shower was understood to have met a stranger in the locker room area. When asked to explain his presence, he said he had been detailed to help guard the area. Yet when the unnamed player finished his shower, the mystery man had gone; and so had the cash and precious personal effects.

Under the headline 'US Rugby Team Valuables Looted', one American report filled in some of the details.

> Paris, May 8 – Sneak thieves today entered the dressing rooms of the American Olympic rugby football team and robbed players of all their valuables, about 5,000 francs, and several hundred dollars in American currency. The jewelry included a number of watches and medals won in athletic tournaments to which the men attach much value.
>
> O'Neill lost 2,000 francs and $200 and Manelli, Turkington, De Groot, Cashel and Cunningham lost everything. Valuable fraternity pins were stolen from two other players.
>
> The police promised to put their cleverest detectives on the case. A workman who has heretofore been entrusted with the task of locking the doors to the dressing room reported that today he had forgotten to do so. He was closely questioned by the authorities.

Perhaps his forgetfulness related to the fact that the Americans shouldn't really have been in the stadium in the first place. At any rate, the inference from the report was that Babe's men had been the victims of an 'inside job'.

For Ed Turkington this must have been quite a blow. He had already risked everything in his personal life for this adventure. It was quite possible that he had lost his long-term girlfriend by then. So when he returned to the dressing room that day, to find that he had lost all his sentimental possessions and all his money too, he must have been close to despair.

On Friday, 8 May, Sam Goodman was still arguing with the French about those film rights for American games. And it seems that Goodman came closer than ever to pulling the American rugby team out of the Olympic tournament altogether at that stage. If it was just an outrageous bluff that Goodman used during negotiations with the Games' hosts, you could be pretty sure that his players would not have appreciated the tactic. Had that bluff been called, and had the Americans been sent home with nothing to show for their ordeal, Goodman might have become one of the most unpopular men in Californian sport.

Perhaps that is why coach Austin seems to have done his best to undermine Goodman's bluff by contradicting him publicly, despite the increased managerial tensions this may have caused. A newspaper report claimed, 'coach Austin last night said that the Americans would go into Sunday's game regardless of the outcome of the discussion of whether or not American photographers will be allowed on the field. It had been previously reported that the Americans would refuse to play should the motion-picture and other camera men be ruled off the field.'

Despite Austin's softer stance, Goodman's hardball tactics had already struck fear into the French. An Associated Press report from 8 May carried the headline, 'GOODMAN WINS OLYMPIC BATTLE – US TO GET RUGBY PICTURES'.

The report went on:

> The deadlock over the question of Americans being permitted to take moving pictures of the Olympic rugby football matches, in which the American team plays, was broken tonight. The Americans have been protesting since Wednesday against the position of the French Olympic committee in giving the exclusive rights for taking the Olympic Games pictures to a private firm.
>
> Tonight Sam Goodman of California, manager of the American team, received from Alan Muhr, assistant general commissioner of sports, the following note: 'The private company enjoying exclusively the right to make pictures will take great pleasure in allowing your official photographers to make pictures of both rugby matches in which the Americans are engaged, under the condition that these pictures are purely for record and educational purposes.'
>
> Today's conference between Goodman and Muhr is said to have been a rather heated one. Goodman objected to the principle of the French Olympic committee's right to sell the exclusive privilege of taking pictures of events in which teams of foreign nations are engaged. Goodman threatened to prevent the French company's men from filming the US rugby matches unless American photographers were allowed the same privileges. Tough-guy Sam is said to have threatened to keep his team off the field unless the idea was accepted; this proved the convincing

argument for the Olympic committee, which promised to break its contract with the moving pictures concern having the concession, or to pay it 100,000 francs forfeit money, in order to allow American photographers to work.

The Americans went through hard practice today. Substitute players will make up the greatest part of the team which will meet the Romanians on Sunday. Most of the 'start' players are being held in reserve for the game with France on May 18, as it is the express determination of the Americans to win this match at all costs.

The American captain, C. E. Slater, will not be in the line-up when the whistle blows. He pulled a tendon slightly in a recent practice and is taking things easy.

Had he read that article, Ed Turkington may not have been so happy about playing in the first match. Did his inclusion in the opening game mean that he would be excluded from the second? Yet Ed must also have known that if he played an outstanding match against Romania, he might still have a chance of forcing his way into the team for the big one against France. Anything could happen. Someone could be injured in training. What mattered was that he was going to be given a platform to show what he could do. He was ready to seize that chance. Whatever happened now, he was guaranteed a medal, by virtue of being selected for at least one of the matches.

Since Rudy Scholz had also been chosen for the first match against Romania, he had effectively secured a second Olympic medal for rugby before he even played. He didn't sound too thrilled by that fact, or the team's last training session before the match. On 9 May, Rudy wrote in his diary, 'Practice all afternoon. Practice is rather hard work; not because I do not like to play, for I really do, but because of the damn selfishness and rotten spirit.'

Would Rudy's reading of the situation hit the Americans hard when it came to serious competition? The Romanians, who were guaranteed a bronze just for turning up, might also have had silver in their sights. They were still considered rank outsiders following their woeful showing against the French. But the match against the USA wasn't a foregone conclusion; and the eastern Europeans had at least enjoyed the opportunity for some much-needed rest, recovery and training following their journey to Paris and the mauling they had received from their hosts. The Americans knew too well what could happen when a fancied side underestimated their opponents. They had won Olympic gold that way in 1920, due to the over-confidence of the French, so they didn't intend to make the same mistake.

One French newspaper warned that the Romanian team,

> has not lost courage, and will present itself against the Yankees in a far superior form than last Sunday. The 'Sky Blues' have worked hard and put their lines in order. Finally the appointment of Nicolae 'Mano' [Maresco], excellent captain and solid athlete, will certainly be of value to their front lines.
>
> With their inexperienced, but courageous rugby, with their forms of attack and style, the 'Eastern French' are capable of achieving against the star-spangled banner, a more advantageous score than against us. They will hurl themselves, this time, at a marvellous team, but which, from the point of view of rugby science and technique, is not in any way superior to them…

For all that, the American management deemed it prudent to give their players some down time before the Romania match. The boys had trained so hard that they were like coiled springs; so they were taken to the Palace of Versailles in order to relax a little before the big day. Adrenalin would surge through their veins again soon enough. Now was the time to refresh themselves and ensure that the pre-match tension didn't become so great that it worked against them.

True to form, Rudy Scholz seemed to enjoy the military aspect of Versailles the most. He wrote in his diary, 'I went around the gallery there with a Major General from the British Army, who didn't know a great deal more about the pictures than I did…In the evening Bill and I went down to the "Latin Quarter" (near Montparnasse) and talked with two American girls. One was studying art and the other was studying mankind I think. Back to hotel at 11pm.'

How much Rudy's late return on the eve of an Olympic match would have been appreciated by coach Austin is difficult to say. Scholz was still up in time to attend Mass the next morning. By the afternoon the photographers were busy recording the build-up to only the second sporting contest of the 1924 Olympic Games at the Stade Colombes. There is a lovely picture of Babe Slater, towering above the two captains of the day, Charlie Doe and Maresco. Slater wore a three-piece suit and one of those huge cloth caps so popular in the 1920s.

When it was the turn of the entire American team to be photographed, along with the referee, the scene became comical. Scholz, sitting on the floor, looks so relaxed that he is actually turning away from the camera and apparently sharing a joke with the match official, David Leyshon. Many of the Americans in the front row are also laughing; but Ed Turkington, pictured in the middle of the back row, couldn't be looking more serious. He was already psyched up and ready to go.

Pretty soon the teams stepped out into the Stade Colombes, where between 5,000 and 7,000 fans had gathered to witness the contest. The French team members were among those spectators, keen to identify any potential threat to their gold medals. The Americans would need to perform well in order to land any kind of psychological blow on the favourites watching from the stands.

Even Rudy was in a serious frame of mind by now. There is a photograph of him standing to attention, military-style, alongside his teammates as the band struck up 'The Star-Spangled Banner'. And once the whistle blew, Rudy was quickly into action as he fed his three-quarters with a huge pass. The first move fell apart and the Romanians were soon on the counter-attack, trying to engineer a shock opening score. The American defence held firm and Dick Hyland seized an early opportunity to show his power and grace. With a trademark feint and a timely pass he released the ball to Charlie Doe. The captain dived over for the all-important first try. When Doe converted his own score, the USA were 5-0 ahead. Within seconds they had extended their lead. Dixon was held up just short of the line but still managed to find Dick Hyland, who duly charged through for the second try.

To the dismay of Scholz and his teammates, however, the crowd jeered them every time they excelled. As team manager Sam Goodman would write later, 'Spectators cheered the Romanians and booed the Americans with great consistency. That attitude seemed to us unnecessary; at any rate, it failed to improve our feeling and love for the French.'

Rudy wrote in his diary, 'The team was booed and hissed thru-out the game for alleged rough play, which was only hard tackling. The French are striving by all means to beat us…'.

In the stands Dud De Groot, who was being rested for the first match, struggled to stay cool in the face of what he regarded as severe provocation. He wrote later,

> To say that the French spectators were unsportsmanlike at that game would be putting it far too mildly. Not only did they clearly evidence the fact that they were for the Romanians from start to finish, but they made matters worse when they booed and hissed us throughout the entire game. If an American made a brilliant play carrying the ball through several Romanians, he was sure to be hissed for his efforts. On several occasions some puny Romanian, in attempting to tackle an American, would be knocked down and laid out for a few minutes, generally with his wind out. The whole stands would rise to their feet thereupon and give the American team the most unsportsmanlike kind of a rasberrying. The few of us who were in the stands had great difficulty in maintaining our tempers, and several times there were near gang fights.

Babe Slater doubtless provided a cool head among all those hot tempers. A fist-fight with French fans was not what the American team needed a week before the biggest game of all. And for all those unsavoury scenes, the Parisian fans couldn't unsettle the Americans on the field sufficiently to alter the course of the first-half action. By now Scholz was regularly feeding Hyland in the centre with outrageously long passes. Hyland wasn't wasting them either. He started to run riot and he set up Jack Patrick for yet another try. Doe, who had missed his last try conversion kick, was accurate this time. Already the Americans were comfortable at 13-0. Hyland and Patrick combined again to extend the US lead to 18-0 by half-time. The French crowd voiced their displeasure, claiming that Patrick had drifted offside before accepting his teammate's scoring pass.

Out on the wing, Turkington was playing a good game without shining quite so brightly as the biggest stars of the show. It was Hyland who caught the eye again at the restart by dancing his way through the Romanians to touch down with apparent ease. But Ed was determined to show what he could do, and his finest moment came soon after a rare Romanian attack had fizzled out. As one American report put it, 'Turkington got away and when on the point of being pulled up [tackled] he passed to Patrick, who scored the sixth try, Doe converting.'

'Turk' might have gone on to tear that tiring Romanian defence to shreds. He might even have found his way onto the list of try-scorers, had he been able to keep his cool. Instead poor Ed allowed himself to be provoked by a late Romanian tackle, and charged straight into a personal disaster with 20 minutes left on the clock. It appears that Turkington called 'mark' having taken a catch while rock-steady on both feet. Rugby rules allowed the catcher a free kick without interference from the opposition as long as the referee had awarded the 'mark'. The Romanian was clearly no respecter of Ed's call; and Turk, in turn, showed the Romanian and his late challenge precious little respect either.

Referee Leyshon, a Welshman who had settled in France, saw Ed punch the guilty Romanian in retaliation. Though Turkington claimed at the time his action was purely defensive, his explanation failed to convince the referee. With the crowd going crazy and calling for Turkington's head, there was only ever going to be one decision. Ed was sent off in disgrace, the jeers and whistles ringing in his ears. In these moments he made the wrong kind of history; for Ed became the first player ever to be sent off in the history of international rugby, preceding the man usually credited with that dubious honour, Cyril Brownlie of New Zealand, by a year.

A priceless American newspaper report was sympathetic to Turkington the next day. It explained, '...Later in the second half Turkington was put out of the game, accused of roughing up a Romanian. He had signaled for a fair catch and was afterward run into by a Romanian, he explained. In putting out his hand to stop the latter Turkington came into violent contact with his face. He went off the field accompanied by unjustifiable comment from the stands...'.

An Associated Press report of the match suggested that Turk's retaliation hadn't stopped with his fist. It claimed, 'Turkington was put off the field twenty minutes before the whistle by the referee for kicking a Romanian player while the latter was down. Turkington argued that the kick was not intentional, and from the stands it appeared to be accidental...'.

On the basis that you don't kick a man while he is down, perhaps Ed didn't think this particular Romanian was a good example of a man. It is unlikely that Turkington was the original aggressor; he had too much to lose personally by being sent off.

Later Ed would admit to at least part of what had happened on the day. 'Yes, he told us that he had retaliated,' revealed his son Ned in 2007. 'But it was with his hand not his boot. He knew he shouldn't have done it, but there was strong provocation.'

Ed would have been distraught in that moment of shame. He had come all that way to make his Olympic dream come true, and now it appeared to lie in tatters. Any chance he might have had of playing in the final seemed to have gone. Just when he was really starting to catch the eye, he was suddenly out in the wilderness.

At least the US team wasn't a man down for long. A newspaper report added, 'Another casualty occurred a few minutes later when the Romanian Bentia, a three-quarter, collided with an American player, then with the referee and then with the ground. He had to be carried off the field, and his departure brought the Romanian team down to fourteen players, and so even with the Americans. Some of the spectators attributed Bentia's fate to the Americans.'

Bizarrely, referee Leyshon seems to have played a part in evening up the numbers too. US domination therefore continued. Patrick scored a try to extend the American lead, while the unstoppable Hyland had saved his most spectacular moment until the closing stages. From the halfway line he swerved right and left until he had the entire Romanian team trailing in his wake. All that remained was to touch the ball down under the posts. Just to rub salt into the wounds, Hyland scored one more try before the final whistle.

The Americans had scored eight tries in all, Hyland running in four and Patrick three. Even so the final score was 'only' 37-0. France had run up 61 points a week earlier, so the Parisian crowd's disdain for American rugby was justified in their view.

A seething Rudy Scholz threatened to return that disdain with interest when he wrote in his diary following the Romania game, 'I don't want to play [next Sunday] but if I play I will play damned hard.'

Yet it is clear from this entry that Rudy's disgust with a perceived the lack of team ethic in the American camp was still stronger than his anger at the way the US players had been treated. It seems incredible that, having gone all that way, Scholz still didn't want to be part of the gold medal game because he thought the Americans might be humiliated. Yet his resentment at the conduct of the French was growing by the day.

Meanwhile it wasn't just the numerical message sent out by the first two games that gave the French press ammunition. They knew their rugby and they were quick to pick fault in the most vulnerable areas of the Americans' game. '...The faults are numerous, in the forwards above all, where they seem quite inexperienced, form a bad scrum and play a mediocre short pass.'

Even De Groot admitted, 'The American scrum, even against the weak opposition of the Romanians, was clearly not yet a success, and time and again they were outhooked.'

It was hardly surprising. Photographs of the American scrum showed players with backs arched and heads pointed awkwardly downwards. This kind of body-shape was never going to achieve the stability the hooker needed in order to heel the ball back to his own side with a clean strike. Clearly uncomfortable, the US forwards were hanging on for dear life instead of pushing for all they were worth. With very few backs straightened as the ball was put in, the so-called tough guys simply hadn't achieved the low, horizontal body positions from which they could look their opponents in the eye and shove them backwards. There was no time to teach the Americans the pushing technique they required to survive and thrive against the French pack.

The three-quarter backs lacked technique too, and one French newspaper seemed to damn them with faint praise when it commented, 'If the Americans were not aware of the finesse of rugby, if their passes are too high, badly made, and their moves somewhat erratic...they play a loyal and sporting game...'

But Rudy won some positive reviews along with Hyland and Patrick. One newspaper which began by praising Hyland and Cleaveland, then added, 'Scholz and Patrick were two other stars who coordinated on the offensive and caused the Romanians no small amount of trouble.' Another said, 'The scrum-half Scholz was very active and his passes were good in general.' Meanwhile *Le Miroir des Sports* called Rudy 'very penetrating.'

A delighted Rudy wrote in his diary, 'Papers gave Hyland, Patrick and myself a fine write-up.'

Yet the American team's leaders all suggested there was room for improvement before the big game against France the following week. 'We are satisfied,' said Sam Goodman, manager of the team, after the match. 'We did not want to swamp these fellows. This game will do us a lot of good.' Meanwhile coach Austin admitted he had 'noticed some weaknesses in the American team,' but that he 'would work hard to overcome them during the week and have the men in perfect condition for the game with France next Sunday.'

Babe Slater warned, 'We will have our regular team in the field next Sunday, and then we shall give even a better account of ourselves.'

But would the French be able to field their strongest team? It appeared not, because *Le Miroir des Sports* claimed that Jaureguy had turned his back on the Olympics yet again. The reporter talked about a trio of stars from the French back line then asked the following question: '…but who will be the fourth man, since Jaureguy, absent from Paris, will not play?'

This news would have angered Babe Slater more than it would have pleased him. Slater had already explained how his team had travelled so far in order to honour the Olympic movement and play against the best teams they could as they defended their title. He had already hit out at the prospect of French absentees when it came to the crunch. Now it appeared that Babe's USA team had been handed the ultimate insult. Jaureguy had turned up to play the Romanians, helped to thrash them, and decided the tournament was beneath him. He had left Paris again, apparently with no intention of giving the USA team any respect by returning to play them.

It appeared that Jaureguy's contempt for the Americans was on a par with that of the Parisian public. They despised the rough, tough tactics the USA team had used to get the better of Romania. This was yet another example of America throwing its weight about, they thought, just as had happened at the end of the First World War.

Even the American photographers and 'cinema-men' had muscled their way into the Olympics, a more visible addition to their French counterparts than one might imagine today. It was quite normal for these photo 'snappers' to run onto the pitch to capture the images they wanted during the match, moving or still. So when these invasions took place, the French crowd for the USA v Romania game would have been reminded repeatedly of the battle of wills that had taken place off the field in the build-up to the match.

The Americans had prevailed, much to the frustration of the French, though there was still an uneasy truce in this particular war. One American report had claimed, 'The truce in the battle over the taking of pictures of the rugby matches extends only for [the USA v Romania match] and a new arrangement will have to be made if American cinema-men are to be allowed to photograph the United States-France game…'.

They could dress it up any way they liked, but the Americans were bound to prevail again, having won the first battle for the cameras, and everyone knew it. It was unbearable to the French that American strong-arm tactics could succeed at their Olympic Games, either on or off the field. Therefore some Parisians decided that they would employ unsavoury tactics of their own in the build-up to the big game. There were isolated examples of Babe, Rudy and the boys being spat at and jostled in the street. Though the American players were too big and strong to allow themselves to feel threatened by such situations, such behaviour was deeply shocking to them nonetheless.

Some of the more responsible French journalists did their best to diffuse the tension in the week leading up to the big showdown. Andre Glarner wrote, 'It is hoped that the crowd will be less partial than it was [for the USA's match against Romania], and will know how to honour the American athletes, who showed a willingness to play in this Olympic rugby tournament even though the game is no longer played in their country.'

Such hopes were hardly realistic, however. If the French crowd had booed the Americans when France weren't even playing, what were they going to do when their favourites were trying to beat the USA? The Olympic organisers were worried; the signs looked ominous. The French Olympic Committee appealed for calm and good sportsmanship from the Parisian public by posting the following message in *L'Auto*, the city's leading sports paper:

The French Olympic Committee addresses the following appeal to the public: One regrets that part of the public present at the Colombes Stadium on Sunday at the Romania v United States game showed very violent sentiments. The French Olympic Committee makes an appeal to the sporting public and to their feelings of equality for the numbers of visitors that are coming to the Olympic Games. In order to help the spectators to conserve their feelings and to show their best sporting spirit the following should be observed: It is sportsmanship to applaud every effort and the nation who wins. It is the first wish of all true sportsmen. Forty-four nations have accepted the invitation to participate in the Paris Games, and we owe to their representatives applause and a cordial reception.

The French Olympic Committee asks the public to abstain from all demonstrations and counts on the good spirit of the public to aid in the success of the Games and they hope this appeal will not be in vain. The Americans play hard, but never brutally or with bad intent. The Californians who have come over 12,000 kilometres [7,500 miles] to play a sport which is not theirs should be granted applause and warmth from the French sporting public.

De Groot summed up the reaction of the Americans when he wrote later, 'It is hard to conceive of a nation so unsportsmanlike that such an appeal is necessary, but it is harder still to try to understand how the people of the French nation could be so hostile to representatives of a country which had so recently saved them from almost certain destruction. Why they harboured such an open hatred for a nation who had done so much for them will never be understood by the members of the American rugby team, but their attitude of jealousy or hostility, whichever it may have been, was always present nevertheless.'

Some papers, in particular the *Petit Journal*, chose instead to turn up the pre-match tension by insulting the US team and declaring them undeserving of their first Olympic title.

The American players who will meet the French on Sunday at Colombes have not, truly speaking, even the most rudimentary knowledge of the game of rugby, which, moreover, they do not practise in California. They took part in the Inter-Allied games in 1919, and they were beaten by France and they beat the Romanians.

In 1920 they did not win the Olympic contest, even though one tries to pretend so, this contest was not played. In September they took part in a match they called 'Olympic', disputed at Antwerp, amid general indifference, against a French team not at all in training, they suffered a heavy defeat. These are the laurels which the American rugby team can claim. As for the method employed, it is that of the pugilist; again that of the pugilist, always that of the pugilist.

The Americans were rightly incensed by this, no one more so than Olympic veterans such as Babe and Rudy, who had fought shoulder to shoulder to land that crown in Antwerp and didn't care to see their achievement being written out of the French record books. But the Americans were now developing a siege mentality. The mood in the camp was defiant. Let the French say and do what they want. Babe Slater's team could not be destroyed by words; perhaps only by each other.

chapter 9

———

BABE, RUDY AND A
MEETING OF MINDS

THE US RUGBY TEAM COULDN'T CONTROL THE MOUNTING
hostility towards them. What they could control was their approach to
winning ball in the scrum-downs during the big final. To achieve any
sense of control, however, they needed to come up with a solution to
their scrum problems in the few days remaining to them. Someone in the
American squad was going to have to be brave enough to spell out just
how serious those problems were. Who was going to stick their neck out
and risk being dropped for rocking the boat so close to the showpiece
game? You've guessed it, Rudy Scholz.

What made the moment all the more dramatic was the fact that
Rudy put his controversial point to coach Charlie Austin right in front
of his captain, Babe Slater. This could have been seen as an act of gross
insubordination. After all, not only was Babe the chosen leader of the
team, he was also the most experienced man in that scrum. If there was
a problem that needed sorting out, surely it was Slater's job to tackle it
and talk to Austin man to man. A discreet conference between captain

and coach would have represented the regular first step towards putting things right. But coach Austin didn't always seek Slater's opinion alone, and Rudy saw his chance.

In 1977, Rudy wrote, 'I was playing at half back and, as a veteran of the '20 team, as was Slater (an outstanding forward), coach Austin (Stanford) would confer with us. Our scrum (mostly American football players) lacked cohesion. I complained and said by the time I got the ball I was surrounded and our stand-off half (we called it first five-eighth) was covered. We had no chance.'

You can just imagine the tension in the air when Rudy said his piece. For weeks he had been complaining in his diary about a lack of team spirit. Though Scholz may not have voiced his opinion publicly before, it probably wasn't lost on Slater that Rudy was unhappy with his leadership. It would have been hard for Babe to remain entirely oblivious to Rudy's festering resentment; and personal tensions between the former friends may already have been high.

Babe could have ensured that Rudy's decision to complain blew up in the little man's face. He could have seen this definitive moment as a disrespectful challenge to his authority. He might have taken this opportunity to remove a dissenting voice from the camp once and for all. A lesser man might well have done so, and under those 'him-or-me' circumstances coach Austin would have had little choice but to do his captain's bidding.

Instead Slater appears to have shown the true strength of his character just as it was most needed. He put the cause of the team before any personal issues. When he might have belittled Rudy, he chose a more difficult route. He supported his teammate from 1920. This moment, he realised, wasn't about Babe and Rudy, or who should have been captain, who had experienced a war and who hadn't. This was about the US rugby team's chances of pulling off one of the most outrageous sporting feats of all time; and those chances weren't looking good. Something needed to be done. Babe knew it, just like Rudy knew it.

You can imagine their eyes meeting in that moment of truth, that make-or-break point in their relationship as teammates. And from Scholz's account of what happened, we learn that Rudy and Babe were suddenly united in the team's hour of need; united in a way they hadn't been for four years. So they talked about the problem with the scrum, and they debated what could be done. Babe and Rudy, the old little-and-large combination, put their minds to solving a complex problem, with coach Austin listening intently. What the three of them came up with was audacious, some would say crazy.

No normal team would contemplate a fundamental change in formation and technique just a few short days before the game for which that team had been created in the first place. But then this was no normal team. If these men had not been adventurous and blessed with that pioneering Californian spirit, they would not have been sitting there in Paris in the first place. Then there was a more simple explanation for what they decided to do; they were desperate and knew they would lose to the French for sure if they didn't gamble.

'So we tried a 3-4 scrum formation', Rudy revealed.

A 3-4 was as rare as rain in Death Valley. Some things would never change in the scrum, of course. It was still full of sweaty men putting their heads and hands in awkward places. But mercifully, with this formation, there were only two rows of them. Fewer pairs of legs for the ball to bounce through when it entered that funny human pin-ball machine. It might not matter if the French scrummaging technique was superior; not if the Americans could heel the ball clean out before the French had time to push. Then Babe and the other big guys could be up in no time and back in the line, ready to be part of those passing rushes with the ball they had just won. That 3-4 sounded like a stroke of genius from Rudy...until they actually tried it.

Scholz added, 'Our hooker John O'Neill (University Santa Clara) was exceptionally fast with his feet but only weighed 156 [lb, 70kg] but he was supported by two fast big men of 220 pounds [100kg] with plenty of weight in the recovery line [second row]. On the 3-4 the ball came out so fast that many times it went straight past me.'

So in training they had suddenly come up against the opposite problem to the one they had encountered in matches. The ball was now coming out of the human pin-ball machine so fast that it flew past Rudy before he could lay his hands on it. If this development hadn't been so alarming, it would have been comical.

But Rudy Scholz was nothing if not stubborn and determined. He would not be beaten by this latest challenge, no matter how long it took to get things right, and he revealed, 'We practiced five or six hours a day.

I would say "hike" and threw the ball in. Simultaneously O'Neil's feet went up and the other two swept…'.

The quick-fingered Scholz soon adapted to the new speed of the heel and began to reach the ball as required, so that he could release the 'speed merchants' further along the line of 'backs' in double-quick time. Suddenly Rudy was happy again, and the whole team began to feel empowered by the new system of play.

De Groot described the change in tactics like this: 'The day after the Romanian game, Monday, we began our final preparations. After much changing our scrum was finally settled to three men in the front row with four in the second row, thus leaving no rear row but at the same time it allowed us an extra man in the backfield. This type of scrum has seldom if ever been played in America and it is not often played in Europe. But upon trial it proved so effective for us, and so mobile, that we decided to stake our all on it, and play it against the admittedly superior French scrum.'

Rudy's complaint had been the catalyst for something quite dramatic. Suddenly the American team felt it had the brains and technique to go with the brawn up front. For the first time they felt like a complete rugby team. It was an outrageous gamble, to change such a fundamental part of any rugby team just days before the biggest day of their lives. But Scholz liked a gamble and Babe could see the value in this one. It might even help Slater to perform better in the scrum, as long as he could shake off that troublesome calf strain in time to play a leading role. And if Babe's brother Norman were to be selected for the final too, it might help 'Nor' cope with the pressure of facing a French pack which had so far demonstrated superior know-how in this particular area of the game.

The more the forwards practiced their audacious 3-4 scrum formation, the more they felt they were onto a winner. No longer was the ball getting stuck among confused feet in the melee. Now the natural relationship between forwards and backs could flow again. And in many respects, this appears to have been a perfect metaphor for the relationship between Babe and Rudy. It had seemed frozen, clogged up with personal baggage. But now, at last, Rudy had been allowed to behave like a leader again. Finally, Scholz could feel important on this Olympic adventure. His chance to take centre stage had come in the nick of time, just days before the climax to the entire trip. He had seized the moment with both hands, just as he now seized the ball as it flew his way in double-quick time from that previously stagnant scrum.

So Babe and Rudy were together again; on the same wavelength as teammates, ready to support each other in the line. Few gave them a chance of success against the French, of course; the betting reflected the wild optimism among the Parisian public.

Rudy later claimed, 'The betting was 20-1 on France to beat the United States, and I don't mind telling you that the Americans hocked everything they owned to put up money on the game. We had a bunch of good old-fashioned American football players, too, and they were out to play for keeps.'

One of those players, Dud De Groot claimed, 'There was plenty of money going begging about Paris giving France victory by twenty points; it was only the newspaper reporters, etc, who watched us work out the last week that took those bets. And so we approached the final contest by far the underdog, in fact we were not conceded an outside chance of victory.'

The Americans needed all the help they could get. On Thursday, 15 May, Madam Luella Melius visited the team at the Colombes stadium. Babe described her as 'an American opera singer who was in Paris'. The soprano had starred as Gilda in Giuseppe Verdi's *Rigoletto*. On that hot, sunny Thursday, Madame Melius had brought with her what Babe claimed to be 'our only mascot. She named it "Cali."'

Presumably short for California, 'Cali' nevertheless appeared to be an African doll with bulging eyes, fuzzy hair and outstretched arms. It was an unusual gift, though the gesture was much appreciated; especially after all the hostility the boys had encountered in the French capital since their arrival. Judging by the photographs taken at the moment of the presentation of the mascot to Babe, 'Cali' caused a certain amount of mirth. Madame Melius, in her stylish long dress, brimmed hat and summer shoes, cut quite an incongruous figure alongside the muddied American players. Babe looked muddier and sweatier than most, his hair ruffled, as though he had just come out of one of Rudy's 3-4 scrums. In sharp contrast, the immaculate Scholz didn't seem to have muddied his kit at all. As the team gave their opera-singer supporter three cheers with one of their typical college yells, Babe and Rudy are caught in the same photograph. Scholz looks stocky and muscular, with only one physical disadvantage alongside his captain. If Rudy were to have shuffled along a little and stood right next to Slater, he wouldn't even have come up to the gentle giant's shoulders.

Whatever their size or shape, every man looked in high spirits, even the team manager Sam Goodman. As he lifted his hat to join in the cheers and revealed his bald head in the process, the suited Goodman was smiling. And he had reason to smile because the referee for the final would not be the French choice, Admiral Percy Royds. Albert Freethy, the Welshman who had refereed the Americans' match against the Harlequins, would officiate instead.

The choice might not have thrilled Babe Slater, who privately believed British referees to be 'crooks'; but Goodman had seen enough during the defeat at Twickenham to believe that Freethy's officiating would give them a fair chance of victory. He had not warned the Americans about their brutal tackling, despite the broken bones it had caused against the Quins at Twickenham. He respected men who had barely played the game and had the courage to face some of the most respected sides in European rugby. He didn't look down on the Americans or believe they should be put in their place. Freethy, from the tough Welsh town of Neath, was prepared to embrace both the elegant European game and the uncompromising American game. He would allow cultures and styles to collide, and may the best team win.

Babe, Rudy and the US team didn't know if they were the best. But for the first time here was a group truly comfortable with each aspect of the game. They didn't fear the French; the biggest fear was being left out of the XV for the final, for there could be no substitutes.

No one knew the line-up that Thursday; and judging by the smile on Ed Turkington's face in the Madame Melius photo, he may just have been told that, despite his dismissal against Romania, he still had as much chance of making the line-up as any other American.

This was now truly a tight-knit squad, with no exceptions. While they could train together they were happy. Off the training field it was harder to deal with the waiting around. With pre-match tensions reaching almost unbearable levels, it is hardly surprising that the young Americans let off steam in ways that didn't always please their hosts.

They weren't going to drink booze so close to the big game; but that didn't stop them from engaging in the sort of pranks you might normally expect after groups had consumed excessive amounts of alcohol. One night they went too far and were very nearly given their marching orders from the Hotel Exelmans. The story of what happened was covered in the topics on which three of the boys were invited to speak at the 1928 reunion. Caesar Manelli's talk was to be on 'The art of hurling p.pots.' Charlie Doe's task was to wax lyrical on 'The art of receiving p.pots.' To fellow squad member Phil Clark fell the trickiest task of all: 'How to pacify an irate hotelkeeper due to his ignorance of the p.pot game.'

The manager of the Hotel Exelmans had reason to feel that he had done everything he could to satisfy the eating and drinking habits of American sportsmen; he had made the group feel as welcome as was possible in a city that had turned hostile to their every word and action. But even he had to draw the line when he found that his hotel bedrooms were being showered with urine in the name of fun. Indeed one account claimed that the American rugby party was told to leave the hotel en masse after 'an unfortunate incident' and move to the very basic accommodation of the Olympic village, which still wasn't even finished. Yet it seems that Clark, probably joined by Goodman and Austin, managed to talk the hotelier out of expelling the team at such a vital time in their build-up for the most important match in American rugby history.

In return for that mercy, we can be pretty sure that the 'p-pot' game was shelved, so to speak; at the very least until after the match.

It was small wonder the squad was going a little crazy, as each member waited for the answer to the question that had been at the back of their minds all the way through those long months of hard work: who was going to play?

The starting XV was due to be announced by the end of Friday. That placed extra pressure on Babe Slater with regard to his own fitness. It wasn't as if he could try to play with a muscle strain and then just allow himself to be replaced if it didn't work out. Babe knew that if he started he would have to finish, come what may. Otherwise he was going to have to pull out and make way for a fitter man.

Everyone was desperate to play, probably even Rudy Scholz by now.

He had already told his diary that he hoped he would be overlooked on the big day. But that was then and things had surely changed. In the vital 24 hours after the victory over Romania, Rudy's status within the group had grown. Suddenly what he said counted for something again. Under these conditions, you get the feeling he would have wanted to play as much as anyone else.

As instigator of the tactical changes, it would probably have seemed outrageous to Rudy that he might still be excluded at the last moment, and Charlie Doe placed at scrum-half instead. But this was the final. Did coach Austin feel he could go with someone who had acted in such a detached manner ever since he had been overlooked for captain and vice-captain on the train east, and fallen out with Sam Goodman in New York? Was his late contribution sufficient to book his place on that Colombes turf for the big game?

Dud De Groot put himself in the shoes of the men whose difficult task it was to pick the team and tell those who had missed out about their fate. 'The last week of practice was a crackerjack, with every man on the squad going at top-notch in an effort to ensure his selection for the final game. Upon coach Austin and captain Slater devolved the mean task of selecting the 15 men to represent the United States and it was not until Saturday night, preceding the game, that these men were definitely chosen.'

In fact most of the decisions had been made by Friday, barring any last-ditch drama, because a newspaper agency report with the dateline 'PARIS, May 16' claimed that 'the lineup of the American rugby football team which will face the French team on Sunday was given out today…'.

When Austin and Slater discussed Rudy Scholz, they knew the factors that counted in his favour and those that might make him a risk. Charlie and Babe didn't harbour any grudges for what had gone before. Scholz looked hungry again and he looked part of the group too. Rudy was back. He was in.

Ed Turkington would have been more of a borderline case. He had performed well against Romania for the hour he was on the pitch. In fact he was just starting to rip holes in their defence when he was sent off. That, perhaps, was part of the problem. If he was going to allow himself to be provoked against the lowly Romanians, how would he react in the emotional cauldron of the final against the French? Then there were matters of size and brute force to consider. Turkington was fast and strong, but he wasn't as physically imposing as many of his colleagues. Did his rugby know-how compensate fully for his lack of bulk in the same way Rudy's did? It would have been a tough call because Ed had been a fine squad member. No doubt Babe and Austin hoped he would continue to demonstrate the same attitude. Unfortunately, however, 'Turk' was out. It was probably Babe who broke the news to the younger man.

Maybe Ed had known deep down that the odds were against him. That wouldn't have diminished his disappointment at being powerless on the sidelines when the most important action began. At least he could console himself with the thought that he had played his part already, both on and off the pitch, in this extraordinary Olympic adventure. And maybe Ed could work out a way to be useful to the team one way or another.

And what about Babe himself? Was that calf strain going to hold up to the rigours of the most competitive match of all? It was one thing to have negotiated his way through training all week. It was quite another to keep a good man out of the team if there was any risk of a recurrence of that pulled muscle. When his replacement might be his own brother Norman, Babe had to think very carefully. He knew his responsibilities and he also knew his own body.

The line-up as announced in the press on 16 May was as follows: Charlie Doe (full-back); W. L. Rogers, Dick Hyland, George Dixon, three-quarters; Robert Devereux, Norman Cleaveland, two-fifths; Rudy Scholz, half-back; Caesar Manelli or Al Williams, forward; Alan Valentine, John O'Neill, Jack Patrick, Dudley De Groot, Edward Graf, Linn Farish and Norman Slater, forwards.

Babe was out. To lose their captain so close to the match would have been a crushing blow to the Americans. Was it a mistake by the reporter, who may not have realised there were two Slaters in the squad? Or was Babe giving himself more time to recover fully? If so he would surely have made it quite clear to Norman that the latter would be required to step aside should Babe feel ready to lead his team after all.

The French management may well have been thrown by the air of uncertainty the Americans had cultivated. Perhaps that was the idea, or maybe the uncertainty was genuine. The French press, meanwhile, were too busy insulting the Americans to read too much into announcements on selection.

Aero-sports, one of the leading sports papers in Paris, summed up the French confidence as the countdown to the match began. On 17 May, the paper's rugby reporter wrote, 'We have arrived at the eve of the day where for the first time the flag of a victorious nation will be raised on the mast at Colombes. Will France be victorious against the force of the redoubtable Americans? Never have our chances been so good; it would be terrible to think that the French should be defeated in this match…'.

The writer dismantled the American game with each word and seemed to think that the same process would take place the following day. He added, 'In the scrum they are not much; dribbling is the only thing they know…The giants of the USA are very quick, more with their hands than with their feet, and their backs are dangerous when they get the ball. But when will they ever have the ball?…With all of these things considered we await now the commencing of the play and only by a miracle can the Americans win, so far superior is our team.'

The man burdened with the dubious task of translating these provocative pronouncements from French to English was Ed Turkington. 'He spoke the language best among the American guys,' said his son Ned many years later. 'He did most of the translating for the team over there.'

Further evidence of Turkington's central role seems to come in the title for his after-dinner speech at that team reunion four years later: 'Translations and highlights of French press.' There can be little doubt that being written off in this way stayed in the minds of the Americans. Every time Ed came out with another French insult, the Americans became just a little more determined to ram those words right back down the throats of their Parisian tormentors. They would use French over-confidence as much as they could where it mattered – on the field.

Doubt seemed to remain, however, over which Slater brother would play – Babe or Norman. It may have been a tense 24 hours for the Slaters in the build-up to the final. And there was further doubt in another key area, as De Groot later explained:

The American squad was still not definitely selected. The uncertainty concerned the men who were to play in the front row of the scrum, for our whole scrum formation for the French game had been shifted to a 3-4 combination.

Sunday morning found the men all down at breakfast early and the first thing that greeted us was the line-up for the game that afternoon. It was as follows:

Front row: Caesar Manelli (Santa Clara), John O'Neill (Santa Clara), Edward Graf (University of California);

Rear row: Linn Farish (Stanford), Dud De Groot (Stanford), Alan Valentine (Swarthmore and Oxford), Babe Slater – captain – (Davis Farm);

Wing forward: Jack Patrick (Stanford);

Backfield: [scrum] half Rudy Scholz (Santa Clara), first five-eighth [fly/stand-off half] Robert Devereux (Stanford), second five-eighth [centre] Norman Cleaveland (Stanford), [outside] centre Dick Hyland (Stanford), wing Lefty Rogers (Stanford), wing George Dixon (University of California), full-back Charles Doe (Stanford).

Babe was back in at his elder brother's expense. Both men knew that Babe was the better player, and Norman must have been prepared for this. Even so, Norman's disappointment must have been felt by both of them. Babe's nephew, also called Norman, said in 2009, 'Babe would have had the team in mind more than his personal feelings, and possibly there were better players than my father, you know? They must have used that criterion to eliminate some of the players. But it couldn't have been easy for Babe because he was very close to my father, that's the way they were the whole time, all the way through their athletic careers.'

Norman senior seems to have never told his son about not playing in the final. 'We only learned about it recently,' he added. 'The French poster for the final names my father as one of the touch judges.' He would get a medal anyway, just like 'Turk' and the other fringe players. But what colour?

Meanwhile Al Williams was the unlucky man to miss out in the front row. Williams and Norman Slater probably consoled each other, along with the others who had missed out, such as Ed Turkington.

For those selected, it was time for each man to think about his job on the field of play, to ensure that he produced his best when it really mattered. There was little point in leaving the hotel, because by now the American team was public enemy number one in Paris. Even some of their fellow-countrymen, residents of Paris, were said to have given the rugby men a wide berth. Pre-match tension had reached fever pitch. In fact this wasn't just tension, it was outright hostility.

At the last moment news broke that Adolphe Jaureguy, the French rugby superstar, had answered the call to arms. Had he remembered Slater's wounding public criticism of the French players, for their apparent indifference to the Olympic tournament and ideals? If so, Jaureguy was now out to make Slater eat his words.

The battle lines had been drawn. Babe Slater, the war veteran, was not afraid of pressure or provocation. He thrived on it. Could Rudy Scholz learn from his loss of discipline the last time these teams had met in Paris? Failure to do so would see the Americans fall apart as they had done in that final tour match four years earlier. Discipline in rugby was everything, as De Coubertin had always emphasised. The Baron would be in the crowd the next day. He had reason to dread what he was about to witness.

chapter 10

THE CAULDRON

THE SUNDAY OF THE BIG GAME WITH FRANCE WAS THE HOTTEST and most uncomfortable day the Americans had encountered during their entire trip. By noon the atmosphere was so sultry that Babe's boys were already starting to perspire. At 2.20pm they rolled up their shirt sleeves as they boarded the bus that would take them to the Colombes Stadium in good time for the scheduled 4.00pm kick-off. By the time they reached the stadium, an hour later, they were soaked in sweat.

According to Ed Turkington, that journey to the stadium was never ideal, even in cooler weather. He said, 'They took us to the stadium in solid-rubber tired buses over bumpy and dusty roads. By the time we got there we were pretty exhausted.' This time adrenalin would carry them on, though they were grateful when they reached shade.

Dud De Groot explained, 'The damp concrete dressing rooms under the stands at Colombes, for the first time, felt comfortable, they were so cool. There was a great hubbub all about the stadium, and an extra force of some two hundred gendarmes had their hands full directing the many hundreds of machines to parking places along the narrow streets.

'All was quiet in our dressing room with very little of the usual kidding going on. In fact I have never seen a team which was as quiet and serious as this one. But considering the stakes perhaps that was natural.'

The obligatory photographs had to be taken, the last thing the Americans wanted. Even so Babe Slater and French captain Felix 'Rene' Lasserre were snapped in memorable pose, Slater looking like a Greek God, while the tough, stocky Lasserre scowled at the camera. Already there was a hint of what was to come, before the US coach had delivered his final instructions back in the dressing room.

Coach Austin revealed only this much about his team talk when asked later: 'I sent them into the game with instructions to play a hard and clean game.'

Before they could leave the dressing room, however, Babe, Rudy and the boys had to wait a little longer. Even from where they were in the bowels of the stadium, they would have heard a deafening roar from above, and one of the most stirring anthems in world sport. As 1920 Olympic Champions, the Americans had been given the honour of going out last. It wouldn't have felt like much of an advantage. When the French team appeared the band, The Fanfare of the Third Regiment of Colonial Infantry, played the 'Marseillaise'. Around 40,000 spectators stood with heads uncovered and sang their hearts out. If they had ever doubted that they were about to enter a cauldron, the Americans knew now. Two minutes later, Babe led his team up onto the field from an underground passageway, and the sound of 'The Star-Spangled Banner' floated out over the field. There were no more than a few hundred Americans to honour their anthem. Otherwise it was greeted with deafening silence, broken only by a tremendous clap of thunder and a flash of lightning. It seemed that even the elements were reflecting the highly charged atmosphere in the stadium, though a short burst of rain eased the mood momentarily.

As they listened to their anthem, dressed in white with shields of stars and stripes emblazoned on their chests, Babe, Rudy and the others would have noticed that the French had increased the height of the perimeter fence around the track and field. Before it had been no more than four or five feet (1.3m) high, now it looked double that. When they saw that fence, the Americans wouldn't have known whether to feel reassured or unsettled. The authorities clearly thought it necessary, just in case the crowd's ill feeling towards their guests spilt over into something more sinister. Did they think the public appeals for sportsmanship would fall on deaf ears?

In the stands Baron de Coubertin, President of the International Olympic Committee, looked on from a sheltered spot. The rugby-loving baron had done more than most to set the right tone for true sporting competition, finding the right words for the Olympic oath. Now he waited to see whether the first final of the 1924 Games would be played in the spirit he had foreseen. As a Frenchman, he would have hoped for something else too – to get the Games off to a winning start for the host nation. Though it had been a long hard season for the Frenchmen, they were still at a distinct advantage...the Americans didn't even have a season.

Jaureguy, Lasserre and the rest of the French players, in their famous blue jerseys emblazoned with their proud, cockerel emblems, could have been forgiven for thinking that all they had to do to win the gold medal was turn up. Yet they might have realised that they weren't going to have it all their own way just before kick-off. Lasserre expected the Welsh referee, Albert Freethy, to play the usual 40-minute halves that all rugby players were used to. But his American counterpart, Babe Slater, came up with a clever psychological ploy as the two captains met with Freethy in the centre of the field. Incredible as it may seem today, Babe suggested that the game be played with 45-minute halves. This sent out a message to the home side that he believed the Americans' level of fitness to be superior.

Lasserre wasn't accustomed to losing mind-games. He had been a fighter pilot during the Great War, and may even have patrolled and skirmished in the skies somewhere above Babe's ambulance. The fact that Lasserre had survived the war, when the average life expectancy of pilots was measured in days or weeks, showed that he won his arguments every time. Who was this American giant, trying to treat the traditions of rugby with such disrespect?

Lasserre had starred in France's 11-11 draw with England two years earlier, in front of 40,000 fans at Twickenham. He was carving out a big reputation for himself in the European game, and he wasn't about to be told what to do by an American who hadn't played any serious international rugby for years. But Babe was not going to be pushed about either, and gently persisted. Freethy was left with a tricky decision to make. What was he going to do? To Lasserre's astonishment, Freethy came down on the side of the visiting underdogs and opted for 45-minute halves. First blood to the Americans.

At 4.05 came the toss of the coin, which Lasserre won and promptly elected to receive kick-off. At 4.08 Jack Patrick, former Stanford and Olympic Club star, raised his hand to signal that he would kick to the left. He did so, lifting the ball 20 yards (18m) into the French forwards. The battle had begun.

The US team showed they meant business from the first whistle. John O'Neill recalled, 'We kicked off and the French player who received the ball was tackled and thrown by our forwards. It was a beautiful play which would have drawn the cheers of almost any group of sportsmen, but that one play started the crowd hissing.'

The Americans refused to give an inch in the early clashes. The problem for Adolphe Jaureguy and his French teammates was that the Americans were angry. They had felt that way for some time and now at last they had the chance to vent their frustrations. The result was always going to be explosive.

Rudy, whose job it was to link the huge 'forward' players and the swift 'backs', had come out with all guns blazing, pumping his little legs for all they were worth as he darted into space and began to punish the French for the disrespect they had shown. With so much fire in his belly, he completely disregarded the increased dangers that existed on a rugby field for anyone of a smaller stature. Unlike the Battle of Paris four years earlier, however, Rudy married that fire with a cold and analytical brain. As Rudy drew on his pace and know-how, Babe led from the front and the US side began to play as one, motivated by a simple thirst for revenge.

Their followers showed similar bravery against the odds. One American newspaper report said, 'Outnumbered thirty to one, the Americans in the huge crowd were on their feet during most of the first ten minutes of play...'.

The Americans quickly adopted a tactic of pinning their hosts in their own half with accurate punts. It proved effective. The US team's towering line-out jumpers threatened to clean up from the start, and Babe Slater began some fearsome charges towards the opposing line, with other big Americans at his side.

Only a fumble or two at the crucial moment saved the creaking French defence in those opening exchanges. De Groot revealed how the rain, though 'short and sweet' had 'made the ball and field quite slippery and treacherous...'. However, after five minutes of mounting pressure, the home team made a handling error of their own not far from their own line. Linn Farish showed an amazing turn of pace over a short distance as he rounded his opponent on the outside to dive over the line and put the underdogs ahead. We know this because the video footage of that opening score has survived to this day. The American fans in the stands forgot the danger they were in and went wild with delight.

Team manager Sam Goodman believed that the opening American try temporarily dented France's self-belief, shattering their status as firm favourites. 'The French were 20-1 favorites – for about five minutes', he commented later.

The French might have fallen even further behind had Charlie Doe managed to convert the try with an accurate kick. His failure to do so from an awkward angle meant that the USA's lead remained a slender one at 3-0. Both teams knew that the first Olympic gold of the 1924 Games was still there for the taking. It would be a question of which team could impose their unique style of play.

The tough-tackling Americans gave an early demonstration of what set them apart from other rugby teams. The first big hit came when William 'Lefty' Rogers levelled Adolphe Jaureguy, the French superstar, with such brutal force that 40,000 fans in the Colombes Stadium fell silent. Although the American seemed satisfied with his work, the crowd couldn't quite take in what they had just seen, and neither could his victim. Having been injured by the English only weeks earlier against the Harlequins, Lefty probably didn't realise the enormity of what he had done. After all, everyone knew that if you played rugby, you risked being hurt. Lefty had been hurt in London and now Jaureguy had been hurt in Paris. So what?

The French didn't see it that way. Jaureguy's lightning speed had given him such a sense of sporting superiority that his face seemed to have settled into a permanent sneer. His fans loved his displays of arrogance and regarded him as untouchable. After Adolphe's four tries against Romania, everyone had assumed it would now be the turn of the US team, with its novices and misfits, to suffer the same fate. Even Babe and Rudy, who had been burned by Jaureguy's blistering speed before, had feared it. Yet Lefty had shown in a violent instant that Jaureguy wasn't untouchable at all. He was a mere mortal and he was suffering.

Jaureguy's sneering expression had given way to a wince as his face hit the dirt with a thud. This declaration of intent from the US underdogs, at 4.15pm on a stifling Parisian afternoon, confirmed one thing – the battle for the first gold medal at the 1924 Olympics would be ferocious.

The majestic Jaureguy wasn't used to being stopped in his tracks. But now he lay writhing as though shot. In the stands, meanwhile, something very ugly was brewing. A nation's fanatics were refusing to accept that the sporting world as they knew it might just be about to fall apart.

Lefty Rogers was only doing what came naturally to a man more used to the crunching impacts of American football than rugby. His chiselled features, and the intensity that took over when he narrowed his eyes into a cold stare, hinted at a certain appetite for this kind of basic conflict. To Parisians, however, this wasn't rugby at all. In the not-too-distant past, French rugby had been the domain of athletic dandies, men more anxious to show off their sprinting and jumping prowess than any appetite for the tackle. Some still believed that the art of bringing an opponent down was something to be executed with finesse, a defensive necessity which ought to result in as little pain as possible for both parties. Tooth-rattling tackles were still deemed to be against the spirit of the game in some well-to-do quarters of Paris. To go in as hard as Lefty Rogers was almost tantamount to a declaration of war, an act that would call for immediate retaliation along a wide front.

The silence in the stadium, as Jaureguy still struggled for breath, soon gave way to howls of anger. More people were watching this rugby match than would witness some of the celebrated track and field events a few weeks later. They had come to see the Americans heavily defeated, the only scenario which would earn them a return on the money they had bet on the result. Many had placed small fortunes on the French team to win by more than 20 points; or else they had accepted odds which would only offer a healthy return if they placed large fortunes on the near-certainty of a home victory.

Rudy Scholz's gambler-friend from Santa Clara, John O'Neill, explained, 'As soon as it became evident that the French team, favorites in betting and backed by many to defeat us by at least twenty points, were up against it, the booing and jeering became terrific.'

Even non-gamblers were already feeling cheated. This was their Olympic Games, and there was no margin in French eyes for anything to go wrong at the curtain-raiser. It was meant to be a party, and the Parisian supporters had come well prepared. Many already seemed to be drunk on the contents of personal hip flasks; and those in the more expensive covered seating along the side of the pitch were becoming particularly aggravated at what they had seen so far. They were hotter than the supporters left out in the open air, and the electrically charged atmosphere was ready to ignite.

Meanwhile the standing spectators at each end of the stadium were now wet and steaming with indignation. They jeered and whistled the Americans, incensed that these no-hopers could apparently believe they might escape their long-anticipated humiliation. Sportsmanship was quickly forgotten, and De Coubertin's recently introduced Olympic Oath, which called for fair play and decency, suddenly appeared meaningless.

Poor Jaureguy was still on the floor and he looked a sorry sight. Normally the loose hair on his high forehead flapped happily in the wind to convey to onlookers the blistering pace of his attacks. Rogers had left that same tuft of hair flopping sadly in the dirt. The scene just didn't seem right somehow.

The 'big hit' from Rogers on Jaureguy only served to sharpen the French crowd's suspicions that the 'Yanks' were going to attempt to strong-arm their way to victory. The common belief was that they didn't know enough about the game to win any other way. If the local hero was seriously hurt as a result of what the French regarded as blatant cheating, there would be pandemonium.

Slowly, however, the much-adored Adolphe did manage to rise to his feet and the swagger began to return. His recovery came as a relief to spectators and left the mood in the stadium simmering steadily. The

French players, however, were ready to retaliate on behalf of the home nation. If the US team wanted to compensate for their inadequacies by using rough tactics, they would quickly discover that their hosts had a mean streak too.

De Groot described it like this:

> The first fifteen minutes of that French-United States game for the Olympic rugby championship was without doubt one of the most terrific struggles that has ever taken place on any football field in any country in the world. The French, right from the opening kick-off, let us understand that they were out to win that game, fair or square, but to win at whatever cost.
>
> At first they did not play unnecessarily rough or 'dirty' football, but as the game proceeded and they seemed unable to get the upper hand and score at will as they undoubtedly figured they would, they began using rather questionable tactics. And from questionable tactics, which the referee warned them about, they turned to downright dirty playing. In the scrum they kicked us while we were down; when they tackled us they added nasty twists and pulls after we were fairly downed and rid of the ball. But worst of all, the very thing which their newspapers had 'roasted' us about before the game they were now guilty of, time and again; and that was use of fists and feet...The writer was intentionally kicked in the face.

So much for the watching baron's Olympic Oath: 'In the name of all competitors, I promise that we shall take part in these Olympic Games, respecting and abiding by the rules that govern them, in the true spirit of sportsmanship, for the glory of sport and the honour of our teams.'

De Groot singled out one French player – full-back Etienne Bonnes – for special treatment. Big Dud wrote,

> The French full-back was a particularly dirty player, persisting in putting his foot in your face after getting away his kicks. We soon found that by tackling him hard and low on the one leg he kept on the ground he soon got over this. But when we tackled him he invariably laid on the ground and moaned and groaned, the whole

audience sympathizing with him. The referee soon got wise to these fake timeouts and refused to allow them. From that time on that full-back couldn't kick the ball when he got it to save his life, he was so busy trying to prevent being tackled. And before the game was over we had gained many yards toward the French goal, because of his downright weakness.

Not all French players wished to avoid a direct physical challenge. Babe Slater had several punches aimed at him, and the French clearly hoped that by encouraging the American captain to retaliate they might be able to get him sent off. They obviously didn't know him. Babe had already been in a real war; he wasn't going to be provoked on a rugby field. Babe and his 'pack' of meaty forwards fought a hard fight as the first half turned nasty; but they kept their aggression largely within the boundaries of fair play.

Learning from past experience, Rudy Scholz also resisted the temptation to show his prowess in physical combat. The Americans had been dismissed as 'street-fighters'. Here was their measured answer. Even so, to achieve self-control was no simple task, because in rugby the line between all-out aggression and illegal play is wafer-thin. It must have felt like walking a tightrope in a storm. By maintaining their discipline, the Americans could hope to weather that storm; yet it was also vital that they held their own, both physically and psychologically, in every part of the contest. If they failed to out-muscle their opponents in the legal battle for possession of the ball, all would be lost anyway.

Rudy later recalled how well-equipped the men in white were for physical confrontation. 'We were in great condition for that game. We'd trained four hours a day and were as tough as nails.'

Not all the Americans had rippling, rock-hard muscles though. Most seriously hurt in the violence on the field was John O'Neill, one of Rudy Scholz's old teammates from Santa Clara. John only weighed 156lb (71kg), and almost looked puny compared to some of his giant teammates on the rugby front line. He was even more vulnerable after the appendix operation he had undergone shortly before leaving the USA. O'Neill played with a great spirit to compensate for his lack of physique, but that also made him prone to injury, and pretty soon his shoulder was dislocated. Painfully it was put back into place, so a French player stamped on his ankle instead. Finally O'Neill received what his teammate Dud De Groot described as 'a deliberate kick in the abdomen.'

Though it was never established just how premeditated these attacks were, it made cynical sense to target O'Neill because of the vital role he played in the American team, heeling the ball back in the scrum. Without an effective hooker, a rugby team struggles to maintain possession of the ball. Now O'Neill had taken a kick in the worst possible place, given his condition.

Until the final, it seemed that his gamble had paid off, because the abdominal wound from his appendix operation had just about healed. But now the fresh scar had been torn open again in an instant.

O'Neill – who already relied on spirit more than power – was in real trouble. Bravely and quietly he got himself patched up as quickly as possible. Still he didn't tell his teammates about the gravity of the situation. Meanwhile thousands of French, who had been baying for blood from the start, jeered and laughed at his pain. They would react the same way every time a US player went down injured that afternoon.

Some American fans objected to the poor sportsmanship of their French counterparts, particularly those in the more expensive, seated areas, where they felt their hosts should have known better. Any such protest was fraught with danger. The wealthier Parisian 'gentleman' was often equipped with a gold-tipped cane, which was the fashion accessory of the day and could also double as a weapon if necessary. The American supporters were about to discover this to their cost.

Still on the field, O'Neill decided to play on despite his seeping stomach wound. He felt he couldn't walk off now, not after what he and his teammates had been through. He only needed to hear the crowd reaction to his suffering to feel his own fighting spirit rise to the next level.

Sensing a moment of American weakness, a second sweeping French move after about 20 minutes released the still-dangerous Jaureguy on a promising run. A few more strides and the French superstar would hit top gear, and then he would be unstoppable. Everyone knew it, and a huge roar rose inside the Stade Colombes to urge him on. This is what the crowd had come to see, and this was the way it was meant to be. Before Jaureguy could find his rhythm, however, he was suddenly knocked clean through the air and flattened onto the running track that surrounded the field. Lefty Rogers, even more pumped up than before, had nailed his man again.

As Jaureguy writhed in pain for a second time, French spectators erupted in fury, calling for more American blood. Mercifully, the high fence around the arena was still holding firm to keep the mob at bay. At this rate, however, the strength of that fence would soon be tested to the full; and if it came down in the clamour, the hundreds of policemen on duty at the stadium would be overwhelmed in no time. How those French police must have hoped their team's fortunes would take an upward turn, or that the US team would finally lie down as it was supposed to do, if only to prevent a possible catastrophe.

But the Americans weren't about to gift the French the glory that would ensure their own safety.

Jaureguy's body, graceful in flight seconds earlier, lay twisted and mangled as if it had just been in a car-crash, which is pretty much what Lefty's second tackle must have felt like. France's prima donna stopped writhing and lay still for a while on the running track until teammates arrived to help him to his feet.

There were fresh howls of protest from the French players and crowd alike, everyone incensed at the treatment to which their favourite was being subjected. How dare the Americans tackle so dangerously? It was one thing to be stopped, but to be sent flying like this seemed to the French like thuggery of the worst kind.

As US captain, Babe Slater would have been unimpressed by the French argument. There was no shortage of thuggish rugby on show in the Stade Colombes, but it wasn't coming from his men. The true hooliganism lay in the punches and kicks already being swung off the ball by frustrated French players, and up in the stands, where small pockets of American fans were now facing overwhelming numbers of attackers.

Years later Scholz recalled, 'We played for keeps, and the few hundred Americans in the stands among the 40,000 Frenchmen, I guess, they made too much noise. There were all kinds of bloody fights, canes, sticks and what not, during the game.'

All Slater, Scholz and their teammates could do was try to concentrate on winning their own fight on the pitch, and leave the French 'gendarmes' to deal with the rest.

In all the chaos, Jaureguy moved gingerly back to his position on the wing. He was fit and athletic, otherwise he wouldn't have survived the hits he had taken. There lurked the suspicion among the Americans that he was still capable of becoming the hero of the day. At 26, he had the experience to understand that his task, tough though it seemed, was to weather these big American tackles until the French got the upper hand. If Jaureguy managed to avoid serious injury and stayed in one piece, he knew that sooner or later his skill and speed could leave his adversaries chasing shadows.

Ten minutes before half-time, flamboyant play swept the Gallic runners through American lines, Andre Behoteguy acting as spearhead. With a superb pass, he suddenly released Adolphe Jaureguy into more space than he had previously been allowed on his favourite left wing. Scholz recalled later, 'He came prancing past Dixon like a shot.' This time the superstar seemed to have found a way past all American defenders, and his stride lengthened as he saw the try-line. If he reached it, he would only need to touch the ball down with customary grace to reassert French authority – and his own reputation. Once their tails were up, the home side could overwhelm even the most stubborn of opponents.

Jaureguy was 25 yards (22m) from his target and almost flying when the move came to a crunching end. It is doubtful whether he saw the juggernauts coming out of the corner of his eye; he had eluded all defenders in his field of vision, and might even have felt he could take his foot off the gas in order to prolong his big moment. What he didn't bargain for was the determination of Alan Valentine, who had watched the crisis develop from his own position on the other side of the pitch.

Valentine had brains as well as fierce good looks and the neck of a bull. During the winter in England he had learned to anticipate such rugby brilliance on the playing fields of Oxford University. As a keen student of the game, he had realised that the very finest rugby players were able to cover not just their own defensive zone, but also those of others when mistakes were made. Even the English reporters present at Twickenham for the game against Harlequins three weeks earlier had marvelled at how fanatical the Americans were at covering each other defensively and chasing lost causes. Now Valentine was alert to what looked like the mother of all lost causes. Rudy Scholz recalled later, 'A

Rhodes Scholar, Valentine was invaluable. (He afterwards became President of the University of Rochester).'

To go with his obvious intelligence, Valentine also had a fearsome physique, which by now was powered by the same controlled anger driving all the American underdogs. None of this offered the prospect of continued good health to a certain Frenchman. The Oxford student reached Jaureguy's torso just before it could glide past him, and launched his own 210lb- (95kg) bulk with enthusiasm. Flying in from the side with all that weight behind his huge shoulders, he hit his opponent with such ferocity that Jaureguy was knocked out. His upper lip was split open and the wound would later need several stitches. This time, the great French hero didn't look in any state to get back up.

According to Scholz's recollection years later, Valentine wasn't alone in tackling Jaureguy, and the French winger was doomed. In 1942 Rudy felt he could still recall the Frenchman's violent end. '[Jaureguy] met three howitzers – Slater, De Groot and Valentine. They hit him from three sides, 600 pounds [270kg] against 165 [75kg], and Europe's greatest rugby player was through for the day.' Most accounts credit the big hit to Valentine alone, and the passing years may have amalgamated several hits from that match into one in Rudy's mind.

The angry mob saw Valentine's tackle as the last straw. The level of fighting escalated in the stands, and some fans made more concerted attempts to scale the fence in order to attack the American players. Though they failed, the Stade Colombes now had a full-scale riot on its hands.

The danger might have dissipated had Jaureguy summoned sufficient strength to carry on. However, this third hit was one too many. As Charlie Doe, the US vice-captain put it later: 'That was the end of him. He was carted off like a sack of potatoes.' The stretcher confirmed that his afternoon was over, though many of the Americans remained unimpressed by his injuries, despite the sight of blood flowing freely from his mouth.

De Groot recalled: 'Of course we received a terrific razzing when France's hero was carried from the field, but if the truth be known, it is the opinion of the American players that Mons Jaureguy could quite easily have finished the game had he so desired, but those few fierce American tackles had completely quelled his desire for battle.'

It may be that De Groot was being harsh on Jaureguy, since other accounts suggest he was concussed, in shock and still not fully in possession of his faculties long after the end of the match. Whatever the French star's true condition, the battle for gold, like the fate of the American players and their fans on this anarchic afternoon in the cauldron of the Stade Colombes, was still very much in the balance. The half-time scoreline of 3-0, thanks to that solitary Farish try, was, in De Groot's words, 'far too small a lead for comfort.'

The Americans' ordeal would become much worse after the interval, and their self-control would be tested to the full. It would all boil down to how much discipline the older heads like Slater and Scholz could maintain among the troops.

chapter 11

———

PAYBACK

J OHN O'NEILL DESCRIBED WHAT HE SAW WHEN THE WHISTLE
blew for the end of the opening half. 'Hardly had the first half ended
when we saw a friend approaching across the field. He had defied all the
authority that France could muster at the stadium, and pushed his way
out of the stands, past the gendarmes, to come upon the field and give
us an American greeting. Who was it but Pat Higgins of Los Angeles.
"Keep going, you've got 'em beat," was the cheering cry of Pat as he
rushed towards us. Say, how Pat Higgins ever escaped the wrath of the
hostile crowd is one of the mysteries of the occasion.'

Much as that brave supporter lifted American spirits, particularly the
injured O'Neil's, most of the squad knew they were going to have to do
more than just carry on as they were. During the break, Turkington and
the other non-playing squad members demonstrated the extraordinary
unity in the American camp when they gave their team a moving and
unselfish pep-talk, imploring the men on the pitch to raise their game
further still if they really wanted gold. Coach Charlie Austin's half-time

team talk was on the same theme. From top to bottom, this squad was singing from the same hymn sheet when it really mattered.

De Groot put it like this: 'Coach Austin and all of our substitutes made us realise as we lay on our backs during the ten minute break that we would have to play harder, faster ball during the last half if we expected to win. We were also instructed to get the ball out to our backs more quickly and start more passing rushes.'

Turkington's great enthusiasm was a tribute to his increasing maturity. Despite Ed's personal heartbreak at being excluded from the American team for the final, he had responded in exactly the right way. He clearly felt as much a part of the team as the players who still had to go out and finish the job. And rightly so; for, if they were to succeed, Turkington, Williams, Cunningham and the rest would also take home those coveted gold medals. Everyone was in it together, even though only 15 players were still in a position to bring gold home for the rest.

No one was showing more bravery than the American supporters in the stands, who had been intimidated and told to be quiet from the start. They took no notice, despite the risk to their own safety, and cheered wildly as their team prepared to receive at the start of the second half. The players took heart from the minority after taking so much abuse from the majority before the interval. The sun came out.

When Jack Patrick caught the French kick-off and signalled for a 'mark', which earned him a free punt downfield, the French jeered and whistled the American star, accusing him of being afraid to run with it. Undaunted, Patrick executed his kick perfectly and gained about 40 yards (36m). He would run when he was ready.

A newspaper report claimed, 'During the first ten minutes of the second half, with one exception and for just a few seconds, the ball was kept by the American players in the French territory.'

Despite being reduced to just 13 men when Clement Dupont was hurt while tackling Hyland, the French suddenly rallied and broke the siege when Rene Lasserrre released Raoul Got for a good gain.

De Groot admitted, 'In spite of their handicap, the French team took that ball from the line-out and by a beautiful kick placed it down into touch in our territory. Another line-out followed immediately, from which the French again got the ball and kicked to touch on our ten yards [9m] line. They were taking us off our feet in this rush for the goal and on the next play, a beautiful passing rush, in which three of the French backs figured, Norman Cleaveland saved a try against us with a beautiful tackle.'

When Dupont returned, the French were back up to 14 men against 15. The home side's confidence, perhaps even arrogance, was growing again. At this point more fighting broke out, the guilty Frenchman a one-eyed forward called Marcel-Frederic Lublin-Lebrere – or 'Lubin' for short. A French newspaper described it as 'a short altercation with fists between Lubin and an American. The referee intervened, but with both being evenly at fault, he only admonished the two players.'

With the game on a knife-edge, the Americans seized the initiative at a scrum on their own ten-yard (9m) line, the forwards kicking the ball up-field temporarily. Those desperate tactics only played into French hands, and it took a thumping tackle from Hyland to prevent a first French try. His big hit caused the attacking Frenchman to fumble, which in turn set off a chain of events in the opposite direction. Vice-captain Doe kicked 40 yards (36m) to the French full-back, who could only kick weakly to touch just inside his own half because three US players closed him down so quickly.

At the line-out O'Neill threw the ball to De Groot, whose impressive charge forward created a platform for Jack Patrick to show off his sublime running skills. A French reporter explained, 'Patrick had the ball, he feinted, went through, passed a poor attempt to stop him from Rene Lasserre, then another by Etienne Bonnes, and scored a try.'

American reporter 'Sparrow' Robertson claimed that even more Frenchmen were left in Patrick's wake: '...then Patrick received the ball about thirty yards [27m] from the French goal and he went through the five that tried to bring him down, knocking them right and left and planted the ball down for a try.'

What helped was the fact that Patrick had been able to touch down right between the posts, leaving Doe with an easy kick on goal. Thirteen minutes of the second half had been played when Doe's conversion made the score USA 8 France 0.

Due to the new 3-4 formation, only seven Americans could scrum-down. Patrick, the eighth man, had therefore been left to run loose as a wing forward. Now he was simply running riot and that further justified the tactical innovation. Rudy Scholz and Babe Slater were the men whose audacious thinking had changed that scrum formation and given Patrick such a superb platform to attack. Now it was their turn to come up with a wonderful moment of interplay and demonstrate the new understanding between them. Rudy and Babe, friends and heroes from the 1920 side, worlds apart for most of 1924, showed they could work in perfect harmony just when it mattered.

De Groot revealed, 'On the very next kick-off Rudy Scholz made a beautiful run for the ball, which was rolling in the loose, scooped it up and passed to Babe Slater, who scored.'

You could just picture Rudy as he darted through the crowd and used his lightning quick hands to gain possession. Babe would have seen his old friend homing in on the ball and must have timed his run to perfection. Seeing Slater, right there on his shoulder, Rudy hadn't hesitated to bring him into play. You could imagine a moment's eye contact between them, a glint of recognition, almost like a shared smile. Then away Babe had raced, using his power and pace to reach the try-line. This was a fitting sporting symbol of their renewed rapport, the biggest and the smallest members of the team combining in perfect harmony. There was only one problem. The try was disallowed. De Groot explained that 'a knock-on was called by the referee'.

What had happened? Babe had already privately accused Albert Freethy and other British referees 'of behaving like crooks' during their English tour. Did he feel there had been another injustice here? Babe's reaction isn't recorded, though he might have been tempted to believe that referee Freethy had wanted to avoid a one-sided romp, with the crowd so volatile. Then again, perhaps Rudy's scoop involved a little nudge forward before he released his skipper for the try-scoring charge. Both men would have been frustrated to see the try disallowed. But at least Babe and Rudy's 3-4 scrum formation still appeared to be providing the Americans with a winning platform.

Babe's disallowed try wasn't the only chance to go begging. De Groot explained, 'A scrum on the French twenty-five yard [22m] line gave us the ball and…George Dixon finally crossed over the line for a try by the sideline. He was unfortunately tackled by three Frenchmen before he put the ball down and was ruled to have been thrown out of bounds, which cost us another three points.'

In a way this squandered opportunity was a reminder to the world of just how naïve some of this American team was, and how new to the game of rugby. Old habits die hard and Dixon, having reached the 'end-zone', seems to have assumed for a fatal second or two that he had already scored, as would have been the case in American football. He must have remembered too late that in rugby you have to ground the ball with downward pressure before a try can be awarded; and the sooner you do it the better. No wonder Dixon's theme for his after-dinner talk at the 1928 reunion was 'Relating the difference between scoring a try at rugby and a touchdown at American football.' His error had not been forgotten.

Luckily the Americans were still so dominant in that 1924 final that they managed to engineer other opportunities to score. And as the Americans tightened their stranglehold on the game, the importance of the 3-4 scrum was never more apparent.

De Groot revealed, 'Our 3-4 scrum worked to perfection and it might also be said that to our own amazement we succeeded in out-hooking the French scrum, a scrum famed throughout Europe for its ability at hooking the ball nine times out of ten. This gave us a decided advantage and for the first time during our European invasion we were able to get the ball out to our backs.'

Sometimes the dominant forwards showed the backs how to carve up the French defence. They sprang up from the scrums to mount lightning-quick raids on enemy territory. The brainwave cooked up by Scholz and Slater paid dividends as a clean heel led to another passing rush from some of the toughest Americans. Patrick, De Groot, Valentine and Manelli, all ran riot before Farish was given another chance to shine. The *Chicago Tribune* wrote, 'Linn Farrish [sic] scored his second try by a fine forty-yard [36m] twisting run.' Doe was denied his conversion because the ball hit the crossbar.

The USA was now 11-0 ahead and Farish had scored two tries to write his name in Olympic history. It didn't mean the Americans were home and dry, though their chances increased further still when a stretcher was called for yet another French casualty. In what sounded suspiciously like American football tactics, one of the French defenders had been hurt as he was blocked. 'Sparrow' Robertson explained, '...one of the French players, when running in an attempt to tackle an American that had the ball, ran into another of the big Yankee players, and he was carried off the field.'

De Groot said, 'A Frenchman, in attempting to stop this rush, laid himself out and was carried off the field, leaving them with thirteen men. This almost caused a riot, for the audience seemed to think we had laid the man out purposely.'

The injured player was the three-quarter, Jean Vaysse, whose elimination with a dislocated left knee-cap was too much for the French crowd to take after Jaureguy's injury. Paul Champ of Parisian paper *Le Figaro* fell short of accusing the Americans of outright foul play and referred to 'the two deplorable accidents in which brutality played no part, although the play of our adversaries was very hard and laced with infringements and voluntary obstructions, which had the effect of exasperating a great number of the spectators present.'

The French, however, were guilty of a far more blatant offence. A Welsh reporter called David Gorry Llewellyn maintained, 'I was watching the game closely and saw but one deliberate piece of brutality. That was when a French forward punched Hyland in the jaw.' It appears that the volatile French forward was again the manic-looking line-out jumper called 'Lubin'.

A Californian newspaper report confirmed, 'Lubin of the French team, who seemed to play an extremely rough game, was cautioned by referee Freethy when he swung a blow to "Dick" Hyland's jaw. The referee was on the verge of putting the Frenchman off the field, but the Americans begged him to allow Lubin to continue.'

If only this moment of supreme sportsmanship from Babe Slater had found a reflection in the behaviour of the French supporters. They had been applauding American injuries, and cheered again at the unprovoked attack on Hyland. This caused outrage among the Americans in the stands. O'Neill explained later:

One of the players was knocked out and the jeering was at its height. One of these boys from home [an American spectator], an art student called (Gideon William) Nelson, from De Kalb, Illinois, stood up and raised his hands to request the crowd to be silent. As he did so, he was cracked over the head with a heavy cane, opening a terrible gash. As he turned to face his assailant, he was rapped over the head a second time, this time behind the ear, and his head was split again.

Another American youth (BF Larsen of Provo, Utah) who rushed to his rescue was also hit with a cane and his head laid open. Then he was picked up, streaming with blood, and thrown down about five rows of seats…Both will be disfigured for life.

One newspaper account claimed that the situation had been exacerbated by previous French objections to the whooping 'college yells' of the American contingent in the crowd. French fans had seen an opportunity to use their metal-headed canes to silence the sources of the irritation. O'Neil's teammate, De Groot, seemed to support this theory that a culture clash in cheering techniques contributed in no small measure to the trouble which broke out. He wrote, 'Several of the more daring American students who formed a rooting section cheered us on in spite of the French hostility, with the result that two of them were attacked by French spectators… Such was the hostile attitude of the French crowd throughout our game and it was a question whether the Americans in the stands or the fifteen Americans on the field received the worst treatment.'

The injuries created a macabre sideshow. Another newspaper report claimed that when Nelson lost consciousness, 'the crowd raised an ironic cheer as the victim of the attack was carried from the stands…Nelson's face was covered in blood and the mob seemed to enjoy the spectacle…

With no weapons of their own, the Americans in the stands became increasingly vulnerable. The *San Francisco Chronicle*'s front page the next day explained: 'The fist fight broke out in the stands and degenerated into a battle royal in which gold-headed canes were freely used. The Americans were outnumbered, and further more they carried no canes with which to retaliate.'

One US player, Norman Cleaveland, told how American fans were being systematically beaten up in the stands, and their bodies passed down to the field to be collected by ambulances. Concentration on the game was sometimes impossible. 'I thought they were dead,' Cleaveland revealed later. 'We were sure it was only a matter of time before they got their hands on us.'

It was just as well that the field was surrounded by that 400 metre (444 yard) dirt track for the forthcoming athletics, and the crowd was further separated from the players by the high perimeter fence. Even so, any American player nearing the crowd to retrieve the ball or throw it back in a line-out was subjected to the most fearsome abuse and intimidation, and was showered with missiles too.

Fired up by what they perceived as the injustice of the block on Vaysse that had reduced them to 13 men, the French team hit back with a fine passing rush. It was finally stopped by Doe at full-back, though the American defence was creaking under the pressure. A high punt landed over the US goal line which neither Dixon nor Doe could catch cleanly. Doe was reduced to spectator by the awkward bounce and Henri Galau only needed to fall on the ball to claim a try for France. The crowd's reaction to their team's attempted comeback was lamentable. They seemed to have written off their own team's chances already, since 13 men against 15 usually constituted a complete mismatch. Instead of encouraging their team they continued to moan. When Behoteguy missed the conversion, the Americans could breathe again because they still had an 11-3 lead.

At this point France seemed to make a conscious attempt to even up the numbers through foul play. John O'Neill claimed, 'Captain Lasserre of the French team five times slugged Captain Slater of our team, and did it so openly that the referee ordered him from the game.' The fighter-pilot had clearly reached a point in this match that he had never experienced in a bi-plane. He had lost all control. Fortunately for the slugger from Bayonne, Babe had not.

O'Neill added, 'But Slater was "game"; and going up to the referee he pleaded that Lasserre be permitted to continue. His wish was granted and as he stepped back from the conference that kept his rival in the game, the crowd jeered him.'

Another newspaper account claimed that Hyland was also a victim of an unprovoked attack from Lasserre. The *Chicago Tribune* wrote. 'Toward the end of the game in a furious mix-up the American star, Hyland, was slugged twice by captain Lasserre of the French team. Hyland made no attempt to strike back, and the referee, realizing the offence, asked captain Slater if the Frenchman should be put out of the game. The referee, A. E. Freethy, stated that the foul play warranted dismissal. Captain Slater, however, replied, "Let him stay in," and the French captain played on.'

It was typical Babe Slater. While Lasserre had lost all personal discipline and was playing well below his best, Slater, also a First World War veteran, had kept calm and produced the rock-solid leadership his team needed in the storm. No wonder he was praised by one American paper for his 'cool, steady game'.

The sportsmanship he showed deserved to go down in Olympic history, and his demonstration of De Coubertin's ethics wasn't over. Lubin, another survivor of the Great War, decided it was his turn to punch Babe. For a man who had lost an eye when he was peppered with shrapnel and bullets during the Battle of the Somme, this was an extraordinary decision. Even to play rugby represented a terrible risk to what vision he retained. A two-way scrap with an American heavyweight could have left him completely blinded. Lubin didn't care as he launched himself once more into a futile fight. He punched Babe so blatantly that he was sent off immediately. Once again Slater appealed to the referee, mindful of the uneven numbers on the field already. 'Lubin' was reinstated. The seething Frenchman with the thick little moustache refused three times to return, until Babe physically lifted his attacker back onto the field of play. This act, and the leniency of referee Freethy, prevented the French numbers from being depleted further. By now the home side could legitimately have been reduced to 11 men, given the repeated violent conduct of Lasserre and Lubin.

Just in case anyone doubted that Freethy had the courage to send a player off if he thought it necessary to restore order, it should be pointed out that he did so the very next year. England were playing New Zealand at Twickenham when he dismissed the All Blacks forward, Cyril Brownlie. Freethy had issued three warnings to both sides already; and his controversial decision meant that Brownlie became the second player in international history to be sent off, after Ed Turkington.

Back in Paris the French fists continued to fly. Yet Babe and the boys showed enough self-discipline to hit back where it would hurt the French most – by playing the game itself to a degree of excellence that couldn't be matched. The athletic Babe rose to win a line-out that should have been claimed by the French, since it had been their throw-in after Patrick's kick to touch. Not only did Slater win the ball, he was also able to unleash Cleaveland to begin a passing rush that swept the Americans all the way down the field. Lefty Rogers finally went over for a glorious try. It was just the reward Lefty deserved for all the bravery he had shown since breaking his nose in London. He had broken a bone in two places, yet he was still prepared to go to those places. And the man who had given Rogers what an American reporter described as 'a marvelous pass' was Hyland, who had come to his senses again after taking Lasserre's punches.

'Tricky Dick' had followed Babe's lead and hit back where it hurt most –
with devastating rugby. Doe had an almost impossible task to convert from
such a bad angle, so the score stood at United States 14 France 3.

With the mood in the crowd worsening, Ed Turkington might still
have allowed himself a smile. Since he was not playing, he had time to
enjoy the fact that he would soon be the proud owner of an Olympic
gold medal. Only if the match was abandoned due to crowd trouble
could he be denied. Perhaps with that scenario in mind, referee Freethy
seemed to be doing all he could to save the French from total
humiliation. The Americans twice charged all the way to the French
five-yard [4m] line, only to be pulled up for mysterious calls of 'knock-
on', when the ball was supposed to have been nudged forward illegally.
Freethy's whistle denied the USA two more scores. But still Babe, Rudy
and the boys kept coming.

Cleaveland also made a beautiful run through the entire French team,
crashing over the goal-line in the corner of the field. Freethy refused to
allow the try, however, claiming that Cleaveland had been bundled out
just before crossing the line. Even then the Americans were not to be
denied one last score, and Rudy Scholz was right in the thick of it. De
Groot explained, 'Another dropout and Devereux, Scholz and Hyland
carried the ball to the twenty-five-yard [22m] line, where the latter was
tackled with the ball and a scrum was called. We hooked the ball out
clean and in a passing rush Caesar Manelli went over for the final try of
the day.' Though Jack Patrick had supplied the scoring pass, Babe and
Rudy's quick-firing scrum was the secret behind the success. It was a
fitting way to end the rout.

Scholz later paid tribute to Patrick. He said, 'Jack Patrick at wing
forward played one of the finest games ever played.' But Rudy knew
they had all played the game of their lives.

Even so, Doe's bad luck with the boot continued when he hit the
crossbar again. It didn't seem to matter. The score-line was now an
emphatic USA 17, France 3.

The leaders ended the game with another passing rush, and when
the shell-shocked French desperately kicked the ball into touch, Albert
Freethy blew the final whistle.

Babe, Rudy and their teammates had done it. Their unlikely dream
had become glorious reality. Would it have happened if Scholz and

Slater hadn't put their heads together to reorganise that desperate scrum? Probably not. De Groot commented later, '...And because we were able to hook that ball and then break up our 3-4 scrum with great rapidity, placing those seven men right back into the passing rushes, we defeated the French.'

It was quite a moment for Rudy and Babe, two very different guys, thrown into the same team and effectively given a choice: work together and win, or be torn apart and lose. It had been a pretty close-run thing at times, but finally the odd couple had found some chemistry again, just as they had back in 1920. Their reward was a second Olympic gold.

Even so, it was hard to celebrate in that tinderbox atmosphere. One report described the moment of victory, which must have felt more ominous than glorious at first. The atmosphere was heavily laden with the threat of further violence. 'As the final whistle blew the crowd appeared for a moment to be stunned. Amid silence the American flag was run up the flagpole. This seemed to awaken a large majority of the spectators from their minute or so of lethargy, for bedlam broke loose.'

Ed Turkington tried to exchange jerseys with a French squad member. It was an act that left him temporarily blinded, as he brought his jersey up over his face. In a stadium where you needed eyes in the back of your head to stay safe, this was not a clever move. Someone – probably the French player – kicked him squarely in the groin while he was unable to protect himself. Ed collapsed in agony. A ladies' man, he might have been worried about the long-term effects of the assault. However, Ed had a more pressing concern – how to recover and get up quickly enough to protect himself from further attacks. If the angry mob had seen one of France's own players provide such a violent lead, they might have taken it as their cue to follow suit. Turkington suddenly looked very vulnerable, especially if the masses breached the perimeter. Even if they didn't lynch him, he might be trampled in all the chaos.

Ned Turkington, Ed's son, said in 2007, 'My father genuinely feared for his life that day. He was kicked in the testicles while swapping shirts. His shirt was over his head at the time. He thought it was the player with whom he was swapping shirts. He went down.'

So picture the scene; here was a man who had left the love of his life to pursue his Olympic dream in what he sincerely hoped would be the most glorious summer of sporting achievement. Less gloriously, he had

204 | FOR THE GLORY

become the first man ever to be sent off in an international rugby match. Then he had experienced the heartbreak and frustration of being left on the sidelines for the final. As if that wasn't enough, he had been subjected to a humiliating assault in his team's moment of glory. Finally he feared that he might be killed. As an Olympic adventure, this wasn't quite what Ed had in mind when he went to the try-outs. Yet for all those tear-inducing twists of fate, he had won gold...if he could stay alive long enough to collect his medal.

Through the pain, Ed rose gingerly to his feet and got his jersey off so that he could see again. Bizarrely, he may even have completed the exchange of shirts, because he was pictured wearing a French jersey on the boat back home. Ned Turkington was understandably sceptical on that possibility. 'I don't know if he got the French shirt and still shook hands', he added wryly. The more likely scenario is that Ed was handed a French jersey later by way of apology. If he did complete the exchange there and then, it was a quite remarkable demonstration of self control in the face of a disgraceful piece of poor sportsmanship from his opposite number.

Despite the obvious danger, O'Neill was determined not to be intimidated either. He was more seriously injured than Turkington thanks to that seeping appendix wound. Yet he explained, 'In accordance with the custom at all Olympic meets, our team lined up and stood at attention as the American flag was raised for the first time in this Olympiad. The band struck up "The Star-Spangled Banner" but so loud were the hisses, jeers and boos that we could hardly hear the national anthem. Though we were standing at attention a very short distance from the band that was playing our national anthem, we could distinguish only occasional notes of it.'

This moment probably completed poor Baron de Coubertin's feeling of shame in the stands. He had brought the ancient Olympic movement back to life in order to promote world peace. Instead it appeared he had created a monster.

For O'Neill and his teammates it felt as though they had fought that monster all afternoon. He added, 'We were happy and proud as we stood there watching the flag ascend. We played a hard game and we fought all the way but we played cleanly and there was no reason for the booing. All about us seemed to be a note of hostility, but above the din made by many thousands of voices we could hear Pete Cunningham on the sidelines, cheering like mad for Uncle Sam. A busted rib had kept Pete out of the game, but it didn't affect his voice. He was there – a real American matching his triumphant yells against those who booed us, the flag and our anthem and I'll tell you that Pete held his own with them.'

The players who won the victory stood proud in defiance as the hundred-strong brass band continued to be drowned out by deafening jeers and whistles. The *San Francisco Chronicle*'s front page the following day revealed, 'An American photographer, while attempting to take a picture of the American flag at the top of the Olympic pole, was hit by various missiles thrown by the enraged spectators, and was compelled to take cover.'

Ed Turkington had recovered just about enough to take part in the ceremony. Later he claimed that the French deliberately flew the Stars and Stripes upside down, though no one else ever talked of such an insult. Perhaps Ed was right; or maybe he still had too much water in his eyes to see clearly.

Vice-captain Charlie Doe had other memories of the moment: 'The medal ceremony took place in front of thousands of people who wanted to rip us to shreds.' Yet in all the chaos it is far from clear that the players were able to receive their medals that day, since it was later reported that it took a good few weeks for those hard-earned medals to reach their rightful owners. Doe may simply have been remembering the US anthem being played instead. There was certainly plenty of confusion as the crowd went crazy.

Enjoying the sight of the flag anyway, John O'Neill said to a teammate: 'That sure looks pretty. Now can you help me to the locker room?' He was about to collapse due to his open abdominal wound. Another US player, Norman Cleaveland, later described his own feelings like this: 'We were sure it was only a matter of time before they got their hands on us. They were throwing bottles and rocks and clawing at us through the fence.'

Men like Slater and Scholz were disgusted by what they saw. Like so many others, they had been ready to risk their lives in the First World War to restore France's freedom. You can imagine the cold rage that came over them, and one look at their teammates was enough to know that everyone felt pretty much the same. Such a display of hatred from a supposed ally was beyond their understanding.

De Groot voiced the team's outrage when he wrote, 'No American team has ever, I believe, been given such an unsportsmanlike reception after having fairly and squarely and cleanly won a game. Certainly we were mystified by such treatment and still more highly incensed against the French as a nation and people. Certainly we deserved somewhat better treatment from a nation which has supposedly always been one of our staunchest friends and compatriots.'

The reasons behind such an unprecedented lack of sportsmanship were probably the same as those behind the hostility ever since the US team's arrival, though doubtless compounded by the injuries to Jaureguy and Vaysse. The events of the day had not helped the French to shake off that lingering post-war inferiority complex, or celebrate France's newfound independence from the foreign forces which had amassed in their country during the war years.

It may be that hard economic times in the wake of that war had played a part in the crowd's actions, though some of the worst culprits certainly didn't have that excuse for their violence, because the 'gold-tipped cane brigade' in the expensive seats had been more violent than anyone, and they were of the highest social standing.

The police certainly didn't think the threat to the Americans had subsided when part of the crowd left the stadium in disgust. The 15,000-strong French mob that remained looked increasingly malevolent. O'Neill added, 'As we left the field, 250 gendarmes formed an escort and protected us from the crowd that surged about the exits.'

Babe Slater looked at the police and the seething mob – then tried to reject the intervention of the gendarmes. 'It will take more than 15,000 Frenchman to lick fifteen Americans', he said proudly.

Others weren't so sure. De Groot said, 'Thousands of people lined the high steel fence which enclosed the field and shut off the people in the stands from us, and it was indeed fortunate for us that we got to our dressing rooms by an underground passage.'

The Americans escaped their would-be attackers because the tunnel back to the dressing room went down under the field before the players neared the stands. Jack Patrick later put a note on a photograph of 'the underground exit that proved a lifesaver following the French game. The crowd was hostile!!!'

Reminders of the day's violence were unavoidable when the

Americans reached their dressing room though. The worst-injured of the American fans, Gideon Nelson, had been placed there temporarily for his own safety before being taken to hospital. De Groot confirmed, 'He was…carried from the stands and into our dressing room, where we saw him after the game, still unconscious.'

One American newspaper reported that, 'Thousands of people were kept at bay by the police while the injured men were being taken to the ambulances…'. Another explained what happened to Nelson next. 'After having his wounds dressed at the first-aid station, Nelson was sent to the American Hospital at Neuilly where it was reported last night that his condition was satisfactory though serious. Larsen refused to go to hospital and returned to Paris with his friends.'

For O'Neill and his friends there was another grim realisation when they reached temporary safety under the main stand. It must have felt like déjà vu. 'When we reached our dressing rooms we found that about everything of value we had left in our clothing was gone. We lost about 16,000 francs worth of valuables.'

Of course it may be that O'Neill, or the reporter quoting him, had attached the robbery of Friday 8 May to the day of the final for simplicity's sake or added another for dramatic impact. It would have been surprising if the Americans had left another 16,000 francs worth of valuables in their dressing rooms after the previous robbery. On the other hand, perhaps they thought that on the day of the big game, and in light of what had happened before, their possessions would be properly guarded this time around. And Ed Turkington did insist 50 years later, 'They robbed us a couple of times.'

Hyland wasn't as concerned about the robbery as he was about settling a personal score. He immediately sought out 'Rene' Lasserre to exact revenge for the punches he had taken from the French captain during the match.

An American newspaper reporter called Frank Getty wrote, '…after the game and the flag-raising, he [Hyland] hurried in search of an interpreter and sought out the French captain in the latter's dressing room in the presence of a hostile group of steaming, sulky athletes. Hyland, a lone American, invited the French captain to finish the affair. The latter was a sportsman. He apologised in the presence of his teammates, through the interpreter, for the blow, explained it had been struck in the heat of combat and the bitterness of defeat, and said he would prefer to shake hands. So Hyland shook and went back to his shower bath.'

Still, according to Scholz it wasn't Hyland or even Babe Slater who received the French leader's jersey as compensation for the punches thrown. Rudy claimed later, 'At least the French captain came in after the game and gave me his jersey, saying I earned it.' Perhaps he appreciated the feisty game played by the smallest man on the pitch. What is certain is that Lasserre publicly paid tribute to the American team soon afterwards. He said, 'We were outplayed by better conditioned men. I don't see what the crowd was kicking up about. I have no complaint to make.'

Meanwhile the American players finally took a moment to savour what they had achieved against all odds. De Groot explained, '…we were a happy bunch in our dressing room and it would have taken far more than that crowd of 40,000 to quell our happiness. We had accomplished the feat which everyone had proclaimed impossible and for which we had worked so assiduously for five long months.'

No one was more delighted than Babe Slater, who had shown the strong leadership that Rudy Scholz had craved when it really mattered. From the moment Babe had spoken so eloquently, yet controversially, about the lack of French commitment to the tournament, he had rallied his troops superbly. He had unified his team in a way that Scholz had never foreseen. He had instilled in them the willpower, the discipline and the sheer bloody-mindedness to overcome all the obstacles that had been set before them. Finally, he had made the French pay for their over-confidence.

Babe declared, 'We were not conceded one single chance of winning by the French paper. After we saw France conquer Romania, we only figured we had a fighting chance. By the old determination to win and the strictest training and hard work, we went into the game with the one idea – to win.

'They were heralded as being so experienced and clever, whereas, we were only novices at the game. As a matter of fact, we outplayed them in every single phase of the game and the score does not indicate how badly they were beaten.'

Babe echoed these thoughts when he wrote home a few days later. 'You probably got all the results of our wonderful victory over France and I mean wonderful too. They were cracked up to be so clever and fast that we were not conceded a chance to win. The fellows worked hard in practice and got in the best physical shape and entered the game with that old determination to win. We outplayed the "Frogs" in every single phase of the game and they only were in our end of the field about six times in the entire game.'

So what did Rudy make of it all? Well, Scholz believed the Americans had won because that elusive team spirit turned up just in time. He wrote in his diary, 'We played the French off their feet due to the fact that everyone went in to win. We fought with such fierceness and determination and together, that I don't think any team could beat us.'

The key word in that diary entry was 'together'. Only in those last few days had Rudy felt a true togetherness in the squad. Perhaps that was because it was only in the build-up to the gold medal game that Scholz wanted to be part of that togetherness.

Later a newspaper report said, 'Rudy Scholz, one of the stars of the American team, claims that the combination used in the final game against France was as good a team as he has ever seen with the possible exception of the Waratahs and the All Blacks...This [US] team played together as a unit and it was the well-organised teamwork, rather than the individual brilliance of the players, that spelled victory.'

Coach Charlie Austin, who had handled Rudy's aloof and sometimes rebellious attitude so brilliantly all tour, was said to be 'beaming with happiness' as he told the press after the game, 'We won because of our determination to do so and because of the great physical fitness of the players. I sent them into the game with instructions to play a clean, hard game, and I believe that everybody who saw the game will agree that the boys carried out orders.'

A 'Scotch international', who may even have been the famous Eric Liddell of *Chariots of Fire* fame, had watched the game carefully. When asked for his opinion he said, 'The Frenchmen developed a fear complex early in the struggle and never recovered. From then on they were a beaten team. The size of the score, however, was quite remarkable.'

The referee, Albert Freethy, made perhaps the most extraordinary claim of all. He said, 'With several more weeks of training, this US team could beat any team in Europe, not barring the best of the British Isles. They play a great game.'

For a man of Freethy's great rugby knowledge to suggest that the USA would have been capable of beating England inside a month was high praise indeed. After all, the English hadn't lost a game in two years. But Freethy had rugby in his blood; he sat on the Wales selection committee at one point during his distinguished career, and his judgement was not to be taken lightly. For the Americans to receive such a high accolade from Freethy in the aftermath of that Olympic victory gave huge credibility to their gold medal triumph.

Whether or not the gentlemen of the Harlequins rugby club or the British Olympic Association would have agreed with the Welshman's verdict is open to debate. However, their delight on hearing the news of America's victory in Paris is easy to picture. The true sportsmen of London, who had entertained and advised the Americans during their stay in the English capital, had reason to feel part of this victory too. The Harlequins had given the Americans the reality check that helped them better to understand the rules of rugby as played in Europe; they had highlighted the threat of Jaureguy and underlined the best way to keep the French at bay. Of course the British could not claim the credit for this glorious sporting upset. The defiance of seemingly overwhelming odds had been a very American feat of sheer self-belief. But the English could feel proud that they had made their small contribution to that success story. They had earned their right to raise a glass to their friends. Why, some of them may even have let out a college yell.

Meanwhile the United Press (UP) sports editor of the day, Henry J. Farrell, gave his reasons why he now regarded Babe's squad as one of America's all-time great teams.

He wrote:

> Rugby is practically extinct in the United States...Many of the players who went to Paris and won the championship by beating the French team 17 to 3 had not played from the time they left Antwerp four years ago until they went out to train for this team.
>
> Under these circumstances the Americans were presented with the same difficulties that a French baseball team would have in beating the pennant winner of the Class A league, let alone the winner of the world's series...What happened to the American

boys in Paris from the time they arrived is well known, and it is too distasteful to be repeated. They got the rawest deal that any team ever got in any country. But they won, and if an American team ever earned glory for demonstrating every trait that America wants the world to regard as American characteristics, those football players won it.

Their victory and their conduct under fire is the brightest entry that has been scored on all the pages of America's international sport records.

The glory of sport held sway, in one little corner of Paris at least. The American celebrations began right there in the dressing room, as gendarmes kept the livid crowd at bay outside. Some brave US supporters had somehow found their way through the lynch mob and the walls of policemen to join the party. And like all conscientious party-goers, they had thought to bring a bottle or two with them. First to congratulate Babe and his team was San Francisco's own ex-Senator Phelan. Next in line came Colonel Johnson, another San Franciscan, and well known among sports-lovers on the west coast. Pat Higgins from Los Angeles, who had boosted the morale of Rudy's stricken friend John O'Neill with his half time dash, found his way through yet again. So did Senator Hollis of New Hampshire, General Charles H. Sherrill, a member of the International Olympic Committee, and an endless string of supposedly lesser lights, who nevertheless beamed as brightly as the rest that day. Most popular among the distinguished visitors to the dressing room were those who arrived with several cases of champagne. Prohibition? What Prohibition! As De Groot put it, 'The strictest training rules had been kept in France and now with the lid off it was a grand and glorious feeling.'

Babe wrote, 'All the Americans in Paris were more than overjoyed and needless to say did considerable celebrating.' The US captain may have felt duty-bound to pop the champagne for his colleagues and take a swig or two. But when he wrote home he confided that it was the French beer that he had loved most. Typically, Babe stayed true to himself and his simple personal likes and dislikes. He always did that, whether he was in sporting heaven or the hell of war.

Even then, the danger at the Stade Colombes hadn't entirely receded. The Americans were brought back down to earth when it was time to consider how to reach their transport from the dressing rooms. It was going to be like running the gauntlet. The *San Francisco Chronicle* of 19 May claimed, 'Police reserves were called out to protect the American players from the crowd massed outside the main entrance to the stadium. The Americans left by a side gate under police protection. This they greatly resented, saying they were perfectly capable of taking care of themselves.'

Babe Slater continued to insist that it would take more than a few thousand Frenchmen to trouble a small but determined group of Americans. He led his team out with his head held high, just as he had done at the start of the match. Some of the French thugs may have taken a look at man-mountain Slater and decided that a fight might not be such a good idea after all. The *Chronicle* simply reported that the Americans 'departed from the stadium without experiencing further trouble'.

Once away from the stadium, the celebrations could step up another gear and an American journalist called Leo Brady described how, 'Frequently they stopped the bus to add a few bottles of champagne to their stock collected on the way, and toasted each other with great eloquence.'

John O'Neill said, 'When we got back to the Hotel Exelmans where the team was quartered, the editors of the various papers in Paris called us up to apologize for the disturbances at the stadium and to assure us that the hostile demonstrations were only made by the rough-neck elements of France.'

One newspaper clipping summed up the mood by then when it claimed, 'The American players were so overjoyed at having won the championship by such a decisive score against one of the finest teams in Europe that they were inclined to "let it go." After they had been cooled off the American players felt so good that they accepted an invitation to attend the banquet given by the French Football Federation.'

The lavish banquet took place at the Palais D'Orsay and the Prince of Wales was also a guest. The Prince was apparently as pleased to see the Americans land such an historic blow to French self-esteem as he was to see Eric Liddell win his race a few weeks later.

Meanwhile US rugby team manager Sam Goodman, basking in the glory of victory as much as the players, didn't lay himself open to accusations of false modesty. Later he wrote, '...it was generally admitted by all the European critics and the famous Welsh referee who officiated, Mr Freethy, that on that day's play the US team was unbeatable and that our wonderful physical condition should be an object lesson to all.'

Frantz Reichel, general secretary of the French Olympic Committee, didn't hold back in his criticism of the crowd, describing their behaviour as 'abominable'. Neither did he hold back in his praise of the gold medalists. He admitted, 'Your boys are wonderful rugby players. They won the match fairly and squarely.'

Meanwhile an American newspaper reporter called George T. Davis revealed that, 'Three members of the American team were honored by a French critic who picked an all-European team. He placed Dick Hyland, Rudy Scholz and Jack Patrick on his selection because of their great work in the Olympic Games.' Rudy later claimed, 'Patrick, Hyland, Valentine and myself were named.' Many other Americans, such as Babe Slater, might have had an equal claim.

That night Babe, Rudy and the boys celebrated further at Kiley's, a famous Parisian nightspot, and didn't return to their hotel until the early hours. Rudy wrote that he finally hit the sack at 5.00am.

The following day Goodman received a cable from William F. Humphrey, president of the Olympic Club of San Francisco. It read, 'Yesterday's victory glorious, but boys won greater honor by their courageous and dignified indifference to the unjust clamor of people who neither represent the spirit of France nor of its people, congratulations to you all.'

That evening the celebrations continued at the Inter-Allies Club, though this time it was more of an All-American – or should that be All-Californian – affair. Babe wrote, 'Senator Phelan gave us a banquet that was hard to beat and a number of prominent Californians attended besides the team.' Slater gave a speech too, thanking his players for their support, their wonderful performance and the spirit and discipline they showed in the face of severe provocation. Coach Charlie Austin and a number of dignitaries also spoke, with Norman Cleaveland, who had played so well, leading the cheers for each man.

Phelan and his wealthy friends even offered to reimburse the players for the money and valuables that had been stolen. Babe Slater and his team decided it would be wrong to accept that generous offer from private individuals. They seemed to believe that it was the responsibility of the American and French Olympic Committees to come up with some form of compensation, though they never did. The objects of sentimental value could never be replaced. So the team was pleasantly surprised that night when fresh awards were bestowed upon them, which would carry great sentimental value for the future.

A newspaper report added, 'At the conclusion of the evening the team was presented with a beautiful bronze trophy showing the victor receiving his laurels. Each man will also be given a handsome bronze medal appropriately engraved.'

Babe Slater was only too delighted to lift yet another trophy, generously donated by the Californian community, though in truth there was only one metal appropriate to this particular sporting triumph – and that, of course, was gold.

When he could have basked far longer in the glory of his second Olympic triumph, Babe Slater left Paris. As the man who had led the USA to its first gold medal of the Olympic Games, Slater could have dined out on the events of that extraordinary battle every night until the closing ceremony in the same stadium. Instead his mind turned to truly deadly battles of times gone by. The Parisian crowd may have forgotten all too soon the difference between sport and war, but Babe hadn't. He remembered that, six years earlier and not far away, he could so easily have lost his life along with millions of others. He wanted to honour his fallen comrades one more time, and show his brother the scene of his worst memories. So while the Olympic party raged, Babe and Norman spent the best part of a week in respectful remembrance of the fallen in a neighbouring country. 'Nor and I just returned from Belgium where we spent a few days in seeing Brussels and the Battlefields,' he wrote on 26 May. 'Expect to go to Switzerland day after tomorrow for a few days and then return to sail on the Leviathan June 3.'

The dramatic purity of the Swiss Alps would have cleansed the soul after the vivid images of war that had doubtless invaded Babe's mind once again. There were no such images in Rudy's head…yet.

LOVE AND WAR

As Rudy Scholz dodged bullets on the Japanese island of Okinawa and threw himself into foxholes lined with human remains to avoid the shells landing all around him, the glory of 1924 might have seemed to belong to another world. But Rudy later claimed that the agility he had honed on the rugby field helped him to stay alive in the midst of the Second World War's worst bloodbath.

What had driven Rudy to find this hell at the ripe old age of 49? The US government had sensibly determined, through the ages of the men they began to call up en masse, that the fighting should be left to younger men, aged 21–35. Even when the age range was extended to between 20 and 44, America's rugby Olympians were mostly too old for action overseas.

Rudy's choice would have been more immediately understandable had the Second World War come along in 1924, just as he returned home from Paris. Back then he was still a restless soul in many ways and looking for personal fulfilment. But 1924 was peace time; and nothing so very dramatic happened to Rudy in those first few months, after he reached San Francisco from the mock battlefield of the Stade Colombes.

The same could not be said of Ed Turkington, the man who had turned his back on his big chance to settle down in order to follow his Olympic dream. Six months to the day after their trial separation has begun, Ed met Elaine Horton as planned outside the Olympic Club in San Francisco – where else? It only took one look into those warm, familiar eyes for Ed to discover that he still loved her. Fortunately for Ed, Elaine still loved him too. From that moment on they were inseparable. Less than three years later they were married at the Horton family mansion on 14th and Balboa, San Francisco. Ed and Elaine had come a long way since a young boy had asked if he could 'wash the baby' downstairs in that same, extraordinary city two decades earlier. As adults, they didn't regret their decision to marry; in fact they stayed married for 69 years. In all that time, they never argued once, at least not in front of their son Ned and daughter Dana. It was a harmony for which their children remained truly grateful.

Looking back, the clarity that came to Ed Turkington through his adventures in Paris probably made him the biggest Olympic winner of all. Sixty-nine years of wedded bliss had to be worth more than a gold medal.

Meanwhile Babe returned to what had always been his greatest love of all, farming, and the tight-knit community around Woodland. In June 1924 the man he farmed with there, Bob Lockhart, held an 'open house' for Babe, in honour of his partner's achievement in bringing home the rugby gold. Anyone from the surrounding area who wanted to come down, shake Babe's hand and hear the story of how the sporting miracle had been achieved could do just that. He had always been popular in Woodland, so we can assume that Bob Lockhart's house was soon filled to bursting point.

Despite all the acclaim he was receiving, it was the doll the team had been given as a mascot during the build-up to the big game that remained on Babe's mind. The tough guy with the soft heart had already thought of a perfect home for that doll – his six-year-old niece Jean's bedroom.

So on 22 June 1924, he wrote to his sister Marguerite and said, '... the doll for Jean is not much for looks but has some sentiment attached to it. It was presented to the team by Madame Melais [sic], an

American opera singer who was in Paris and was our only mascot. She named it "Cali." I will enclose a clipping, the picture taken at the presentation during one of our practices…'

When he wrote that the doll was 'our only mascot', Babe seemed to be remembering just how isolated the rugby team was in Paris. Their treatment had caused outrage back home in the US and became front page news from New York to San Francisco. With the main part of the Olympic Games yet to start, the abuse of Babe, Rudy and the boys had turned into a diplomatic incident.

The First World War remained the reason for much of the ill-feeling. One newspaper explained indignantly, 'The dispatches state that the American players were booed and hissed throughout the game and that when the American flag was raised at the close of the game the crowd went into a spasm of fury. The American flag was not received that way by Parisian crowds in 1917 and 1918.'

Another went even further: 'If the team representing the Stars and Stripes is going to be hissed every time it wins an Olympic title, it would be better for the Americans to return home, and concern themselves no longer with international athletics.'

That didn't happen, fortunately for the red-faced guardians of the Olympic movement. But the disgraceful events of that rugby final were not forgotten; for they set the tone for many more examples of bitter controversy at the 1924 Olympics. There was the 'Olympic Tennis Scandal' as the English newspapers described it. British, American and Belgian officials threatened to withdraw their players unless the organisation of the tournament improved. There was no water for the tennis stars, no towels, no lavatory near the Colombes Courts, builders at work in the women's shower block and crooked umpires aplenty.

Then there was the case of the Italian fencer, Signor Oreste Pulitti, who was given such an easy ride in the individual sabre contest, when he took on three of his fellow countrymen, that a Hungarian judge by the name of Georges de Kovacs disqualified the entire Italian team for collusion. Pulitti later slapped Kovacs twice in the face and Brigadier-General Reginald Kentish, who had helped to entertain the American rugby players in London as Honorary Secretary of the British Olympic Association, was called to an International Olympic Committee meeting to endorse the Italians' expulsion from that and future Olympic fencing tournaments. Pulitti was said to have wounded Kovacs in a dual that followed a further altercation on their way home from Paris.

When crooked boxing judges tried to allow a French middleweight called Roger Brousse to bite his way to quarter-final glory – to the dismay of his British opponent, Harry Mallin – all English-speaking contestants in the 1924 Olympic boxing tournament had seen enough. The decision was successfully appealed after Great Britain, the United States, Canada, Australia and South Africa threatened to withdraw as one. Mallin even went on to win the gold medal. Yet the Olympic boxing event still ended in scenes of uproar when Italians tried to attack judges after decisions didn't go their way. The British Olympic Association instructed the International Olympic Committee that they would never allow their boxers to compete at an Olympic Games again.

These disgraceful scenes in the boxing arena were described by the highly-respected and authoritative *Times* of London as 'a culmination of what has been going on since the first free-fight [free-for-all] broke out in the French-American Rugby Football match.' The 1924 Olympic Games were not even over on 22 July, when the *Times* published the verdict of its 'Special Correspondent' under the headline 'OLYMPIC GAMES DOOMED – FAILURE OF THE IDEAL.' This was supported by a 'Leader column' which carried the headline: 'NO MORE OLYMPIC GAMES.' It added, 'Unhappily the experiences of the present Olympiad have confirmed, with dreadful clearness, the long-felt misgiving that the tendency of these Games is to inflame international animosities rather than to allay them…'.

A situation that had already seemed precarious back in 1919 had now reached crisis point. In the aftermath of the 1924 Olympics, Dud De Groot of the American rugby team claimed 'a bulletin has been issued to the effect that the British are considering a recommendation of their committee that they withdraw from future Olympic Games, because, instead of furthering good sportsmanship and a friendly and advanced international feeling, it is tending to create, instead, a spirit of antagonism, animosity and now even open hostility…Perhaps with a person of some other nationality as chairman of the Olympic committee, some means of punishment for poor sportsmanship can be worked out, but at present, with a Frenchman at its head, of course, little progress can be made.'

That was a little unfair on Baron de Coubertin, who adored sportsmanship and must have shaken his head in despair at what he had witnessed on that opening day of the Paris Olympics in the Stade Colombes and since. Yet De Coubertin's involvement with the Olympic Games was effectively over, and so was rugby's. The sport that had set the tone for so much ill-feeling and controversy at the 1924 Games was never seen at an Olympics again.

Dick Hyland tried manfully to mend Franco-American relations almost single-handedly. He stayed in Paris after the Olympics to study at the Sorbonne, and joined the Stade Francais rugby team – where he became a close colleague of none other than Adolphe Jaureguy. Parisian fans who had been baying for Hyland's blood months earlier were soon cheering for him instead. Hyland and Jaureguy became great friends and set up many a try for each other. It was an unforeseen twist to the story.

In 1925 came another. The most exquisite porcelain vases turned up at the US Olympic offices in New York. Part of the relief sculpture in white depicted the bare torso of a rugby player reaching out with the ball, as two tacklers try to pull him down. The image was set against a background of deep blue with golden leaves. The vases were a gift from the City Council in Paris to each American rugby gold medal winner. It was almost as if they were still trying to make up for the terrible treatment the players received in the French capital. Delicate beyond belief, they provided a stark and stunning contrast to the bloody brutality which was seen on the day the vases were earned. Somehow they acted as a reminder that there was still beauty to be found in sport and the Olympic movement itself, if only the world would let the Modern Games live and evolve. As we all know, the world showed mercy, and preparations began for Amsterdam 1928 and beyond. As a testament to those powers of survival, Rudy Scholz's vase can still be seen in the 'de Saisset Museum' at Santa Clara University, lit up in the basement. The vase is a fitting tribute to the 'glory of sport' referred to in the Olympic oath.

Two years after that vase arrived, Rudy was struck by more stunning beauty and delicacy – of the human kind. In 1927 he heard a woman called Mildred Sophey sing in a choir in the St Rose Church in Santa Rosa. Spellbound, he fell in love with the voice and then its owner, who was half French and half Irish. With his idealistic view of romance, Scholz had been waiting for this moment all his adult life. Suddenly he understood why his romance with Cecilia, which had distracted him at times during his first Olympic adventure, had not brought lasting happiness. He had been destined to meet Milly, the woman of his dreams. She was more than just a very pretty face, she was musically gifted too. There was real spirit in her eyes, which sparkled when a warm, expressive smile spread across her face. She had dark hair, cut quite short in the style of the day, she was slim with great legs. Rudy was mesmerised by this young woman, though not so tongue-tied that he didn't introduce himself just as quickly as he could.

Scholz never had been short of a word or two and right away the little guy made a big impression. At 24, Milly was seven years younger than Rudy. Neither of them cared; it just felt right from the start. The courtship began and they both already knew where this was heading. That same year they became engaged to be married.

And 1927 had been a memorable year for Babe Slater, too. Woodland Legion went unbeaten all season thanks to his prowess on the American football field. Babe and Woodland won the northern California championship with a 6-0 victory over Merced in San Francisco's Kezar Stadium. Slater was still a sporting god at the top of his game, even though by now he was 31 years old.

For Rudy Scholz, sport took a back seat over Christmas and New Year as wedding preparations gathered pace. The ceremony took place on 22 January 1928, in the same Santa Rosa church where Rudy had first heard Milly sing – St Rose. Pretty soon Milly was pregnant with the first of their four sons, Rud. Three more, Rich, Ron and Dave, would follow in time. So now there was French blood in the Scholz family, another nice little irony after what he and the team had been through in Paris.

In 1932 it was Babe Slater's turn to hear wedding bells, at the Clarksburg Community Church, California. By coincidence, like Rudy, he too had chosen an Olympic year in which to tie the knot. Though he had once admitted that French girls were 'a good treat for sore eyes', there was no exotic flavour to this union. Babe had moved to Clarksburg five years earlier and had fallen in love with a local woman called Virginia Cave. She was pretty and dependable and brought out Babe's softer side. Virginia must have been extra special, because the strong, silent Babe had never been short of female admirers. Yet he was 36 by the time he chose Mrs Right and declared himself ready to settle down.

Like Rudy Scholz and Ed Turkington, Babe never had any reason to regret his decision. The following year their daughter, Marilyn, was born. She was to be their only child, and the source of much joy.

Neither fatherhood nor middle age had dampened Rudy's passion for sport. In 1938 he turned out for the Olympic Club in San Francisco – a side coached by his old teammate, Jack Patrick. When he cracked a small bone in his shoulder, a reporter suggested to Rudy that it might be time to retire.

'Retire, hell, I'm just getting good,' he replied. 'I used to play wing-three-quarter in college, but I'm so fast now that coach Jack Patrick makes me play half-back for the Olympic Club. And I'll be back there in my position by March. The doctor says I'll be ready to go again by then.'

When asked how old he was, Rudy confessed, 'Let's see, how old am I? I was born in 1896. That makes me what – 42? Yes, that's right, 42 – but don't tell anybody.'

Sadly the time for wisecracks was almost over, especially in Babe Slater's community, where a lot of Japanese immigrants had settled. His nephew, Norman recalled, 'Babe used to get along just fine with them. Before the war, a Japanese family even farmed some of Babe's land, because they could farm onions better than we could. We had a Japanese family right across the road from our house. It contained a general and an admiral. They disappeared right after Pearl Harbor and we learned they were highly-ranked officers in the Japanese military.'

On 7 December 1941, without declaring war on America, the Japanese attacked Pearl Harbor in Hawaii. US President Roosevelt said the day would live in infamy throughout history. Some 353 Japanese aircraft struck the US Navy in two waves of destruction. On that shocking day, 2,402 were killed and 1,800 wounded. This outrageous act of provocation soon backfired on the Japanese because it brought America into the Second World War.

In Clarksburg, the Japanese community, whose members were Babe Slater's friends and neighbours, were suddenly regarded with suspicion. 'We were worried there were more Japanese around us like that, who were a secret part of their military.' Norman Slater explained. 'It turned out they were the only ones, but after Pearl Harbor we approved of, even if we were not overjoyed by, the decision to transport most of the Japanese to what we termed concentration camps.'

Those camps were not sinister places like the Nazi death camps in eastern Europe. The Japanese were not being led away to their deaths. Not all were even transported to the camps. Some Japanese Americans, who successfully convinced their adopted country of their loyalty, came in very useful for the US campaign in the Pacific. Babe's nephew revealed, 'I had four Japanese boys in my class at school and three of them were later decorated by the US side for their work as translators. That was important work because Japanese was a lousy language for someone who needed to learn it quickly.'

With Pearl Harbor the reality of the Second World War was brought home to the USA. Due to the age of the 1924 gold-medal winners, none were going to be called up unless they wanted to be; and even then they were highly likely to be kept away from the front line. Babe Slater stayed on his farm, knowing he could still make a very important contribution to the war effort. Food was to be rationed and much of it was sent to Europe. Farmers like Babe were therefore as vital to the USA as any soldier. So Slater did his bit for the war, even though he experienced it from a far more peaceful environment than last time around.

Rudy didn't want a peaceful environment. When people got over the shock of Pearl Harbor, there was still a general sense of outrage on the West Coast about what the Japanese had done. Scholz shared that outrage. Rudy's son Rud said, 'Those on the west coast at the time had no love for the Japanese "sneak attack." I did not think Dad was an excessive hater of the people themselves, but the regime that sponsored it…Emperor Hirohito, Japanese Prime Minister Hideki Tojo, et al – against which the US had to fight…I would NOT put Dad down as any more outraged than all the average citizens.'

But Rudy was going to do something about it, unlike most citizens his age. He was determined to find a way to go to war at last. If Rudy was fit enough to play rugby, he was fit enough to fight. And in a newspaper interview in 1942 he claimed he was certainly fit enough to play rugby. Rudy explained, 'Well, I have kept up with athletics year after year, and I've never actually been out of condition. Then I've had enough [rugby] experience to save a lot of steps. You see I can foresee a great deal of what's going to happen.'

Though the same would not be true in combat, it was a risk he was prepared to take. Scholz had missed the First World War and he wasn't going to miss the Second. He was desperate to see action, just as Babe Slater had done about a quarter of a century earlier. The idea of listening to the stories of homecoming men all over again, without some stories of his own to trade, would not have appealed to him. If a new generation of war veterans were about to command the respect of the nation, Rudy wanted to be one of them. Babe Slater had commanded enormous respect in the early 1920s. It was Rudy's turn now.

No one would sensibly suggest that Babe Slater was the reason why Rudy still wanted to go to war. And Dave Scholz didn't think his father was envious of Babe as such. He argued, 'Rudy was an adventurer, a risk-taker, high on the self-confidence chart, who was supremely competitive, liked to challenge himself and loved the military. Those traits are what compelled him to find a way to go into combat. Not envy. Given Dad's long-term commitment as an Army Reserve Infantry training officer, it's easy for me to speculate that he was anxious to test himself and his training in combat.'

Yet it is also hard to resist the idea that part of Rudy was still competing with Babe on some subconscious level. The frustration of missing the First World War had always stayed with him. And who had unwittingly magnified that sense of frustration in Rudy, due to his own participation in the Great War? Babe Slater, the man he had shared a room with in post-war Brussels in 1920, the hero of the Belgian battlefields and the Antwerp Olympic final, the Mr Perfect who had also taken the team captaincy that Rudy surely wanted four years later.

Rudy's eldest son, Rud, said of his father in 2009, 'He stayed in the reserve in the 1920s and 1930s because he liked the army – the uniforms, camaraderie and esprit de corps. He wiggled his way to the Pacific to see the fight he missed in World War One, I do believe.'

The First World War and Babe Slater; were they ever completely separated in Rudy's mind? We can only speculate. Whatever the truth, Rudy Scholz wasn't intending to play second fiddle to anyone this time around. He had received promotion to captain during the 1930s, according to customary Army Reserve policy of the time. Rudy was put on active duty and promoted to major in 1941. After Pearl Harbor he was assigned to San Francisco's High School 'Junior Reserve Officer Training Corps.' There he formed the only ROTC Ski Battalion in the United States.

In July 1942 he was promoted to Lieutenant Colonel; and in 1943 Rudy was put in command of the First Replacement Depot in Banning, California. This was most likely his last post prior to going overseas. If he was going to war at last, he was going to be ready. If he ever found himself in a 'him-or-me' shootout, he wasn't planning to be the guy who missed.

Rudy's official military 'Report of Separation' later revealed that his arms qualifications meant that Lt Col Scholz was:

> Expert in:
> .45 caliber pistol
> .50 caliber machine gun
> .30 caliber carbine
> Sharpshooter with .30 caliber rifle M1

Since he was already in his late 40s, however, there was no guarantee that Rudy would ever see combat, even though he had recently made a little more local rugby history by playing a full match for San Francisco's Olympic Club against the University of California (Berkeley) at the tender age of 47.

Lieutenant Colonel Rudy Scholz found himself in a similar race against time to the one he had lost in the First World War. History might still have repeated itself, because the war could have ended before Rudy reached it. Indeed an event was being organised in his home city that hoped to ensure an end to all wars. The birth of the United Nations was soon to take place in San Francisco. And the security for that momentous conference was to be overseen by Scholz's old 1924 teammate, Ed Turkington, in his latest capacity as Chief of Police for San Francisco. So which was to come first, Rudy's war or world peace?

Rudy's official 'Report of Separation' states that he reached the 'Asiatic Pacific Theater' on 19 January 1945, which would have seen his arrival on Saipan well after the US invasion of that island the previous summer. After missing the fighting on Saipan, however, Scholz was very much part of preparations for an event that would prove to be even more horrific. For the island of Okinawa was the next target. It lay just 340 miles (544km) from the Japanese mainland, and would provide a vital launch-pad for any future push towards Tokyo. The invasion came on the last day of March and the first day of April. From that moment the survival of Rudy Scholz hung in the balance. Many of his comrades would not live to see their loved ones again.

There were at least seven sustained kamikaze attacks from above, when some 1,500 Japanese pilots tried to plough their planes into the astonished and vulnerable ships of the US Navy. No wonder the Navy saw more killed (4,907) than wounded (4,874) as this dreadful tactic reaped its harvest. Like anyone sailing towards Okinawa at the start of that bloody summer, Rudy ran the gauntlet of these kamikaze raids. Once on the island he also witnessed the Japanese embracing death like an old friend. A mixture of suicidal 'Banzai' charges and dogged defending of foxholes and caves meant that survivors among the Emperor's forces were a rarity. They usually saved the last bullets for themselves.

While the mass-slaughter began on Okinawa, tragedy also struck back home in the USA. President Roosevelt died, just days after drafting his speech for the United Nations Conference on International Organization in San Francisco. The powerful words he chose were almost like the triumph of life over death, because they were quoted long after he was gone. 'The work, my friends, is peace; more than an end of this war – an end to the beginning of all wars...'.

Despite Roosevelt's death, the meeting of 50 countries in San Francisco went ahead, just as Roosevelt would have wanted it to. There was a UN charter to be drafted and a lasting peace to be engineered. There would be 282 delegates and 1,444 more people accredited for various roles at this monumental occasion. For Ed Turkington, the organising of security for this inaugural UN event would be no small challenge, though by now he was Police Commissioner of San Francisco. Therefore the responsibility would not have come as any great surprise to him. The conference rumbled on until 26 June when the UN Charter was agreed and signed. Yet without Japanese involvement or surrender, two months of talking had little short-term effect.

Many thousands of people were losing their lives horribly on Okinawa during that time; and the end of the Second World War was still a few more months away. Stubborn Japanese resistance in the bloodbath of the Pacific had given Rudy Scholz the chance to achieve a lifetime's ambition and taste combat in the Pacific. The only question was whether or not he had bitten off more than he could chew as the body-count on Okinawa reached sickening new levels.

The US military sustained around 50,000 casualties between March and June, with over 12,000 killed in action against a determined and suicidal Japanese army. Among the defending forces on Okinawa, over 100,000 sacrificed their lives, though that total was almost certainly eclipsed by the number of civilians who died. There was rarely time to find and bury the dead. With so many bodies out in the open, a grizzly concoction began to spread across the island, which was 66 miles (105km) long and just seven miles (11km) wide. When the rains fell, human gore mixed with the mud, maggots multiplied and anyone unlucky enough to fall into this slop would be literally covered in the filthy effects of war. The stench was unbearable and clung to everything, until slowly the soldiers became accustomed to it. By all accounts, the memory would never leave anyone who was there, and the assault on the senses was virtually indescribable.

Even more grotesque was the way in which the civilians of Okinawa were terrified and bullied into mass suicide by the Japanese army. Indoctrinated with the belief that US soldiers would commit terrible atrocities against women and children, entire families leapt to their deaths from cliffs on the south of the island. Otherwise they used grenades – thoughtfully donated by the Japanese forces – to blow themselves and their loved ones apart. Instead of taking their chances with Rudy and the rest of the invading forces, between 100,000 and 150,000 locals killed themselves. So it is no exaggeration to estimate that over a quarter of a million people died on that narrow island in the summer of 1945, including Japanese and Americans.

Against this backdrop it is extraordinary to consider that Rudy Scholz actually went looking for trouble. On the face of it Rudy might have had a higher than average chance of survival. That's because he seems to have become a Special Staff Officer in the 10th Army. His military record was destroyed in a fire, but we know that he had previously acted as a Liaison Officer between General MacArthur's HQ and the Navy and Marine HQs. One of Scholz's sons, Rud, recalled, 'Mother said that Dad was a member of General Buckner's staff in the Pacific and that he went over "without portfolio", in other words that he was not attached to any specific unit.' Rudy wasn't expected to put himself at the sharp end of the fighting. That didn't mean he would choose to stay clear of danger, though. He preferred to lead from the front and seek it out.

Due to the destruction of those war records, we must rely mostly on anecdotal evidence from Rudy, passed down to his sons, to understand the sort of charmed life he led at times. Since the stories don't always reflect perfectly on Rudy, we have no reason to suppose that he was telling anything other than the truth.

On one occasion Scholz led a highly risky reconnaissance patrol – not something that Lieutenant Colonels were supposed to do. His son Ron takes up the story. 'As best I can recall, Dad told me that he was going out on a patrol and he asked a Sergeant to load his .45 caliber pistol prior to leaving. During the patrol Dad said he took out his pistol and went into some of the caves the Japanese were using on the island. As it turned out, these caves were empty. When Dad got back to base he discovered that his pistol had not been loaded.'

During a further patrol, Rudy apparently did save the lives of his men. His .45 pistol was loaded this time. One of Rudy's sons, Rich, revealed: 'When Dad returned home, being 13 years old I asked him if he had ever killed a "Jap". As best I can remember he said he was going through the jungle with the troops when a sniper opened fire; he immediately raised his .45 and shot the sniper.'

If anyone doubted that Rudy's survival depended on who was first to fire – his patrol or the Japanese – then evidence exists in his son Dave's garage in Sunnyvale, California. Tucked away there is a Japanese rifle, neutralised along with its owner by American bullets on Okinawa in 1945. There is damage near the rifle bolt, where one of those American bullets struck home. On the heavy wooden rifle butt is written a new name, far more prominent than the Japanese Emperor's chrysanthemum symbol on the bolt. That name is 'Scholz.'

Rudy's son, Rud, said:

> For many years Dad stored a Japanese bolt-action rifle in the attic. That rifle was unusual in that it had a smashed trigger guard that appeared to have been caused by a bullet strike from someone else shooting at whoever was holding this rifle at the time. From the extent of damage to this weapon, it certainly seemed whoever had been carrying it surely suffered a lethal hit.

One day I was in the attic with Dad and finally got round to asking him about it. I recall he said that he saved it as a souvenir from one of his recon patrols (on Okinawa, I guess). He was doing a jungle scouting mission with about a squad of men under a sergeant as lead NCO. I understood the sergeant was a little behind and to one side of Dad, but had more jungle experience than Dad. I presume Dad only had a .45 pistol (almost useless), while the sergeant had an M-1 Garand, much more accurate and effective because it held eight, 30-caliber rounds. At any rate, the danger was the presence of Japanese snipers – and one was there where they were at a particular spot. I do not remember Dad saying who fired first, but the sergeant saw the sniper and did kill him – 'ruining' the sniper's Japanese rifle in the crack-shot process.

Rudy was often under fire and later told his sons that he managed to dodge the bullets partly due to the agility and speed he has retained from his many years on the rugby field. Rudy's son Rich added, 'Regarding dodging bullets via athletic ability, I remember Dad saying that he was out somewhere in Okinawa and a Japanese machine gun opened up on him…and how athletic experience gave him the capability to instinctively fall and roll down a small hill and fortunately into a small shrine…This gave him the needed cover.'

Scholz was undoubtedly brave on Okinawa. Indeed Rudy's son Ron has a story about how he might have been more highly decorated had he been of a lower rank. Ron explained, 'Dad told me about a conversation he had with his superior officer after he had returned from another outing. His superior said, "The action you took today deserves a medal, but because what you did is expected of an officer, I'm not going to put you in for one."'

The greatest prize of all was survival itself. No hell on earth could be worse than Okinawa; just as no hell on earth could have been worse than the horrific vision of Passchendaele in its skeletal aftermath, as witnessed by Babe all those years earlier.

Slater put what he saw and experienced into words. So did Scholz, though he didn't tell anyone. His son Dave didn't find out until 2005. Dave explained, 'I was prompted by others to really start digging into a

box containing my father's memorabilia collection. I was lifting out
from the box a couple of old scrapbooks when this small piece of paper
fell to the floor.' This is what Rudy had jotted on that piece of paper:

The Song of the Infantryman
in the Pacific

My clothes are soaked in sweat.
The leather on my shoes
is moldy green and wet.
The smell like rotten booze
That permeates the air,
it comes from the heaven's sons
who from their caves did dare
to brave the torrent guns.

My boots a home for bugs
The typhus germ and coots
and am-pha-lis-tic chugs
I'm mud from head to foot
which covers me all day
The 'trines are always bad
(if only I could pay
for one we used to have).

I've heard the bullets whine
the sniper's deadly song
on rations C we'd dine
until the time's too long
I've heard the sirens call
the ka-mi-kaze dark raid
I've seen the tracers ball
of flaming red – then fade.

I've seen the trucks be mire
in deep unyielding muds
I've seen the fields on fire

with booby traps and duds
I've hid in foxes' holes
(amid the human gore)
like crawling sightless moles
to 'void the mortar's pour.

It's more that might be told
but note the distant sight
the thoughts – that turn to gold
and music fills the night
and soothes the torpid mind
(so cares – that 'fest the day
and endless seems in time
do slowly steal away).
At rest – no more to pine.

(Lt Colonel) Rudy Scholz
At Yonabaru
Jeep stuck in the mud
27 July '45

Rudy Scholz had stepped out of Babe Slater's shadow. He had also learned from first-hand experience the terrible human cost of war.

Due to the simple, abrupt rhythm of the poem, Rudy's granddaughter, Lynn LaRue thought it

> sounded as if he had some of his illusions shattered. Though we never talked about it, I think my grandfather was someone who went into battle with some preconceived ideas that war was a glorious adventure, a noble struggle of bravery and heroism, good versus evil. However, after witnessing first-hand what war really is, I think he had come to realize that it wasn't necessarily glorious or noble; that real battles are horrible, painful, frightening, filthy events where humans are torn apart on the outside and inside. What he and so many other marines saw and went through during that time is almost impossible to comprehend.

Babe would have understood, as a fellow war veteran, albeit from a different global conflict. He had also dodged mortars and seen men blown up all around him. Now they had both experienced pretty much the same horror, war in grim reality. And this Second World War couldn't go on. It was estimated that 1.5 million would die in an invasion of Japan; so the last resort – the dropping of atom bombs on Hiroshima and Nagasaki – was given the green light. Hiroshima and its people were largely obliterated on 6 August, and Nagasaki was subjected to the same treatment on 9 August. Although over 220,000 people died as a result, and that action will always be regarded as barbaric by some, there can be little doubt that a million or more were saved in the long run. The suffering Rudy and the others on Okinawa had endured effectively brought a swifter end to the war. No wonder he is regarded as a military hero as well as a sporting hero.

Japan offered to surrender on 10 August. The Americans accepted that surrender two days later. The Japanese Emperor Hirohito broadcast to his nation that he had surrendered on 15 August. Rudy Scholz left the Asiatic Pacific Theater on 18 August. He had answered the desperate pleas of his wife Milly to come home. To do that, Rudy had respectfully declined a very tempting offer from General MacArthur to stay out in the Pacific in an administrative role.

Rudy won two campaign service medals for 'Battles and Campaigns' in the Eastern Mandates and Ryukus. When a Bronze Star arrived through the post, there was some doubt over whether this had been officially awarded to him, or merely sent by that superior officer who had decided that Rudy deserved the honour after all. But there was something simpler that perhaps Rudy prized even more highly. Dave Scholz explained, 'Of all the awards he received in his lifetime, Dad's "Combat Infantry Badge" was the one that I believe he was most proud of.' To say that about a man with two Olympic gold medals in his trophy cabinet was some statement. Yet the stakes on Okinawa had been higher than in Antwerp or Paris, the nature of the conflict more fundamental.

Babe Slater had never been a combat infantryman, but he had dodged bombs and seen the worst effects of the First World War. And it appears that part of him also wanted to know just how devastating the Second World War's bombs had been – and how people were recovering from their frightening force.

Babe's nephew, Norman Slater, suggested, 'Babe was probably curious to see what the bombs did to Japan and what the country was doing to recuperate, whether the Japanese people had straightened themselves out.'

So Babe visited Japan in the early 1950s, a perfect time to go, because this marked the true moment of reconciliation between Japan and its former enemies, the Allied powers. Once again San Francisco played host to the men striving for a lasting peace. The Treaty of Peace with Japan was signed by 49 countries on 8 September 1951 and came into force on 28 April 1952.

Slater and those who went with him from his local Farm Bureau in Yolo County became part of that general spirit of reconciliation. Babe certainly went to Tokyo, though it is less likely that he ever reached Hiroshima or Nagasaki. However, his nephew recalled later, 'He talked about seeing severe damage, he described it in devastating terms, so I would guess that one of those cities may well have been among his destinations. I can't recall his precise words after all these years but he had seen total destruction because that's what he talked about.'

In truth, Babe Slater didn't have to go to Hiroshima or Nagasaki to witness some of the worst devastation caused by Allied bombs. Tokyo had been bombed so heavily that on one night alone, that of 9–10 March 1945, 16 square miles (25 square km) of the city had been destroyed. Estimates put the loss of life between 88,000 and 100,000, with anything from 41,000 to 125,000 wounded. Some 286,385 buildings were destroyed by the B-29 raid on that night alone. By the end of the war over half of Tokyo had been raised to the ground. So it isn't hard to imagine the urban wilderness Babe might have seen, even six or seven years later.

It is extraordinary to think that, while Rudy remained on the outside of Babe's war, but was keen to survey the barren scene when it was all over, so Babe went through exactly the same process with regard to Rudy's war. Perhaps for the first time they were equals in life experience. Of course they were still opposites in so many ways – they hadn't even fought in the same war. Yet Rudy had caught up with Babe, and come to understand for himself what Slater had already experienced before their Olympic adventures together.

Babe and Rudy would have had plenty to talk about, had they seen fit to meet up later in life. And if they had grown bored with swapping stories about close shaves and bloody wars, they could always have talked about rugby. It's a shame that meeting didn't happen, because Rudy had plenty of new rugby stories to tell.

Incredibly, as he and his former Olympic teammates reached their mid-60s, Scholz was still active on the sports fields of California. Herb Caen, a highly respected columnist in the *San Francisco Chronicle*, wrote wittily about the city's social scene. On 16 April 1962, he admitted,

> We have joked occasionally that there are no bohemians in the Bohemian Club and no athletes in the Olympic Club who can lift anything heavier than a martini, but we are ready to amend that slightly. Saturday ago, the Olympickers managed to scrape together a rugby team to take on Oregon State College's tough young team at G'Gate Park. Midway, the Olympic's fullback was injured, and since there was nobody else on the bench, coach Rudy Scholz quickly suited up and dashed into the game, promptly getting off two great punts and all manner of slashing tackles. Coach Scholz, a lawyer, is sixty-five years old. Final score: Olympic Club 11 Oregon State 0. Martinis for everybody.

While Rudy was still flexing his muscles on a rugby field, Babe's life was drawing to a close. He stayed happily married to Virginia until his death from a heart attack at home on 30 January 1965. He was a few months short of his 69th birthday. A great man and a kind man, Babe Slater had lived the dreams and nightmares of so many and he had done it with dignity.

Rugby stayed so close to Rudy Scholz's heart that he simply refused to hang up his boots entirely. He became president of the Bald Eagles Rugby Club of San Francisco, with the emphasis on the 'bald'. Even so, you didn't have to be ancient to turn out. It was an over-40s side and in 1977 they played the Whoi-Whoi club – the official over-40s team from British Columbia – at Pebble Beach, California, in the Monterey National Tournament.

Al Moss wrote in the *San Francisco Chronicle*:

> Scholz, who played for the 1920 and 1924 Olympic teams that won gold medals, was scheduled to play five minutes in the

second segment; he wisely kept his nose out of the loose rucks, but showed good foot around the field and a serviceable pass from his scrum-half position. He got a great hand when he came out, but his stint wasn't over. Graham Budge, the great old Scottish prop who captains the Whoi-Whoi club – himself a mere stripling in his middle fifties – came to the sideline, put his arm around Scholz and led Rudy back to the middle of the field, stripped off his jersey, presented him with the white Whoi-Whoi shirt – and Scholz played another ten minutes for the other side. Seems reasonable to have him play for two teams. After all, he is 40 twice. The Americans, surprisingly, won the game 14-9, but that really made little difference.

A player wouldn't have swapped sides like that in Paris more than half a century earlier. You couldn't even swap shirts at the end of the game back then without risking a kick where it hurts. But Rudy's Bald Eagles and Canada's Whoi-Whoi club had developed a healthy respect for each other and agreed to play again.

Rudy's wife, Milly, seemed to understand Rudy's desire to play rugby almost until he dropped. She went with him to Vancouver, British Columbia, in that same year of 1977, and the two over-40s rugby clubs were enjoying a banquet after playing each other again. The MC was having trouble keeping the rowdy crowd quiet until Milly stood up and brought the house down by singing a moving rendition of 'O Canada' – the Canadian national anthem. It was the same voice that had so enchanted Rudy back in 1927.

Rudy Scholz was photographed still playing rugby at the age of 83. His final match was against a veteran Irish club called Instonians. The game finished 28-10 to the Irish, though a Bald Eagles newsletter later paid tribute to Scholz senior at the expense of his rugby playing son, and team captain, Dave. The reporter wrote that Rudy took Dave's place on the field 'with no loss of leadership and only a small amount of speed'. It didn't seem to matter how brittle his bones were by then. He was still prepared to take the risks. And that old Tommy Cooper joke springs to mind again, the one about breaking bones in two places. Whether doctors advised him against it or not, Rudy Scholz was still going to those places.

Milly had already thanked him for their life together in a note she wrote for his birthday on 17 June 1975. It read, 'TO RUDY, There was not time in the crowded years for the immediate acknowledgement of love's thoughtfulness; there is leisure now to pen my heart's response; and more, there is the satisfying glow because, without the need of words, YOU KNOW.'

Rudy Scholz died of cancer in 1981, aged 85. To say he had lived a full life and done it his way would be an understatement. Marriage, as we have seen, was pretty good to Rudy, as it was to Babe. Along with their 1924 teammate Ed Turkington, they clocked up more than 150 years of matrimony between them.

Amazingly Ed lived until 1996, just three years short of his hundredth birthday. Had he survived until the new millennium, he would have become one of the few men in history to have lived in three different centuries. Still, Ed Turkington had been extraordinary enough, as had Babe Slater, Rudy Scholz and all the others. Fittingly, their place in Olympic history is secure. For when the Games reach London in 2012, Babe, Rudy and the boys will still hold the rugby crown. As the last rugby gold medal winners, they are eternal champions of a sport they graced with their brilliance, when it would have been so much easier for them to stay at home.

Was it just a coincidence that one rugby team had spawned so many remarkable characters? Did the trials and tribulations of Paris, 1924, help to make them that way? Take Linn Farish, who scored two tries on that day of the riot: he operated behind enemy lines in Yugoslavia during the Second World War. He rescued downed Allied airmen before he was killed in a plane crash in September 1944. Farish was awarded a Distinguished Service Cross posthumously. Later he was also revealed to have been a Russian spy; though he appears to have been given this dubious label simply because he shared certain information with Josep Tito's communist partisans while working alongside them during the war. Patriotic Farish would never have done anything to harm his beloved USA.

Meanwhile William 'Lefty' Rogers became a pioneer in the field of chest surgery – which was a little ironic given that he seemed to spend most of his time trying to cave in the chests of opponents on the rugby field. And Dud De Groot went on to coach the famous Washington

Redskins American football team. There were so many heroes alongside the two who took centre stage in this true story.

Above all, however, it was Rudy and Babe who showed how sport has a way of prevailing beyond wars. If played in the right spirit, the true Olympic spirit, sport has an ability to bring out the best in people. It can even bring entire countries together for a while; so Baron de Coubertin was certainly on to something.

Despite what Scholz went through on Okinawa, those who knew him best reckon he would have been as pleased as anyone had he lived long enough to see the USA play Japan in a magnificent match at the first Rugby World Cup in 1987. Rudy would have been even happier that the Americans won a nail-biting game 21-18 in a dramatic finale.

His son Dave suggested, 'I think Rudy would subscribe to the "time heals all" philosophy. He would also most heartily endorse confining all "wars" to the sports fields.'

Scholz might not always have felt like that; but having seen the horror of war for himself, maybe he knew it was worth looking for another way. Babe Slater probably came to the same conclusion a few decades earlier.

They may have been very different, Rudy and Babe, but they didn't disagree on everything. Finding common ground; that was the key. Perhaps it always will be.

Appendix I

1920 Olympic Games US Rugby Team

Daniel B. 'Danny' Carroll (Playing Coach)* # +	Australia / Stanford U.
George W. Fish # +	U. of California
James Fitzpatrick +	Santa Clara U.
John Muldoon # +	Santa Clara U. / Olympic Club
John T. O'Neill # +	Santa Clara U.
John C. 'Jack' Patrick # +	Stanford U.
Cornelius E. 'Swede' Righter # +	Stanford U.
Rudy Scholz # +	Santa Clara U.
Robert 'Dink' Templeton # +	Stanford U. / Member US Track Team
Charles Tilden, Jr. (Captain) # +	U. of California
Morris Kirksey # +	Stanford U. / Member US Track Team
Charles W. Doe # +	Stanford U.
Matthew Hazeltine	Stanford U. / U. of California
Joseph Garvin Hunter # +	Beliston Club
William S. Muldoon (older brother of John)	Santa Clara U.
Colby 'Babe' Slater # +	(UC) Davis Farm / Olympic Club
Heaton Wrenn #	Stanford U.
Davis M. 'Dave' Wallace	Stanford U.
Charles T. 'Red' Meehan # +	U. of California
James Duarte Winston	Santa Clara U. / U. of California
George E. W. Davis	Stanford U.
Harold Von Schmidt	Barbarian Club

NOTES

* Danny Carroll was a member of the gold medal 1908 Australia / New Zealand (combined) Olympic Games rugby team

\# Played against France according to www.rugbyfootballhistory.com

\+ Played against France according to Rudy Scholz correspondence

Compiled by David Scholz 2009

Appendix II

1924 Olympic Games US Rugby Team

Charles Austin (Coach)	Stanford U.
Colby 'Babe' Slater (Captain)*	(UC) Davis Farm / Olympic Club
Charles Doe (Vice Captain)#*	Stanford U.
John T. O' Neill#*	Santa Clara U.
Joseph Garvin Hunter#	San Mateo High / Beliston Club
John C. 'Jack' Patrick#*	Stanford U.
William S. Muldoon#	Santa Clara U.
Rudy Scholz#*	Santa Clara U.
Norman Cleaveland*	Stanford U.
Dudley De Groot*	Stanford U.
Linn Farish*	Stanford U.
William 'Lefty' Rogers*	Stanford U.
Richard 'Dick' Hyland*	Stanford U.
Robert H. Devereux*	Stanford U.
Phillip Clark	Stanford U.
J. Cashel	Palo Alto Club
Caesar Manelli*	Santa Clara U.
H. Cunningham	Santa Clara U.
Alan Williams	Cornell U. / Olympic Club
George Dixon*	U. of California
Edward Graff*	U. of California
Norman Slater	Berkeley High
Edward Turkington	Lowell High / Olympic Club
Alan Valentine*	Swarthmore College / Oxford

NOTES
\# Member, 1920 Olympic Games US Rugby Team
* Position played in 1924 Games final v France

Compiled by David Scholz 2009

ACKNOWLEDGEMENTS

THE BIGGEST THANKS of all must go to Dave Scholz, the son of one of the book's heroes, Rudy. Dave helped with extensive research and some fine early editing. He even came up with the title, taken from the Olympic oath and cleverly shortened by his perceptive wife Charlotte. To have met you both and worked with you for so long on this, Dave, has truly been a pleasure and an honour.

Emmense gratitude also goes to Pall 'Boomer' Andrew, whose knowledge of and passion for American rugby history were second to none. Just imagine: Boomer was so enthusiastic about doing a book on these reigning Olympic rugby champions that he offered to house the author for a week in the beautiful San Francisco Bay area before he had even met me – and despite the fact that he was still recovering from a major stroke. I hope he and his beautiful wife Ginger didn't come to regret that touching generosity because it was a very special time for me. Boomer and Ginge, you are a class act. Your son Paul volunteered to help me too, which was much appreciated.

Another lovely couple, Ned and Alexandra Turkington, were also a great help and generous hosts in the enchanting Nappa Valley. Ned's father Ed also features strongly in the story. For all Ed's achievements, however, it is Ned's courage as he battled Parkinson's disease that I will always remember because he too was determined to forget his personal troubles and help with the story.

Dave Scholz's brothers, Rud, Rich and Ron, deserve a special mention for their assistance; and Rudy's granddaughter, Lynn LaRue gave generously with her own observations on Rudy's experiences on Okinawa. Like Dave, you all do Rudy proud.

Thanks must also go to Dick and Marilyn Slater-McCapes for playing host when I visited UC Davis. Everyone should know the great work you have done to preserve 'Babe' Slater's story in the 'Babe Slater Collection'. Thanks also to Norman Slater, nephew of Babe Slater, for his natural warmth and humour on the occasions he chose to help me face-to-face or by phone to increase my knowledge of this book's other great hero.

Daryl Morrison, Head of Collections at UC Davis, which houses the wonderful Babe Slater Collection, had the unpleasant experience of finding out that someone else wanted to do a book about Babe Slater, when she had thought about doing a similar project herself. The character she showed by helping me anyway is a great testament to her spirit and personality.

Jack Clark – former World Cup coach of the USA rugby team and more recently doing a great job with 'Cal Rugby' at the University of California, Berkeley – was a wonderful help in so many ways. The scrapbooks from the 1920–1924 era were vital, as was the spectacular rugby photo he so kindly sent for the front cover. Jack and his small but brilliant team of helpers at 'Cal' typify the rugby spirit of Northern California. Here's wishing you even more success, guys. If this book helps boost the profile of American rugby then no one will be more delighted than me.

More great characters helped me to understand what makes San Francisco tick, such as the charming Stu McKee and the tenacious former front-row tough guy, George Reppas. Bet you still pack a punch, George.

Maggie Kimball, University Archivist at Stanford, was instantly warm and generous in providing photographic assistance from the 'Lefty Rogers' collection there. The 'Cal' – Stanford rivalry may still be bitter but you put it on hold for this project, guys, and I am truly grateful.

In England I must give a big thanks to Jeremy Robson of JR Books for seeing the potential in the story, Lesley Wilson for assisting, and Chris Stone for telling it like it is at copyediting stage. That was fun, Chris.

Alice Constance at the British Olympic Association in London couldn't have been more helpful; and Anna Renton at the RFU in Twickenham also showed what fine people these organisations have working behind the scenes.

Ann Bissell at Midas PR showed great enthusiasm as she sought to bring this story to a wider audience.

And last but definitely not least, my wife Victoria and four-year-old son Luca put up with me spending more hours at the computer and on the phone than was reasonable. Luca, I hope you enjoy sport all your life son – and don't ever have to experience war.

INDEX